ORIENTALS

**Asian Americans
in Popular Culture**

In the series:

Asian American History and Culture

edited by Sucheng Chan, David Palumbo-Liu, and Michael Omi

ORIENTALS

ASIAN AMERICANS
IN POPULAR CULTURE

Robert G. Lee

 Temple University Press PHILADELPHIA

Temple University Press, Philadelphia 19122
Copyright © 1999 by Temple University
All rights reserved
Published 1999
Printed in the United States of America

ⓧ The paper used in this publication meets the requirements of
the American National Standard for Information Sciences—Permanence
of Paper for Printed Library Materials, ANSI Z39.48–1984

Library of Congress Cataloging-in-Publication Data

Lee, Robert G., 1947–
    Orientals: Asian Americans in popular culture /
Robert G. Lee.
        p.   cm. — (Asian American history and culture)
    Includes index.
    ISBN 1-56639-658-1 (cloth : alk. paper)
    1. Asian Americans—Cultural assimilation.   2. Racism—United
States.   3. United States—Race relations.   I. Title. II. Series.
E184.06L48   1998
305.895′073—dc21   98-25853
                                                              CIP

For Jennifer, Luz, and Max
and for all the folks who were there
when the chips were down

Contents

Preface
Where Are You From?

"Orientals are rugs, not people," says my student, summing up Asian American history. As she knows, it is the common experience of all Asian Americans—recent immigrant or fourth-generation American born, university professor or garment worker—to be asked by other Americans, "Where do you come from?" My student knows that the question, while often benign, is never completely innocent. "Oakland" or "Oshkosh" is never the acceptable answer, and its rejection reveals at once that the question is not about hometowns. The repeated question always implies, "You couldn't be from here." It equates the Asian with alien.

The assumption that Asians are alien to America is, of course, anachronistic. Notwithstanding prehistoric migrations, or ancient sea travels, Asians have been a historical presence in the Americas since Filipino sailors abandoned Spanish galleons to settle in Louisiana and Texas in the mid-eighteenth century.[1]

The anachronism of the assumption that Asians are indelibly alien is occasionally revealed in a way that provokes more embarrassment than anger. In November 1996, the board of the Association for Asian American Studies held its business meeting in San Diego. After a long day of discussing the mundane affairs of state in the academic profession, academics from half a dozen universities across the country adjourned to a nearby Thai restaurant where the conversation was relaxed and lively. As the food arrived, another patron of the restaurant, a silver-haired, Caucasian gentleman in tweeds, strode over to the table and asked the inevitable: "Where are you from?" After a moment of acute silence, the answers rolled back: "New York, Chicago, Providence, Ann Arbor, Irvine, San Diego." Clearly bewildered that these Orientals did not understand his question, their fellow American shook his head in disbelief before exiting.

All too often, the assumption is deadly. A few months before this business meeting, in Tustin, about an hour north of San Diego, Thien Minh Ly was brutally murdered in his hometown. Two white drifters, Gunner Lindberg, 21, and Dominic Christopher, 17, were arrested for the murder. Lindberg had written a letter describing the murder in grisly detail:

> Oh I killed a jap [sic] a while ago I stabbed him to Death at Tustin High school I walked up to him Dominic was with me and I seen this guy Roller-blading and I had a knife. We walk in the tennis court where he was I walked up to him. Dominic was right there I walked right up to him and he was scared I looked at him and said 'Oh I thought I knew you' and he got happy that he wasn't gona get jumped. then I hit him.[2]

Thien Minh Ly was not a "Jap." He was a twenty-four-year-old Vietnamese American who had graduated from UCLA with bachelors' degrees in biology and English. He had just returned home after finishing a master's degree in biophysics and physiology at Georgetown. He was thinking about going on to law school. He was rollerblading on the tennis courts of his hometown high school. When his body was found, Thien Minh Ly had been stabbed more than forty times. His throat had been slashed, and his face had been kicked in.

These two events do not seem comparable. The first is ironic, amusing, at worst embarrassing; the second is brutal, horrifying, and tragic. Yet both encounters attest to the everyday tenacity of the assumption that Asians are an alien presence in America. In some quarters, Asian Americans, their dedication to upward mobility combined with safely familiar exoticism, are trumpeted as the success story of American multiculturalism. Elsewhere, Asian Americans are deeply resented as alien intruders whose presence threatens the economy and corrupts society. Hate crimes against Asian Americans have been rising at an alarming rate over the past two decades. Just between 1993 and 1995, racial violence against Asians rose from 335 to 461 incidents across the country, a 38 percent increase in two years. In 1995 the violence of attacks on Asian Americans increased dramatically, with assaults rising by almost 11 percent, aggravated assaults by 14 percent. There were two murders and one firebomb attack.[3] The idea that Asian Americans are a threatening alien presence can also be heard in the cry for resurrecting racial and ethnic barriers to immigration and in alarums over the influence of "foreign" money in American politics.

This book is about the ways in which Asians in America, immigrant and native-born, have been made into a race of aliens. The representation of the Oriental constructs the alien as a racial category. The concept is deeply imbedded in American ideologies of race, class, gender, and sexuality. Its complicated connections to the wide skein of American culture means that while the images that constitute the Oriental at any given moment are frequently contradictory, often to the point of appearing mutually exclusive, and sometimes mutable, they are stubbornly resistant to eradication.

The student's quip about rugs and people touched the heart of the matter. As Marx observed long ago, while people make their own histories, they do not do so in a world of their own making.[4] The history of Asians in the United States has been a continuous struggle against racial exclusion and subordination as Orientals. Asian Americans have waged fierce battles on the railroads, in the mining camps, in the courts, in the fields, in the factories and the universities, to assert their claim to be American and to define what "American" means. This book attempts to map the history of the Oriental in hopes of helping to clear the way forward.

Scholarship is a social construction. Despite the necessary solitude of writing, the joy of scholarship comes in the sharing of ideas. This book is the product of shared ideas. The Department of American Civilization at Brown University has been a nurturing environment, and my colleagues have been a tremendous intellectual and personal resource. Many of the ideas in this book were conceived in lively discussions in my reading group on American Orientalism, a outstanding group of young scholars which over the years included Oscar Campomanes, Matt Jacobsen, Yuko Matsukawa, Melani McAlister, Mari Yoshihara, Jennifer Ting, and Kathleen Zane.

More specifically, I want to thank Jennifer Ting for insisting early on that sex was central to understanding Asian American history and for demonstrating the importance of the insights of queer theory to this study; and Laura Santigian for pointing out the importance of popular music as a medium for the construction of race and the treasure trove of nineteenth-century songsters under my nose at the John Hay Library of Brown University.

Very special acknowledgment needs to be made to Joanne Melish. Although her own scholarship has focused on the construction of race in the early republican era, the two of us have spent the better part of a decade reading, talking, and debating the meaning of race in American history. Joanne's close reading and her suggestions for improving the text at each stage have been innumerable and invaluable. I am also grateful for the keen eyes of Susette Min and Mari Yoshihara in correcting the many errors of form and substance in earlier drafts of the text. Josephine Lee, Gary Okihiro, Michael Omi, Susan Smulyan, Kevin Scott Wong, and an anonymous reader for Temple University were all generous with their time and gracious with their comments. All remaining errors of fact, judgment, and style remain my responsibility. My last (by convention) but very large acknowledgment is to Janet Francendese, executive editor at Temple University Press, who saw promise in this book and who has been my steadfast and patient supporter in ushering it into print.

ORIENTALS

**Asian Americans
in Popular Culture**

Introduction

Yellowface

Marking the Oriental

n March 1997, the cover of *National Review* featured President William Jefferson Clinton, first lady Hillary Rodham Clinton, and Vice President Al Gore, all in yellowface. The president, portrayed as a Chinese houseboy—buck-toothed, squinty-eyed and pigtailed, wearing a straw "coolie" hat—serves coffee. The first lady, similarly buck-toothed and squinty-eyed, outfitted as a Maoist Red Guard, brandishes a "Little Red Book," while the vice president, robed as Buddhist priest, beatifically proffers a begging bowl already stuffed with money.

In using the yellowface cartoon to illustrate a story about alleged political corruption, the editors of *National Review* simultaneously emphasized their racial point and revived a tradition of racial grotesques that had illustrated broadsides, editorials, and diatribes against Asians in America since the mid-nineteenth century. The cover story summarized allegations that the Clinton administration had solicited campaign donations from Asian contributors in exchange for policy favors. These allegations virtually ignored the much larger illegal campaign contributions of non-Asians and focused almost exclusively on Asian and Asian American contributors.[1] Like most of the mainstream media, *National Review* was silent on the broader questions: the impact of multinational corporations on American politics and the baleful influence of big money on big politics. *National Review* instead played the race

1

card. Focusing only on the Asian and Asian American campaign contributions, *National Review* made it clear that it was not corporate money, or even foreign money generally, but specifically Asian money that polluted the American political process. In the eyes of the *National Review* editors, the nation's first family (with Al Gore as potential heir) had been so polluted by Asian money that they had literally turned yellow.

Yellowface marks the Asian body as unmistakably Oriental; it sharply defines the Oriental in a racial opposition to whiteness. Yellowface exaggerates "racial" features that have been designated "Oriental," such as "slanted" eyes, overbite, and mustard-yellow skin color. Only the racialized Oriental is yellow; Asians are not. Asia is not a biological fact but a geographic designation. Asians come in the broadest range of skin color and hue.

Because the organizing principle behind the idea of race is "common ancestry," it is concerned with the physical, the biological, and the reproductive. But race is not a category of nature; it is an ideology through which unequal distributions of wealth and power are naturalized—justified in the language of biology and genealogy. Physiognomy is relevant to race only insofar as certain physical characteristics, such as skin color or hue, eye color or shape, shape of the nose, color or texture of the hair, over- or underbite, etc., are *socially defined* as markers of racial difference.

The designation of yellow as the racial color of the Oriental is a prime example of this social constructedness of race. In 1922, the U.S. Supreme Court denied Takao Ozawa, an immigrant from Japan, the right to become a naturalized citizen. In its ruling, the court recognized the fact that some Asians, including Ozawa, were of a paler hue than many European immigrants already accepted into the nation as "white." Race, the court concluded, was not a matter of actual color but of "blood" or ancestry, and Ozawa, being of Japanese "blood," could not claim to be white, no matter how white his skin.[2]

What does Yellowface signify? Race is a mode of placing cultural meaning on the body. Yellowface marks the Oriental as indelibly alien. Constructed as a race of aliens, Orientals represent a present danger of pollution. An analysis of the Oriental as a racial category must begin with the concept of the alien as a polluting body.

The cultural anthropologist Mary Douglas argues that fears of pollution arise when things are out of place. Soil, she observes, is fertile earth when on the ground with tomatoes growing in it; it is polluting dirt when on the kitchen table. Pollutants are objects, or persons, perceived to be out of place. They create a sense of disorder and anomaly in the symbolic structure of society. Douglas observes that pollution is not a conscious act. Mere presence in the wrong place, the inadvertent crossing of a boundary, may constitute pollution.³ Aliens, outsiders who are inside, disrupt the internal structure of a cultural formation as it defines itself vis-à-vis the Other; their presence constitutes a boundary crisis. Aliens are always a source of pollution.

Not all foreign objects, however, are aliens—only objects or persons whose presence disrupts the narrative structure of the community. It is useful here to distinguish between the alien and the merely foreign. Although the two terms are sometimes used interchangeably, they carry different connotations. "Foreign" refers to that which is outside or distant, while "alien" describes things that are immediate and present yet have a foreign nature or allegiance. The difference is political. According to the *Oxford English Dictionary*, as early as the sixteenth century "alien" referred to things whose allegiance lay outside the realm in which they resided, as in "alien priories"—monasteries in England whose loyalty was to Rome. This early definition of "alien" emphasized the unalterable nature of the foreign object and its threatening presence.

Only when the foreign is present does it become alien. The alien is always out of place, therefore disturbing and dangerous. The difference between the alien and the merely foreign is exemplified by the difference between the immigrant and the tourist. Outsiders who declare their intention of leaving may be accorded the status of guest, visitor, tourist, traveler, or foreign student. Such foreigners, whose presence is defined as temporary, are seen as innocuous and even desirable. On the other hand, if the arriving outsiders declare no intention to leave (or if such a declared intention is suspect), they are accorded the status of alien, with considerably different and sometimes dire consequences. Only when aliens exit or are "naturalized" (cleansed of their foreignness and remade) can they shed their status as pollutants.

Alienness is both a formal political or legal status and an informal, but by no means less powerful, cultural status. The two states are hardly synonymous or congruent. Alien legal status and the procedures by which it can be shed often depend on the cultural definitions of difference. In 1923, a year after it denied Takao Ozawa the right to naturalize, the Supreme Court stripped Bhagat Singh Thind, an Indian immigrant who was already an American through naturalization, of his U.S. citizenship.⁴ In *Ozawa v. United States,* the court had ruled that no matter what the actual color of his skin, nor how much he could prove himself culturally assimilated, Ozawa's Japanese "blood" made him "unamalgamable" by marriage into the American national family. In *United States v. Thind,* despite the ethnological evidence presented by Thind that he, a high-caste Hindu, was a descendent of Aryans and hence white by "blood," the court ruled that he was not, holding that race was not a scientific category but a social one, and upheld the revocation of Thind's citizenship.

In both *Ozawa* and *Thind,* the Supreme Court tacitly recognized race to be a product of popular ideology. In both cases, Chief Justice Sutherland, writing for the court, cited the existence of a "common understanding" of racial difference which color, culture, and science could not surmount. The important thing about race, the Supreme Court held, was not what social or physical scientists at the time may have had to say about it, but rather how it was "popularly" defined.

Not until 1952, after more than a century of settlement in the United States, were Asian immigrants finally granted the right to become naturalized citizens. Even so, long after the legal status of "alien" has been shed, the "common understanding" that Asians are an alien presence in America, no matter how long they may have resided in the United States nor how assimilated they are, is still prevalent in American culture. In 1996, the immediate response of the Democratic National Committee to allegations that it had accepted illegal campaign donations from foreigners was to call Asian American contributors to the party's coffers and demand that they verify their status as citizens or permanent residents. One such donor, Suzanne Ahn, a prominent Houston physician and civic leader, reported to the U.S. Commission on Civil Rights that DNC auditors threatened to turn her name over to the news media as "uncooperative" if she did not release personal financial information to them. Ahn concluded that she had been investigated by the DNC, the FBI, and the news media simply because she had contributed to the DNC and was Asian American. Even public figures do not escape the assumption that Asian Americans are really foreigners in disguise. When Matthew Fong, a fourth-generation Californian, ran as a Republican candidate for Secretary of State in California—a position his mother March Fong Yu had held for the better part of two decades—he was asked by news reporters whether his loyalties were divided between the U.S. and China.[5]

In the run-up to the 1996 presidential elections, a cartoon by syndicated cartoonist Pat Oliphant played on the persistent "common understanding" of Asian Americans as permanent aliens in America. It showed a befuddled poll watcher confronted with a long line of identically short Oriental men with identical black hair, slit eyes behind glasses, and buck teeth, all wearing identical suits and waving ballots. Referring to the Asian American DNC official who was made the poster boy of the fundraising scandal, the caption reads, "The 3,367th John Huang is now voting." Echoing the public comment of presidential candidate Ross Perot that none of the Asian names brought out in the campaign finance scandal thus far sounded like they belonged to "real" Americans, one of

'THE 3,367TH JOHN HUANG IS NOW VOTING...'   11/4/96

Oliphant's signature nebbishes asks from the margin, "Just how many John Huangs are there? How many you want?"[6] The cartoon plays on the "common understanding" that Orientals are indistinguishable as individuals and thus ultimately fail as "real" Americans. How could Oliphant's poll watcher, the yeoman guardian of the American political process and embodiment of "common understanding," possibly hope to distinguish among all the Orientals flooding into the nation's body politic?

Popular Culture and Race

The Oriental as a racial category is never isolated from struggles over race, ethnicity, sexuality, gender, and national identity. The Supreme Court's "common understanding" is a legal fiction. It gives popular convention, the common sense of "real" Americans, the power to define race. The "common understanding" of the Oriental as racialized alien therefore originates in the realm of popular culture, where struggles over who is or who can become a "real American" take place and where the categories, representations, distinctions, and markers of race are defined. Some studies attribute hostility toward Asian immigrants directly to economic competition and the creation of an ethnically defined segmented labor market. They provide us with an economic framework for

understanding the dynamics of class and race and a map of the economic terrain on which anti-Asian hostility has been built. By themselves,
however, those studies do not account for the development or functioning of specific racial images of Asians in American culture.[7]

This book takes up popular culture as a process, a set of cultural practices that define American nationality—who "real Americans" are in any
given historical moment. American citizenship and American nationality
are not synonymous; citizenship carries with it an implicit assumption
or promise of equality, at least in political and legal terms, while nationality contains and manages the contradictions of the hierarchies and inequalities of a social formation. Nationality is a constantly shifting and
contested terrain that organizes the ideological struggle over hierarchies
and inequalities.

The nature of popular culture is the subject of much debate.[8] Popular
culture is most often identified as having its roots in the organic culture
of the common folk or peasant life, in opposition to court or bourgeois
culture. Popular culture, then, is often characterized by politically resistant, if often nostalgic, qualities. Ever since the rise of industrial capitalism in the early nineteenth century, popular culture has been in reality
complex, increasingly shaped by the capitalist processes of its production
and circulation. Nevertheless, popular culture, albeit sometimes recon-
stituted as co-opted or deracinated mass culture, continues to be identified with subordinated groups, as opposed to the dominant ruling class.

The mobilization of national identity under the sign "American" has
never been a simple matter of imposing elite interests and values on the
social formation, but is always a matter of negotiation between the dominant and the dominated. Subordinated groups offer resistance to the
hegemony of elite culture; they create subaltern popular cultures and
contest for a voice in the dominant public sphere.[9] The saloon vies with
the salon, the boardwalk with the cafe, and the minstrel theater with the
opera house as an arena for public debate and political ideas.[10]

Although it mobilizes legitimacy, the cultural hegemony of dominant
groups is never complete; it can render fundamental social contradictions invisible, explain them away, or ameliorate them, but it cannot resolve them.[11] However deracinated, whether co-opted, utopian, nostalgic, or nihilist, popular culture is always contested terrain. The practices
that make up popular culture are negotiations, in the public sphere, between and among dominant and subaltern groups around the questions
of national identity: What constitutes America? Who gets to participate
and on what grounds? Who are "real Americans?"

Since popular culture is a significant arena in which the struggle over
defining American nationality occurs, it also plays a critical role in defining race. Race is a principal signifier of social differences in America. It

is deployed in assigning differential political rights and capital and social privilege, in distinguishing between citizens presumed to have equal rights and privileges and inherently unequal, subordinated subjects.[12] Although race is often camouflaged or rendered invisible, once produced as a category of social difference it is present everywhere in the social formation and deeply imbedded in the popular culture. The Oriental as a racial category is produced, not only in popular discourse about race *per se* but also in discourses having to do with class, gender and sexuality, family, and nation. Once produced in those discourses, the Oriental becomes a participant in the production and reproduction of those social identities.[13]

The Stereotype and the Family

The racist humor of portraying Bill and Hillary Clinton and Al Gore in yellowface works only because the first family is always presumptively white—an enduring, if anachronistic, symbol of America as a white nation in the popular imagination. Yellowface transforms the first family, historically and symbolically white, into the Oriental family: Bill, Hillary and Al have, through the pollution of Asian money, become alien, yellow, and Oriental.

The family is the primary metaphor of the nation. The idea of Americans as a family is the discursive basis for an imagined nationhood. The family as a symbol of nationhood structures nationality as fictive kinship, a common ancestry. One need only recall that the most common terms in which the nation is invoked ("brotherhood," "mother tongue," "fatherland") all reference terms of kinship. These are terms also shared by race. The fiction of common ancestry (both biological and cultural) has been made central to the construction of both race and nation. Indeed, historically, the two categories have been interchangeable. For example, it was common in the early decades of this century to speak of national groups—the American, French, or Japanese—as "races."

The family is also the primary ideological apparatus, the central system of symbols, through which the state contains and manages contradictions in the social structure. It is the principal social unit through which the individual can become a national subject, a member of the community through birth, adoption, marriage. The family is a primary site in which labor power and class relations, gender and sexual relations, ethnic and racial identities are produced and reproduced. It is also the symbolic system that gives meaning to and organizes the closest psychological, economic, and sexual relationships among people and within a community.[14]

Although the family has often been considered a private sphere, even a haven from the marketplace and from public life, in fact the family unit has been a key entry point for state intervention in every area of daily life.[15] In the realm of economics, the state enters the family via taxes and estate laws. The state regulates gender relations in the family via marriage and divorce laws. It regulates sexual relations through family laws regarding age of consent, sanctioned and prohibited sexual behaviors, pornography and marriage. It regulates the familial relationship between parents and children via custodial, child welfare, and adoption law. It regulates race relations through laws prohibiting interracial marriage and addressing housing, education and public accommodations.

In the "crisis of the family" and the struggle to "restore family values" that has been trumpeted for the past two decades, the Asian American family, portrayed as "intact," "disciplined," and patriarchal, has been presented as the model for economic success in a period of economic decline.[16] This representation is quite recent; Asians have been cast as an economic, social, and sexual threat to the American national family throughout their history in the United States.

The pollution of the nation's first family did not only come about through a suspected exchange of money for policy. The Clinton administration's hands-off policies toward human rights violations by the Indonesian government in East Timor, or the superexploitation of workers by Nike in Vietnam in the interest of free trade, to name only two instances, has barely scandalized the American press or public. What the press seems to have been most interested in is the number of times Asian contributors and fundraisers came for coffee at the White House. Although the White House logs of overnight guests show no Asian or Asian American guests save the governor of Hawaii, press reports that big contributors to the Clinton re-election campaign might be invited for overnight stays at the White House were usually printed next to, and often illustrated with, pictures of Asian American fundraisers. The idea that the Lincoln bedroom might now be slept in by (wealthy) Orientals seems to most offend the "common understanding." The alien body present in the national bedroom can now be imagined as the deeper source of pollution.

The Six Faces of the Oriental

Six images—the pollutant, the coolie, the deviant, the yellow peril, the model minority, and the gook—portray the Oriental as an alien body and a threat to the American national family. From each of these racial paradigms emerges a wide array of specific images. Each of these representations was constructed in a specific historical moment, marked by a shift in class relations accompanied by cultural crisis. At such times American nationality—who the "real Americans" are—is redefined in terms of class, gender, race, and sexuality.

The representation of the Asian as pollutant originated in mid-nineteenth-century California. For white settlers from the East, Chinese settlers from the West disrupted the mythic narrative of westward expansion. The Chinese constituted an alien presence and a threat of pollution which earlier fantasies of exotic but distant Asia could not contain. In the popular imagination, California was a free-soil Eden, a place where small producers, artisans, farmers, and craftsmen might have a second chance to build a white republic, unstained by chattel slavery or proletarian labor.[17] In this prelapsarian imagery, the Chinese were both identified with the moral chaos of the Gold Rush and portrayed as the harbingers of industrial wage slavery. As the national debate over slavery, abolition, and statehood came to a boiling point in the late 1860s, the ideal of establishing California as both free and racially pure demanded the removal, or at least the exclusion, of both Chinese and African Americans.

The representation of the Chinese immigrant worker as a coolie came about as the U.S. working class was formed in the 1870s and 1880s. Although they had come to America as free (albeit highly proletarianized) workers, Chinese immigrants found themselves segregated into a racially defined state of subordination as "coolie labor." The Chinese "coolie" was portrayed as unfree and servile, a threat to the white working man's family, which in turn was the principal symbol of an emergent working-class identity that fused class consciousness with gendered national and racial identity. The coolie representation not only allowed the nascent labor movement, dominated by its skilled trades, to exclude Chinese from the working class; it also enabled the skilled trades to ignore the needs of common labor, which it racialized as "coolie labor" or "nigger work."[18] Irish immigrants who were in the process of consolidating their own claim to Americanness and a white racial identity led the popular anti-Chinese movement.

The Oriental as deviant, in the person of the Chinese household servant, is a figure of forbidden desire. The deviant represents the possibility of alternative desire in a period during which middle-class gender roles and sexual behavior were being codified and naturalized into a rigid heterosexual cult of domesticity. In the West, the Chinese immigrant played a central role in the transition from a male-dominated, frontier culture shaped by the rituals of male bonding to a rigidly codified heterosexual Victorian culture. In the 1860s and early 1870s, hundreds of Chinese women were brought to San Francisco and forced into prostitution. By the end of the decade, thousands of Chinese immigrant men were driven out of the mines and off farms and ranches and were hired into middle-class households as domestic servants. Both of these situations opened up possibilities of interracial sex and intimacy. Middle-class whites regarded the Chinese with ambivalence. On the one hand, the Chinese were indispensable as domestic labor; on the other, they represented a threat of racial pollution within the household. A representation of the Oriental as both seductively childlike and threateningly sexual allowed for both sympathy and repulsion. The representation of the Oriental as deviant justified a taboo against intimacy through which racial and class stability could be preserved.

By the turn of the century, Asian immigrants were represented as the yellow peril, a threat to nation, race, and family. The acquisition of territories and colonies brought with it a renewed threat of "Asiatic" immigration, an invasion of "yellow men" and "little brown brothers." At the moment when the United States prepared to pick up "the white man's burden" in the Caribbean and the Pacific, "Asiatic immigration" was said to pose "the greatest threat to Western civilization and the White Race." [19] Domestically, the triumph of corporatism, the homogenization or de-skilling of industrial labor, urbanization, and immigration had all contributed to massive changes in both middle- and working-class families. These changes contributed to the construction of a culture of consumption, reflected in new gender roles as well as new sexual attitudes and behavior among men and women of both classes. In the aftermath of the First World War and the Bolshevik Revolution, these domestic social and cultural transformations were accompanied by deep anxieties about racial suicide and class struggle.[20] Through its supposed subversion of the family, the yellow peril threatened to undermine what Lothrop Stoddard, a popular advocate of eugenics and racial geopolitics, called the "inner dikes" of the white race.

The representation of Asian Americans as a model minority, although popularly identified with the late 1960s and 1970s, originated in the racial logic of Cold War liberalism of the 1950s. The image of Asian Americans as a successful case of "ethnic" assimilation helped to contain three spectres that haunted Cold War America: the red menace of communism, the black menace of racial integration, and the white menace of homosexuality. In place of a radical critique calling for structural changes in American political economy, the model minority mythology substituted a narrative of national modernization and ethnic assimilation through heterosexuality, familialism, and consumption. By the late 1960s, an image of "successful" Asian American assimilation could be held up to African Americans and Latinos as a model for nonmilitant, nonpolitical upward mobility.

Since the 1970s, the model minority image has coexisted with and re-inforced a representation of the Asian American as the gook. The shift in the U.S. economy from large-scale industrial production to flexible accumulation and the global realignment of capital and labor have brought about new crises of class, race, and national identity. In the context of these contemporary crises, the "intact" and "traditional" Asian American family is promoted as a model of productivity, savings, and mobility, not just for African America or Latino families but now for all American families, including those of the white middle class. Simultaneously, however, in post-Vietnam and post-liberal American popular culture, the Asian American is represented as the invisible enemy and the embodiment of inauthentic racial and national identities—the gook. The Vietnam War is replayed in popular culture as the narrative of American decline in the post-industrial era. The received wisdom of the Vietnam War narrative is that America's defeat in Southeast Asia was brought about by a faceless and invisible Asian enemy, aided and abetted by an American counterculture. The rapid growth of the Asian American population and its apparent success render the model minority, like the now-mythic Viet Cong, everywhere invisible and powerful. In the narrative of American decline, Asian Americans are represented as the agents of foreign or multinational capital. In this narrative of national decline, Asian American success is seen as camouflage for subversion. The model minority is revealed to be a simulacrum, a copy for which no original exists, and thus a false model of the American family. In the dystopic narrative of American national decline, the model minority resembles the replicants in the science fiction book and film *Blade Runner*—a cyborg, perfectly efficient but inauthentically human, the perfect gook.

The cultural crises in American society that give rise to these representations of the Oriental come in the wake of economic change, particularly in what economic historians Gordon and Reich call transformations of the structure of accumulation.[21] The transformation of the social relations of production and the organization of work and segmentation of the labor market have profound effects on the structures, relations, and meaning of families, gender, and race. At each stage of capitalist development, new "emergent" public spheres are constituted and new demands arise for participation in the dominant public sphere.[22] The popular discourse of race in which these constructions of the Oriental were produced and deployed is not a transparent or unmediated reflection of the economy, but rather an expression of social contradictions drawing on images of the present, visions of the future, and memories of the past.

As a historical analysis of the construction of representations of the Oriental and a study of racial ideology, this book asks how these representations were constructed and what ideological tasks they performed. Racial images and stereotypes are ideologically active, and thus contradictory and unstable. The Oriental appears in various guises throughout American popular culture, in pictures, songs, paraphernalia, books, and movies, and no single image represents the totality of the representation. Therefore, rather than focus on any single genre or medium, or the technology of a genre, or its reception, this book looks at popular songs of the nineteenth century, magazine fiction and illustrations, silent movies and pulp fiction, and Hollywood musicals and dramas. The principle criterion for selecting these "texts" has been the extent to which each helps to illuminate the social contradictions of its production, the internal complexities of the Oriental representation, and the way in which the Oriental is imbedded in the discourses of race, gender, class, and sexuality in America.

Yellowface: Stereotype and Discourse

The reappearance of the yellowface grotesque on the front pages of a national magazine was deeply unsettling, particularly to those Asian Americans who had bought into the myth of the model minority. Since the mid-1960s, the national media had popularized an image of Asian Americans as the perfectly assimilated and presumptively accepted ethnic minority in the United States. Among many Asian Americans, the emergence of the model minority image led to a popular preoccupation with "good" stereotypes vs. "bad" stereotypes.

This preoccupation with "positive" and "negative" stereotypes reifies and inadvertently legitimates the racial discourse of the Oriental that produces both the coolie and the minority. It shifts attention from a critical analysis of race toward a narrow utilitarian calculus in which specific images are measured in terms of their usefulness to strategies of upward mobility.[23] Discussions of "good" and "bad" stereotypes have, more often than not, focused on the distance between image and reality. However, stereotypes of Asian Americans are not simply distorted versions of Asian lives in America. The Yellowface coolie and model minority, despite their apparent contradiction, not only coexist but, in fact, can become mutually reinforcing at critical junctures because neither is created by the actual lives of Asians in America. What produces these stereotypes is not just individual acts of representation, but a historical discourse of race that is embedded in the history of American social crises.

On the other hand, a concern with these images as the product of and agent in a complex racial ideology can lead us to an understanding of racial representation as a social practice. The Oriental is a complex racial representation, made up of contradictory images and stereotypes. This complexity and ambiguity gives the Oriental its ideological power, its connection with the broadest web of social concerns. In turn, this con-nectedness reinforces the representation and gives the racial stereotype its power to survive, mutate, and reproduce.

Resisting the Oriental

Asian Americans have not been passive in the face of the production and reproduction of the Oriental stereotype which has barred them from immigration, citizenship, and participation in American society and cul-ture. A century before John Huang became a celebrity in the annals of American political scandal, Asian Americans challenged their exclusion from America both through the legal system and in the realm of culture.

The historical struggle of Asian Americans to achieve full citizenship in the United States has challenged and revivified every aspect of citizen-ship in a liberal democracy, including the right of entry and naturaliza-tion, equal protection and economic rights, and the right to participate fully in the public culture.[24] Asian names dot the landscape of constitu-tional jurisprudence: Yick Wo (equal protection), Fong Yue-Ting (im-migration), Wong Ark Kim (citizenship through birth), Toyota (land ownership), and Fred Korematsu (internment) are only a few of the most widely cited. Historian Sucheng Chan has identified almost 200 cases that Asian Americans have brought before the U.S. Supreme Court and more than a thousand cases that have come before lower federal courts and whose written decisions have warranted inclusion in the *Fed-eral Reporters*.[25] Chan estimates that this number represents only about 10 percent of the cases actually brought before Federal courts.

One need only recall such books as Younghill Kang's *East Goes West,* Carlos Bulosan's *America Is in the Heart,* or John Okada's *No-No Boy* to be re-minded that culture has also been an arena where Asian Americans have contested their exclusion as Orientals, critiqued the unfulfilled promises of democracy, and mapped alternative visions of American identity. Cul-tural critic Lisa Lowe observes,

> Asian American culture is the site of more than critical negation of the U.S. nation: It is a site that shifts and marks alternatives to the national terrain by occupying other spaces, imagining different narratives and critical his-toriographies, and enacting practices that give rise to new forms of subjec-tivity and new ways of questioning the government of human life by the na-tional state.[26]

The film *Mississippi Masala* is a contemporary example of Asian Americans' resistance to their racial subordination as Orientals in popular culture. Directed by Mira Nair, the film is ostensibly about an interracial love affair between an Indian American woman and an African American man, but maps a critique of the contemporary racial landscape in America shaped by class, gender and immigration. *Mississippi Masala* simultaneously calls our attention to the transnational character of contemporary Asian American immigration and to the multiple statuses of Asian Americans, as both bourgeoisie and working class and as a "middleman minority" within local racial and class hierarchies. The film rejects both the evasion of liberal multiculturalism and the essentialism of ethnonationalism in favor of a political consciousness shaped by an understanding of contradictory histories and the complexity of power. Only the full consciousness of these global histories and local positions make possible class alliances and trans-racial coalitions. In its utopian vision of a racial democracy, *Mississippi Masala* stands with Carlos Bulosan's *America Is in the Heart* in the Asian American tradition of resisting the Oriental.

1

The "Heathen Chinee" on God's Free Soil

What Was Your Name in the States? Nostalgic California

> Oh, what was your name in the States?
> Was it Thompson or Johnson or Bates?
> Did you murder your wife
> And fly for your life?
> Say, what was your name in the States? [1]

The popular song "What Was Your Name in The States?" invoked the often shadowy, sometimes tragic, background of many an American who fled to the California gold country. It also established California as a place sufficiently distant to destabilize personal histories, a space for rehabilitation if not redemption. In the 1850s, California was constructed in the popular mind as a Jacksonian community of independent small producers, miners, and pioneers. These men imagined California as a place where a lost American organic community could be reconstructed and their own identities remade. Mid-century California, on the fringe of the American core economy, was the site of a nostalgia wrought by a sense of collapsed space and time. Its distance from "the States" and its position at the farthest reach of the continent represented both the expanse and the limits of continental expansion.

According to the *Oxford English Dictionary*, James Cook, the British explorer of the South Pacific, first used the word "nostalgia" in its pathological sense as "a form of melancholia caused by a prolonged absence from one's home or country, severe homesickness." In 1770, Cook noted in his journals of his voyages to the South Pacific, "The greatest part of them [the ship's company] was now pretty far gone with the longing for home which the Physicians have gone so far as to esteem a disease under the name of Nostalgia." A mid-nineteenth-century meaning of nostalgia is the "sense of loss of time," and this temporal sense is extended to the "regret or sorrowful longing for the conditions of a past age; regretful or wistful memory or recall of an earlier time." The dictionary's definitions remind us that nostalgia can be traced to the dislocation that resulted from early capitalist expansion.

> I remember, I remember when the Yuba used to pay,
> With nothing but a rocker, five hundred dollars a day.
> We used to think 't'would always last, and would, with perfect ease,
> If only Uncle Sam had stopped the coming of Chinese.

"California As It Was and Is," published in 1855 in *Put's Original California Songster*, laid the blame for the passing of California's "golden" era squarely on the arrival of immigrants from China. "Put" was the pseudonym of John A. Stone, who wrote the largest number and most popular of California gold rush songs, including "Sweet Betsy from Pike." Stone had come to California in search of gold and discovered a single quartz boulder that contained a vein of gold worth $15,000. Put immediately retired to write songs as a full-time occupation.[2] The subtitle of his collection, *Giving in a Few Words What Would Occupy Volumes, Detailing the Hopes, Trials, and Joys of a Miner's Life,* explains the cultural project of the publication. The songster constructs a popular narrative of California from the vantage point of its imagined past. Like many of the other songs in the collection, "California As It Was and Is" is a lament mourning the passing of an earlier California, imagined as a pre-capitalist idyll. The singer is called to "remember" his cabin "still among the sugar pines" and a time when "we hadn't any laws/ We could live in peace among the diggers and their squaws."

In the pastoral image of "California As It Was and Is," the Chinese immigrant represents the entering wedge of disruptive capitalism. After the arrival of the Chinese, independent placer mining on the Yuba collapsed and, the song complains, "We're compelled to pay a tax which people say is gambled off. . . . And certain ones are trying to give our mineral lands away/ to build a railroad from the States to San Francisco Bay." The song goes on to lament the state of party politics—"But now its Whigs and Democrats, and Know Nothings of late/All fighting after office, with a chance to rob the State"—and in the face of rampant corruption mourns the loss of a more direct system of justice: "When Captain Lynch was boss, we had no use for prison brigs. . . . But now it's thieves on every side, political thieves in flocks."

Virtually all the song's claims are false. The arrival of Chinese miners in the mining districts of California had nothing to do with the decline in gold prices. Miners and other Anglo settlers carried out a ruthless extermination of the largely peaceful coastal Indians of California. Even the song's picturesque image of the bucolic miner's cabin "beneath a sugar pine" was more likely to have been a ragged tent in a rock-strewn arroyo. Like "California As It Was and Is," a score of popular songs published between 1855 and 1882 portrayed the Chinese immigrant as an agent of economic decline and social disorder for free white workingmen and their families.

"California as It Was And Is" differed little from the hundreds of songs that popularized a nostalgic pastoral vision of California for nineteenth-century American audiences. The music historian Nicholas Tawa pinpoints the 1820s as the period in which a mass market for music developed and songwriters began to craft tunes for a popular audience. By the 1850s, musicians could speak of "the people's song" or "a music for the millions" that was distinct from the opera and art songs intended for a musically sophisticated and trained elite. Rooted in American and British sentimental ballads and the minstrel show, the new music was simple and straightforward, its message immediately and reassuringly identifiable. A writer for the *Musical Review* in 1855 remarked, "By the people's song we mean a style so simple and easy (yet pure and chaste) as is ever within the reach of all, including the uncultivated and unlearned."[3]

Popular music offered a powerful medium for an ideology of nostalgia. As a ritual that both reflects and produces group solidarity, popular song is in the broadest sense liturgical.[4] Popular songs were not to be passively consumed in the listening, but were intended for singing around the campfire, in the boardinghouse parlor, in the saloon and music hall, and at the political rally. As oral ritual, popular music provided social identity and encouraged group solidarity. The lyric imagery, symbolism, and metonymy of popular songs evoked memory and emotion, linking the atomized present to the collective past. The very simplicity of its form, its use of fixed chord progressions, its emphasis on strong, unadorned melody, assured effortless and immediate accessibility to "the uncultivated and unlearned." An emphasis on harmony brought the individual into the group's voice. At once audience and performer, the singers not only apprehended the lyric of the song but enacted its narrative as performance.

Despite its simplicity, this "music for the millions," with all of its references to a pastoral past, rarely came out of a folkloric or oral tradition in an ethnological sense. Although many of these popular songs were set to traditional tunes and melodies, songs published in songsters relied on lyrics or melodies pirated from currently popular tunes or minstrel songs.[5] "California As It Was and Is" derived from an older favorite, "I Remember When," a nostalgic lament for lost childhood innocence. Produced by urban writers and publishers for consumption by a largely urban audience, these songs were written in the first instance for the saloon, minstrel show, or musical stage before finding their way into the songster.

In the decades between 1820 and 1860, the nation's population tripled, going from just under 10,000,000 to more than 31,000,000.[6] By the 1850s, when the publishing of inexpensive songsters became a truly national business, American printers had already been turning out inexpensive collections of popular songs for more than a century.[7] In 1846 the development of the "Lightning Press," a steam-powered rotary press, allowed printers to increase their output by 400 percent and lower the price of reproduction. In the 1850s songsters could be bought for a dime; by the 1880s, for as little as a nickel. Songsters like *Put's Original* were published in cities throughout the country in inexpensive and portable pocket editions, primarily for the millions of new city dwellers.

In the two decades before the Civil War, the Hutchinson Family Singers, natives of New Hampshire, became the premier troupe of family singers in America. The Hutchinsons had been deeply moved by the religious fervor of the "Second Great Awakening" that swept through rural New England in the 1830s. By the late 1840s they had become the musical voice of moral reform, singing of salvation and temperance. The Hutchinsons received their greatest notoriety for bringing the Free Soil and Abolition messages to the popular musical stage. One of their Free Soil songs, "Ho for California," brought together two visions of California as an earthly paradise. In the first few stanzas of the song, California was portrayed as a "promised land" where gold could be had for the picking up.

> We've formed our band and are well mann'd,
> To journey afar to the promised land,
> Where the golden ore is rich in store,
> On the banks of the Sacramento shore.
>
> As we explore that distant shore,
> We'll fill our pockets with the shining ore.
> And how 'twill sound, as the word goes round.
> Of our picking up gold by the dozen pound.

In another stanza, California embodies the prophesied golden City on a Hill, a providentially ordained land reserved for Free Labor.

> Ho for California!
> In the days of old, the Prophets told
> Of the City to come, all framed in gold,

Peradventure they saw the day
Now dawning in California.

O! the land we'll save, for the bold and the brave
Have determined there never shall breathe a slave;
Let foes recoil, for the sons of toil
Shall make California GOD'S FREE SOIL.

Then, ho! Brothers ho! to California go,
No slaves shall toil on Gods' Free Soil,
On the banks of the Sacramento.
Heigh O, and away we go
Chanting our songs of Freedom, O.[8]

Ironically, this popular Free Soil vision of California was sung to the tune of Dan Emmett's blackface minstrel song "De Boatman Dance."[9]

Thousands had flocked to the Sierra Nevada foothills after gold was found at Sutter's Mill. For the many men who lacked experience, skills, or capital, prospecting for gold was the more alluring alternative to becoming wage workers in the rapidly industrializing Northeast or to farming on the prairie.[10] For such men, prospecting for gold represented a return to the small producer economy. Henry George, in *Poverty and Progress,* his magnum opus defense of the white small producer, "remembered" gold mining in California during the early years of the gold rush as a pastoral pursuit strikingly similar to that memorialized in "California As It Was and Is."

The placer miner, who found in a river bed or surface deposit the glittering particles accumulated for ages by a slow processes of nature, picked up or washed out his "wages" (as he called them) in actual money— coin being scarce, gold dust passed as currency by weight—and at the end of the day had his wages in a buckskin bag in his pocket. There can be no dispute as to whether these wages came from capital or not. They were manifestly the produce of his labor.[11]

California imagined as a small producer economy—free of slavery, free of the cash nexus of capitalism, and free of the Chinese, "when the Yuba used to pay, with nothing but a pan and pick, five hundred dollars, in a day," represented the nostalgic heart of Free Soil California.

The great economic transformation that took place between 1815 and 1855 was experienced culturally as a collapse of both space and time.[12] The effects of capitalist expansion were at once global and local. The rise of factory production created both an industrial metropolitan core and a huge rural periphery that was tied to the core through a web of commerce. Industrial capitalism fundamentally changed the relationship between town and country, between master and servant, and among age-old relationships within the family; and it loosened the web of social relations, mores, and values that had, as tradition, for centuries held village and family life together. Connections were forged between places that had not previously been linked; age-old links were sundered. Distances, measured as travel time, between these newly linked places were shortened by roads, rail, and steamship routes, and by the monetarization of labor, which could pay for travel. Individuals often experienced the effects of these profound transformations as an inchoate sense of loss.

Among immigrants from the industrializing Northeast, nostalgia for a pre-industrial pastoral was already part of the cultural vocabulary. Historian Herbert Gutman finds that female millworkers writing in the *Lowell Offering*, a journal published during the mid-1840s, showed a deep "attachment to nature [that] was the concern of persons working machines in a society still predominantly 'a garden.'" In neighboring New Hampshire, mill workers petitioned their employers not to cut down an elm tree to make room for an additional mill. They wrote that the huge tree "belonged to a time when the yell of the red man and the scream of the eagle were alone heard on the banks of the Merrimack." [13]

One Eastern transplant who noted the nostalgic sensibility even in the earliest days of the American settlement of California was Hubert Howe Bancroft. In 1849, while in his early teens, Bancroft accompanied his parents to California from Springfield, Mass. In 1856, the young Bancroft established H. H. Bancroft, a trading and publishing house, one of whose projects was to amass material for documenting virtually every aspect of California life. Although its founder was not university-trained, H. H. Bancroft would become, over the next three decades, the preeminent historian of California.

Bancroft's description of San Francisco's "steamer days"—the two or three times each month when the mail steamers arrived and departed from San Francisco, connecting it with the States—evokes the intensity of the nostalgia at the heart of the California imaginary. Steamer days stirred up anxiety about the collapsing structure of time and space. "It is difficult," Bancroft writes, "for one who has not lived it through to realize with what nervous pulsations these vessels were watched as they came and went." Nervousness gave physical expression to the sense of dislocation, the sense of being "beyond the pale of civilization, of Sabbath and home influence, of all the sweet memories and amenities that make life endurable." Americans in Gold Rush California were "voluntary exiles, cut off from friends and all congenial society, doomed for a period of life of self-abnegation and hard labor." Even as Steamer Days reminded Americans of their exile, the arrivals and departures of the mail packets and clippers were "links in the life-chain that was to bind the future to the past." [14]

Steamer days, for Bancroft, seemed to represent the intensity of early California capitalism. They captured the complex amalgam of nostalgia, hope, and memory, the collapse of space and time that California, at the intersection of core and periphery, represented. On these occasions the past and future seemed to mingle with the present, and hope, regret, and dogged determination filled the heart with longings indescribable.[15] In this state of nostalgic funk, Bancroft wrote,

> The present went for nothing, or worse than nothing, perhaps; for it might be a nightmare, a horrible dream, something to be blotted from the memory as soon as it ended. When the steamer came in . . . what a flood of tender recollections rushed in upon the soul![16]

Bancroft observed that just beneath the surface "flood of tender recollections" resuscitated by the arrival of the mail packet lay the unrelenting cash nexus of a burgeoning capitalist economy.

> Steamer-days . . . were the great tickings in social and commercial time. Bills were made to fall due on those days, letters must be written on that day and collections and remittances made. . . . They were feverish fidgety days . From morning till night collection clerks with a package of bills in one hand, and the mouth of a canvas coin-bag slung over the shoulder in the other, were rushing about the streets, and seldom was the office lamp extinguished before twelve or two o'clock.[17]

Americans in California did not only pine for "the States" but almost immediately constructed a nostalgic narrative about California itself. Bancroft noted the tendency of even the earliest of Americans settlers to speak of San Francisco in nostalgic and pastoral terms. Bancroft cited at length William Van Voorhies' address to the Society of California Pioneers in 1853.

> I can well remember . . . when the bay of San Francisco afforded ample room and verge enough for easy and unobstructed passage of the largest class mail steamers. . . .
>   I can remember well also when an unobtrusive *casa*, compared with the immense structures which now rise here and there at magnificent distances, was all that met the eye; when the Parker House, the old Portsmouth house, the United States Hotel, Howard's Store, the venerable adobe on the Plaza, then a customs house, afterwards a broker's shop and now no more, with one or two other shanties, looked to us immigrants of '49 like palaces; when seraped natives chased the wild bullock over the surrounding hills, satisfying a lean lank traffic, not commerce, with the offering of a hide or horn; when a Chinese was a *lusus naturae,* and a woman on the street—which was an imaginary line drawn in red and blue in on paste board—an absolute and unmitigated wonder.[18]

By this time Chinese were no longer freaks of nature in San Francisco. Between 1848 and 1853, some 22,000 Chinese had arrived in California. Their number would double in the next two years. A handful of Chinese arrived in San Francisco prior to the gold rush, but substantial numbers of immigrants from Guangdong Province set out for California after the news of the gold strike reached South China. In 1850 and 1851, advertisements in Hong Kong newspapers attracted passengers for ships returning to America.[19] By 1851 the rush from Guangdong to California was on in force.

Between 1848 and 1851, the great majority of Chinese immigrants to California were import-export merchants, shopkeepers, and tradesmen.[20] Skilled craftsmen were also among the Chinese who came; the first stone buildings in San Francisco were built by Chinese stonemasons with stone imported from Guangdong.[21] Peter Parker, the U.S. consul in Canton, reported that between January 1, 1851, and January 1 of the following year, 14,000 Chinese embarked for California. The following year the number of immigrants jumped to 20,025; it leveled off to an average of roughly 4,000 immigrants per year for the next decade.[22] This initial surge seems to have been a response to the lure of gold; immigrants came primarily from the farming districts outside Canton, and many headed into the mining districts in search of gold. By the mid 1850s California seems to have lost its allure for the Chinese. Only in the late 1860s, when China coast newspapers again carried advertisements for workers on California's railroads and in agriculture, was there another wave of immigration from China.[23]

The arrival of the Chinese disrupted the nostalgic image of pastoral California evoked by Put's song or Van Voorhies' orations by providing a visible reminder of the capitalist enterprise at the heart of the American settlement of California. But long before the Chinese arrived in large numbers in the 1850s, American merchants from New England and the Northeast had begun to pull Spanish and Mexican California into the trade orbit of the United States.

At the beginning of the nineteenth century, Boston traders had begun to see San Francisco as an outpost in the web of commerce that tied Boston, Canton, and Hawaii. By 1820, Bryant, Sturgis and Co. had made San Francisco a key port in its China trade and had made huge profits in the trade in sea otter pelts. When the Mexican government authorized trade in hides and tallow at California ports in 1822, Bryant Sturgis, along with other American and British firms, seized the opportunity to tap a new supply of raw material for the growing shoe and harness industry in New England. Alfred Robinson, the first Bryant Sturgis agent in San Francisco, is estimated to have shipped a half million hides to New

England ports alone. The San Francisco trade was immensely profitable; during the peak of the hide trade in the mid-1830s, American merchants could sell their manufactured goods for prices that averaged 300 percent above the Boston cost.[24] San Francisco merchants expanded their trade so quickly in the four years after the discovery of gold at Sutter's Mill that only three cities—New York, Boston, and New Orleans—could claim a larger share of the nation's foreign commerce. California merchants developed a near-monopoly on the Hawaiian and Philippine trade, built a respectable trade with Japan, and shared the China trade with New York. California agriculture in the 1850s and 1860s fed a coastal shipping trade that outstripped the shipping trade to Eastern ports. By the time of the Civil War, San Francisco was the nation's sixth busiest port.[25]

Chinese immigration was part of a global working-class migration that fueled San Francisco's explosive population growth in the 1850s and 1860s. Compared to the country as a whole, an extraordinarily ethnically diverse population settled in San Francisco. In 1850 only one in ten Americans had been born overseas, but fully half of San Francisco's residents had been born abroad. In 1860 San Francisco trailed after only New York and Boston as a center of immigration. California attracted not only old-stock Anglo-Americans displaced from farms and workshops in the Northeast, but also immigrants from the hinterlands of Europe, Latin America, and Asia.

The transition to the market economy in capitalism's periphery was likely to be experienced as economic hardship and social dislocation. This was as true in Andalusia, Norway, or the Mezzagiorno, or the West Counties of Ireland, as it was in South China, where between 1830 and 1930 more than 70 percent of the peasants lost their land.[26] The hope of millions of peasants and laborers was to migrate toward the economic core. Money, now earned as wages from the landlord or borrowed against future wages in the metropole, became the key to travel along the new steamship and railroad lines that connected the world's countryside to its cities. Labor historian David Montgomery observes,

One thing was clear to immigrants from the periphery. Their own world had become monetized. . . . By the turn of the century, however, rural laborers in those countries knew well that they could earn in one day in the United States what they could in five or six days at home.[27]

The California Ball: Crisis and Chaos

Those who were fortunate enough to take gold from California's Free Soil, or to extract it from others who had, filled the forward compartments of the steamers, "going home with all the prestige of travel and

adventure in strange lands," Bancroft observed. He noted that these sojourners were careful to project a suitable image of themselves as pio-
neer miners.

> It is matter of pride with many to be seen by their friends in their mining
> costume; so the bushy hair and the long beard are protected with care, and
> every hole in the battered hat, every patch in the woolen shirt, every dirt
> stain on the greasy pantaloons, are regarded with affection.[28]

For many others the fevered search for gold led to failure, frustration,
and ruin. Economic growth in California in the middle decades of the
nineteenth century was chaotic, and prosperity wildly uneven. During
the 1850s, the San Francisco–based economy experienced four separate
cycles of boom and bust related more to local supply and demand problems than to the national business cycle. Although working-class men
from the East continued to arrive in San Francisco to fuel California's
population growth, only one person in ten stayed for more than thirty
years, and three out of four left within eight years of arriving in the city.[29]

Bancroft also observed hundreds of these less successful sojourners
boarding the same steamers for "home."

> In the steerage also were many penniless persons, broken in health and
> spirits going home to die. There were those . . . already morally dead; there
> were self-pitying unfortunates, whining and complaining; . . . and there were
> those who had manfully fought the battle and had been beaten. Faithfully
> and patiently these last had toiled and suffered, hope and fear alternating
> between fortune and disease, unwilling to give themselves the needed rest
> and care with wealth and happiness just within their grasp; and so, with
> their pale faces, and sunken eyes, and hollow cheeks, they feebly drag them-
> selves about with hope crushed, and this world forever lost to them.[30]

One such failed sojourner was Hinton Rowan Helper. His family, like
many of the others in the area, were non-slave-holding small farmers in
Rowan County, in the Piedmont region of North Carolina. Although his
father died when Helper was young, the family managed to send him to
a well-known local academy. From there, Hinton Helper apprenticed as
a clerk in Salsbury, N.C., and then went north. When fortune eluded him
in New York, he left for the gold fields of California.

Although he had not killed his wife, Helper, like many another immigrant to California, arrived with something of a shadowed past in "the
States." While an apprentice in North Carolina, he had embezzled several hundred dollars from his employer, but he voluntarily paid off this
"debt" after he settled in New York. In 1850, he quit the city for the gold
fields.

Failing to find gold or any other financial success in California, Helper left California five years later to embark on a career as a writer. Hinton Helper would become infamous for his white supremacist antislavery tract, *The Impending Crisis of the South.* Published in 1857, the massive volume was an argument in favor of abolition as a solution to a greater problem than slavery—"miscegenation." *The Crisis* became the center of heated debate on the floor of an already deeply divided U.S. Congress and is credited as much as Harriet Beecher Stowe's *Uncle Tom's Cabin* with bringing about the Civil War.[31]

After his stint in the mining country, Helper failed to find suitable employment in San Francisco; before leaving he wrote *Land of Gold,* a book intended to lay bare the myth of California as paradise regained.[32] Helper excoriated California, from the weather to the land itself, as barren and unproductive. But what most appalled him was the abandonment of moral rectitude in the feverish search for gold. Helper wrote obsessively about the scarcity of proper white middle-class women in California; without these natural bearers of moral order, righteous young men like himself could not survive, let alone prosper. Hinton Helper left California frustrated and angry, unable to realize its golden promise of redemption.

Put's song "The California Ball" gave a somewhat humorous voice to the feeling of social and moral dislocation that many men like Helper experienced in the rapidly expanding capitalist economy of California. In a parody of California society at play, it relied on the trope of the ball common to popular music, especially minstrelsy. As a signifier of race and class, the ball suggested the formality and hierarchy of the social elite and alluded to the minstrel songs that poked fun at elite rituals for the benefit of working-class audiences. In minstrelsy, the ball was most familiarly brought into song as the "Negro Ball." This juxtaposition of the subordinated racial Other and elite culture was calculated to strike its audiences as incongruous, unnatural, and hilarious.

In much the same way that Helper had described the collapse of a moral system as a result of gold fever, Put saw the distinctions rooted in social class washed away in California.

> T'would make our eastern people cave to see the great and small,
> The old, with one foot in the grave, all "splurging" at a ball.

In California even women were unmoored; so much so that their "natural" instincts for motherhood itself seemed to be lost to the feverish pleasures of the Ball:

> A dozen babies on the bed and all begin to squall;
> The mothers wish the brats were dead for crying at the ball.

Similarly, sexual prohibitions based on age seemed also to have dissolved.

> Old women in their Bloomer tights
> Are fond of "balance all!"
> And "weighty" when it comes to jigs
> And so on at the ball!
>
> A yearling miss fills out the set
> Although not very tall;
> "I'm anxious now" she says, "you bet,
> To proceed with the ball!"

Just as Hinton Helper was horrified that marriage relationship was degraded in California, Put saw marriage vows abandoned in the "California Ball."

> A married woman—gentle dove—
> With nary tooth at all,
> Sits in the corner making love
> To some "pimp" at the ball!

In Put's California, sexual license, naked aggression, and disregard for "proper" ethnic distinctions are openly displayed and condoned.

> A drunken loafer at the dance,
> Informs them one and all
> With bowie knife stuck in his pants,
> "The best man at the ball! . . .
>
> The Spanish hags of ill repute,
> For brandy loudly call:
> And no one dares their right dispute,
> To freedom at the ball! [33]

For Hinton Rowan Helper, the fevered race for gold had led to a disastrously uncontrolled, willy-nilly settlement of California by a "motley crowd" of nations and peoples, so that "the tattooed [sic] islander, the solemn Chinaman, and the slovenly Chilian [sic] mingled with the more decidedly white and black from Europe and Africa" and now were "thronging in the streets." [34]

Helper wrote with bitter irony that gold, capitalism's "mighty talisman, had transformed a wilderness into a busy place of industry, a barren peninsula into a blooming city." The incessant and unrelenting search for gold had battered down the Chinese Wall between nations, "harmonizing the antagonistic elements of this strange brotherhood." By this Helper did not mean a universal brotherhood of man but an unnatural admixture of races that deterred the immigration of True [white] Womanhood to the moral wilderness that was California. [35]

In one respect Helper's observation was correct; a motley crew had settled in San Francisco. Between 1850 and 1870 San Francisco experienced a dizzying rate of population growth. By then only nine cities in the country were larger. When the opening shots of the Civil War were fired, there were more than 3,000 Chinese and almost 2,000 African Americans among the 57,000 residents of San Francisco. There were even more European immigrants in the city, principally from the British Isles and Germany. By the end of the war the city's population had doubled, to more than 100,000; and by the end of the decade, one out of every three San Franciscans had been born in Ireland, Germany, China, or Italy.[36]

The well-known minstrel performer Billy Rice evoked this diversity in his song "The Chinese Ball," published in his *Ethiopian Comic Songster*.

I'll tell you something that happened
Going to 'Frisco o'er the plain;
May I be clubbed in three different languages
If ever I go there again.
I met a jolly Irishman,
An ambassador from France,
Who invited me to go down to a hall
And take in a Chinese dance.

When we arrived down the hall
They were dancing the jigglewig,
their hair hung down three feet behind
Like the tail of an Irish pig.
They were dancing society polka
All round the room,
Until one great big fat Japanese
Fell into a swoon.

I started to dance at the Chinese ball,
Along with a Chinese rough,
Her front name it was Hannah
and her back name it was Snuff
I tried to take her on the pinch,
But found she couldn't be bluffed.
And when we sat down at the dinner table
You'd swear to yourself she was stuffed.[37]

Orientalism and Race: From Chinese to Chinaman

Edward Said has argued that Orientalism is an imaginative geography and history which "helps the mind to intensify its own sense of self by dramatizing the difference and distance between what is close to it and what is far away."[38] In this respect, Orientalism reifies the relationship of power between the West and Asia by constructing the Occident and Orient as cultural polarities defined by (real or imagined) distance. Although scores of Chinese had settled in the United States, mainly on the Eastern seaboard, in the decades before the California gold rush, these early settlers, scattered among the waves of European immigrants coming to the United States, were viewed primarily as curiosities embodying the exotic difference of the Orient. The arrival of thousands of Chinese settlers in California, however, undermined the definition of Oriental difference, which relied on distance. This construction of racial difference as distant and exotic was displaced (but not completely replaced) by a construction of racial difference as present and threatening. Once thousands of Chinese lived in the United States, they could no longer be imagined as simply foreign, made strange by their distance. Chinese in America were now alien and threatening through their very presence.

Before the arrival of Chinese immigrants in substantial numbers in the mid-nineteenth century, the representation of China had enjoyed a long career in American popular culture. In 1784, Peale's Museum in Philadelphia opened a display of Chinese curiosities among its collections of objects from Africa and India.[39] Peale's Chinese collection opened in the same year that the New York clipper *Empress of China* docked in Canton, opening the fabled "China Market" to American merchants. The Peale Museum displayed Chinese items of trade, everyday utensils, weapons, and bric-a-brac, but what attracted the greatest curiosity was the collection of wrappings used to bind the feet of Chinese women and the tiny shoes and slippers that fit bound feet. In 1799, the East India Marine Society opened its museum in Salem, displaying many artifacts from the China, India, and Pacific trade circuit. In addition to curios and other items of trade, the Salem museum featured life-size clay models of Chinese officials and the Cantonese Hong merchant Yamqua, in effect putting Chinese people on display.[40] By 1805 Peale's, which had been renamed the Philadelphia Museum, had introduced life-size figures in "life group" dioramas as a way of displaying its Chinese collections. In the Philadelphia Museum, Chinese artifacts were displayed on wax models, side-by-side with models of Native Americans and other "exotic" peoples

> drest in their real and peculiar habiliments, viz.—Chinese laborer and Gentleman; Inhabitants of Oonalaska; a Kamaskadle; an Aferican [sic]; a Sandwich Islander; an Otaheitan; a South American; and Blue Jacket and Red-pole, celebrated Sachems of North America.[41]

Public interest in such displays inspired Nathan Dunn to open the Chinese Museum in conjunction with Peale's Philadelphia Museum in

1838. Dunn had been a merchant in Canton, where he had amassed a huge collection of Chinese clothes, everyday utensils, and tools, as well as prints and *objets d'art*. Peale, a Quaker, had also been a merchant in Canton for many years. Peale particularly wanted to use his collection of memorabilia to refute negative portrayals of the Chinese as barbaric heathens—being circulated by frustrated Christian missionaries—and instead to promote a positive image of the Chinese as potential trading partners. In the Chinese Museum, well over a thousand Chinese items were on display, but the central attraction were the eleven dioramas or "life groups." These groups of life-size clay figures dressed in Chinese costumes represented the hierarchy of Chinese society: high- and low-ranking mandarins, literati, ladies of rank, actors, teachers of the main Chinese religions, itinerant craftsmen, a man being carried in his sedan chair, visitors to a wealthy residence, and farmers. According to the museum's catalogue,

> The visitor finds himself, as it were, transported to a new world. It is China in miniature. The view is imposing in the highest degree. The rich screenwork at the two ends of the saloon, the many-shaped and many-colored lamps suspended from the ceiling; the native paintings which cover the walls; the Chinese maxims adorning the columns and entablatures; the choice silks, gay with a hundred colors, and tastefully displayed over the cases along the north side, and the multitude of cases crowded with rare and interesting sights, form a *tout ensemble,* possessing a beauty entirely its own, and which must be seen before it can be appreciated.[42]

The Chinese museum was a huge attraction. An estimated 100,000 people visited it between its opening in December 1838 and the summer of 1841, when the collection was moved to London. Fifty thousand copies of *Ten Thousand Chinese Things,* one of the two catalogues of the Chinese museum, were sold. However, the Chinese museum was a financial failure, and in 1849 it was sold along with the Philadelphia Museum to Phineas T. Barnum, who had opened his own American Museum in New York.

In 1834, Barnum's American Museum had introduced a live Chinese woman, one Ah Fong Moy, to its audience. Although not an actress in the theatrical sense of the word, Ah Fong Moy was far from the ethnologically "correct" but inanimate clay figures of the Chinese museum dioramas. Unlike the invasive and dehumanizing treatment of Sarah Bartman, the so-called Hottentot Venus, who had been exhibited naked to a scandalized and fascinated Paris and London two decades earlier, Ah Fong Moy was presented as a "Chinese Lady," always robed in resplendent silks and often seated among luxurious Chinese furnishings."

"The Chinese Lady" was displayed against a backdrop of various dioramas and was featured in a wide variety of narratives as far from China as the Battle of Waterloo. By the time Ah Fong Moy returned to China in 1837, she had performed "Chineseness" at the American Museum, the Brooklyn Institute, and the City Saloon in New York, and in Peale's Philadelphia Museum.[43]

By far, Barnum's most intriguing display of the Oriental had been Chang and Eng, the "Siamese Twins," who combined the exotic with a rare physical anomaly. Chang and Eng joined Barnum in 1860, late in their stage careers, having originally had been brought to the United States in 1829 by Robert Hunter, a British merchant who had "discovered" the ethnically Chinese twins in Siam (now Thailand). After touring the United States and England for a decade with great success, the twins retired to Wilkesboro, a county seat in western North Carolina, where they established themselves as landed Southern gentry by purchasing two farms, building two separate residences, and becoming slaveholders. In 1843 Chang and Eng married the Yates sisters, Sarah and Adelaide, and between them fathered twenty-two children. Although an 1849 return to the touring circuit in the company of two of their daughters was not successful, Chang and Eng had better results from an 1853 tour of Canada and Nova Scotia along with a son and a daughter. During their stint with Barnum, the twins and two of Eng's sons performed in October 1860 at the American Museum in New York. Although they embarked on a profitable tour of California, the Civil War brought a hiatus to their tours and ruin to their plantations. After the Civil War, Chang and Eng again took to the stage circuit with their children. After Chang suffered a stroke in 1870, the twins retired permanently, and in 1874 they died. The twins' forty-year career established them as international celebrities; indeed, their fame gave their physical condition the popular name of Siamese twins.[44] Chang and Eng are among the best-remembered humans to be displayed in the nineteenth century, an era in which collections and curiosities (human and otherwise) fascinated the public in the U.S. and Europe.

The relationship among the categorical imperative of the natural sciences, ethnology, and imperialism has already been well established.[45] Although the United States had yet to expand its political jurisdiction overseas, by the middle decades of the nineteenth century it had extended its reach across the continent and developed commercial interests around the globe. This expansion demanded the cataloguing—the identification, description, and above all creation of a hierarchy—of peoples and things within the national inventory. The dioramic museum display of the Oriental categorized and naturalized cultural difference for a predominantly middle-class audience for whom a new visual experience of the nation and the world had been made possible by scientific, military, and commercial expeditions.

While the museum diorama might locate China as a distant exotic object (simultaneously desirable and repulsive in its difference) in the geographic imagery of a middle-class eager to expand its commercial horizons, the immigration of "ordinary" Chinese people to the United States had an altogether different significance. The principally working-class (formerly small producer) American settlers in California experienced the large-scale settlement of Chinese in the United States as a boundary crisis. In the minds of white immigrants from the East, Chinese who settled California from the West were anomalous; they broke the chain of westward historical progress. Immigration from China changed the meaning both of China and of California for white Americans. China could no longer be imagined simply as a distant destination to which Americans ventured to seek their fortunes in trade. It now had to be taken into account as a place from which workers came to America in search of gold and wages. The presence of Asian immigrant workers in the West meant that California could no longer be seen as a stop in a one-way trade between America and Asia. The vision of California as a place for restoration of the White Republic now had to accommodate another California, not only a point on the circuit of trade relations but also a center of capitalist production.

Not all foreign people or objects are pollutants, only those whose presence disrupts the narrative structure of the community. Pollutants are anomalies in the symbolic structure of society, things that are out of place and create a sense of disorder. A mere presence in the wrong place, the intentional or unintended crossing of a boundary, gives offense.[46] Douglas' observations about pollution help clarify the distinction between ethnicity and race. In ethnicity, boundaries of difference are constructed as permeable, and therefore ethnic differences are conceived as assimilable and nonpolluting; in race, boundaries are constructed as impermeable, and therefore racial difference is conceived as unassimilable and polluting.

Much as the "anomalous" condition of "free" persons of color in New England at the beginning of the nineteenth century constituted for whites the negative meaning of their blackness, the idea of Chinese "settlers" in California was an equally impossible anomaly, and the Chinese were constructed as pollutants.[47] Identified with the entering wedge of industrial capitalism, the Chinese came to embody all of the dislocations of Western settlement. The coming of the Chinese became a symbol for the break between a pastoral past and the commercial future that Bancroft had written about in his description of furious "steamer days" and that Helper had mourned as the collapse of moral order. Chinese immigration became a metonym for the collapse of time and space produced by the transition to industrial capitalism, a collapse that constituted a boundary crisis within the symbolic or ideological structure of American society. This boundary crisis demanded the transformation of Chinese cultural difference from exotic to pollutant. Unlike the Chinese visitor, the Chinese settler could not be contained within the category of the Oriental in the order of commerce and empire but had to be assigned a new position as a person of color in the racial state.

The forty-year career of Chang and Eng suggests both the shift in the signification of the Chinese from object of curiosity to symbol of racial crisis and the shift in the popular sites of that signification from museum to minstrel show. Chang and Eng were first exhibited in 1829, at the peak of the popularity of Peale's Philadelphia Museum. By 1860, when Chang and Eng played Barnum's gaudy and theatrical American museum and left on their tour of California, the twins were widely identified with the minstrel show. Many minstrel shows had made "Siamese twins" part of their comedy routines; the accompanying illustration from Charley Fox's *Minstrel Songster* shows the well-known minstrels Charley Fox and Frank Dumont playing "Siamese Twins."

Human bodies, their parts and functions, are always culturally constructed. Mary Douglas has argued that as a cultural construction endowed with social meaning, the body can be read as a representation or map of the social system. She observes that the body becomes a particularly salient symbolic referent in the context of boundary crises, the physical body mirroring the boundaries of the social body. In this regard, Chang and Eng, conjoined at the chest by a five-inch fleshy mass, signified nature's failure to properly define the boundary between two individuals. In addition, Chang and Eng's marriage to the Yates sisters was a *cause celebre,* as was their fathering of twenty-two children. Both facts occasioned reports in the national newspapers. Indeed, acknowledging the public interest in their progeny, the twins in their tours of the 1850s and 1860s always included several of their children. In Chang and Eng, the Siamese twins who had become Southern slaveholding gentlemen touring with their Eurasian children, East and West had indeed met. As an embodiment of boundary crisis, symbolic of the collapse of racial, class, and sexual order, the Siamese twins were mind-boggling.

Minstrelsy was a powerful vehicle for constructing the Chinaman as a polluting racial Other in the popular imagination.[48] From the 1850s onward, the character of John Chinaman and, to a somewhat lesser extent, Japanese characters were played in yellowface on the minstrel stage. Dozens of songs, comedy skits, and stump speeches (monologues

Charley Fox Minstrel Show cover.

that featured caricatured languages and "dialects," including spurious Chinese, Irish, Dutch, Hebrew, and African American) featured "John Chinaman." So prominent was the Chinese theme in comedy theater and minstrelsy that the famed Buckley Family minstrels (originally the Buckley Ethiopian Melodists) made their home stage in New York at the Chinese Theater.

In 1849, only a year after the discovery of gold at Sutter's mill, minstrel theater arrived in San Francisco, where it met immediate success. By the mid-1850s San Francisco had become a destination for all the major minstrel companies in the country. It was such a center for minstrelsy that E. P. Christie's already famous Christie Minstrels changed their name to Christie's San Francisco Minstrels to add to their luster when traveling around the country.

Unlike the museums, which catered to an emergent middle-class audience, the minstrel show began as an entertainment for the new urban working class. Blackface minstrelsy made a place for itself on the American stage in the 1820s and -30s when production was shifting from workshop to factory and proletarianization of labor was in full swing. These were decades of deep economic and social insecurity for small producers and a new class of wage earners, both in the cities and on the farm. Blackface minstrelsy attended to the class anxieties and animosities of this nascent and stratified working class, unsure of its position and prospects. Alexander Saxton has shown that most of the major minstrel performers had come from artisan or petty bourgeois families in the urban Northeast. Reflecting their own class background as well as an affinity for the class interests of their audience, many of the most prominent minstrel performers—Daniel Emmett, E. P. Christie, Stephen Foster—were all prominent in the Northern wing of the Democratic Party.[49]

In San Francisco, minstrel theater was closely identified with its principal impresario, Thomas McGuire. An Irish immigrant, McGuire had been a saloonkeeper and entertainment promoter in New York, where he had joined a volunteer fire company, at that time a base for urban working-class politics, and was a strong supporter of the Democratic party machine at Tammany Hall. One of McGuire's closest colleagues, Mike Walsh, another Irish American Democratic Party leader, was an outspoken proponent of class radicalism and white supremacy.[50]

For its audience of urban workers who were being shaped into a working class, the minstrel show constructed and displayed a line-up of racial and ethnic characters. Blacks, Jim Crow, and Zip Coon, Indians and John Chinaman were compared and contrasted with European Americans, Tommy the English sailor, Mose the Irish fireman, Siegal the German. Even as these characters interacted on the stage, the minstrel show drew sharp boundaries around racial difference and made clear the unacceptability of racial amalgamation. By distinguishing between funny but acceptable behavior among various white characters and ridiculous and punishable behavior among colored characters, these minstrel shows enacted the bounds of acceptable working-class behavior and resistance. In this regard, minstrelsy can be understood as a ritual response to boundary crisis. As such, minstrelsy was called upon to distinguish a category of anomalous and polluting (hence non-assimilable) racial difference from a category of normal and nonpolluting (and hence amalgamable) ethnic difference.

The power of the minstrel show as a ritual of race-making lay in the ambiguity of laughing with and laughing at Zip Coon, Jim Crow, and John Chinaman. Although in the 1850s blackface minstrelsy would mount a nostalgic defense of slavery in the face of the abolition movement, in its beginning decades of the 1830s and -40s, it made the urban free person of color, in the caricatures of Zip Coon and Jim Crow, its principal object of ridicule. Constructed as a trickster, the citified dandy Zip Coon represented freedom without the self-control needed for republican virtue. The tricks that Zip Coon played on his always pompous oppressors could be appreciated for their spirit of resistance by the "b'hoy boy," the epitome of a newly emergent white working-class urban youth culture whose brash behavior and style in many ways mirrored the dandified, urban, free black. At the same time, the white journeyman turned factory worker might be nostalgic for the sense of freedom from restraint that Jim Crow was depicted as enjoying. While Zip Coon's or Jim Crow's antics could be applauded, their ambitions to move outside the boundaries of their black world had to be sharply thwarted through ridicule.

The ideological effect of the blackface minstrel show lay in its dual message to a nascent working class consolidating its own white racial identity. The minstrel show featured Zip Coon's stump speeches, parodies of political campaign speeches, academic lectures, or sermons, replete with exaggerated elocution and littered with malapropisms to emphasize that, however "free," the African American could only masquerade as a citizen. While the malapropism of the hilarious stump speech warned that the anomalous freedom of persons of color represented a danger to the republic, it served to remind its working-class and immigrant audiences of the utter seriousness and responsibilities of citizenship.

The minstrel representation of the Chinese immigrant as a racial Other relied on a trope of insurmountable cultural difference. Unlike the minstrel characterization of free blacks, who were represented as fraudulent citizens because they were supposed to lack culture, the

Chinese were seen as having an excess of culture. This excess had led them into a state of degradation and cultural degeneration. Excess and degeneration, of course, carried with them connotations of disease, contagion, and pollution. In a culture dominated by virtuous republicanism, which held self-control in highest esteem, excess was also closely identified with moral sloth. Mary Douglas has observed that when external boundaries of the social system are perceived to be threatened, attention is paid to the orifices of the body and the bodily functions of ingestion, digestion, and excretion as symbols of entry and exit into and out of the social system. The minstrel construction of Chinese racial difference around cultural excess focused on three such natural symbolic systems, each closely related to boundary crises: language, food, and hair.[51]

Chinese "pidgin" fascinated white Americans and was widely imitated on the minstrel stage. For fifteen cents, DeWitt Publishers offered *"Bones" His Gags and Stump Speeches: Nigger and Dutch Stories and Dialogues; "Broken Chinee" Dialect Pieces and Queer Conundrums.* The "dimester" booklet was advertised as a must "For the Professional Burnt Cork Man; Every Amateur Dabbler in Darkey Doings; Everybody that Likes Genuine Fun" featuring the "best hits of the Ethiopian Stage."[52]

Canton English was only one of many languages spoken in nineteenth century California. This pidgin English attributed to Chinese speakers in California was in actuality a trade language, with its own linguistic and symbolic codes, syntax and vocabulary rules. The origin of this language dates back to early English-Chinese trade relations in the late seventeenth century; some of its vocabulary had even earlier antecedents in Arab, Portuguese, and Spanish trade relations with China from the fifteenth and sixteenth centuries. For example, Zayton, the Arab name for Yangzhou (an earlier Chinese name for Guangzhou) lends itself to the English name "Canton." "Joss" meaning "god" is derived from the Spanish "dios"; the English term "mandarin" is derived from the Portuguese "mandarim" to rule; the Canton English term "Yankee" is derived from the Dutch "Jan Kees," and so forth.

John Dillard has argued that a variety of pidgins and creoles were in widespread use throughout the nineteenth-century American West, where speakers of Native American languages, French, Spanish, English, American creoles, and Canton English all came into contact.[53] The common use of pidgins and creoles threatened to subvert the hegemony of Anglo-American English-language-based culture and undermine its teleological myth of nationhood.

Minstrelsy's response to such a crisis was to reinforce the hegemonic power of standard English, setting the linguistic standard for participation in citizenship. Comedic skits centered around miscommunication based on ethnic accents, dialects, and creoles. Malapropism and the exaggerated elocution of the "Nigger stump speech or gag" were commonly used to ridicule the ambitions of African Americans for full participation in social or political life. On the minstrel stage, Canton English and nonsense words were often deployed together in the construction of John Chinaman. The collapsing of linguistic difference between pidgin and nonsense dislocated language and collapsed meaning, echoing the collapse of time and space in the secular world of capitalist social relations. The conjoining of pidgin with nonsense simultaneously diminished the status of Canton English as an important commercial language and infantilized its speakers.

This effect is immediately apparent in the song "Hong Kong" as it appeared in Nick Gardner's *Two Ring Circus Songster.* Both the first stanza and the refrain make extensive use of pidgin and pidginized English, and the meaning of the lyric can still be understood.

> My Name is Sin Sin, come from China
> In a bigee large shipee, commee long here;
> Wind blow welly muchee, Kick upee blubelly
> Ship makee Chinaman feelee wellee queer.
> Me fetchee longee a lillee gal nicee
> She com longee to be my wife
> Makee bigee swear to it all her life.
>
> Me likee bow wow, wellee goodee chow-chow,
> Me likee lillee gal, she likee me
> Me fetchee Hong-Kong, whitee man comee long,
> Takee lillee gal from a poor Chinee.[54]

In the same song sung by Charles A. Mason under the simple title "Chinese Song" and published in Charles A. Loder's *Hilarity Songster,* the chorus is heavily inflected with nonsense words, making the meaning of the song itself incomprehensible.

> Ki, Ki, Ki, Ching, Ching, Ching,
> Hung a rung, a chickel neckey
> Suppe, fatte hung
> Eno Posa keno Posey, keno John,
> Chinese manee goode manee from Hong Kong.[55]

In the refrain to "The Heathen Chinee," sung by the famous minstrel performer Luke Schoolcraft, nonsense words combined with pidgin to present the yellowface singer of the song as childlike.

> Hi! hi! hi! Ching! ching! ching!
> Chow, chow, wellie good, me likie him.
> Makie plentie sing song, savie by and bye.
> China man a willie man, laugh hi! hi![56]

Minstrel songs paid great attention to Chinese foodways; indeed it is uncommon not to find some reference to Chinese eating habits in a minstrel song. Food habits, customs, and rules are central symbolic structures through which societies articulate identity; you are, symbolically at least, what you eat. In her study of regionalism in antebellum political culture, Anne Norton argues that eating was the primary metaphor of the West. She writes,

> Eating provides an archetypal expression of the mythic process of regeneration through violence. . . . Prominent features of Western politics—the importance of charismatic authority, the significance of territorial expansion, and the legitimacy of authority obtained through conquest—also become more intelligible in the context of the Western preoccupation with consumption, digestion and elimination.[57]

In her analysis of the construction of Davy Crockett as a mythic hero of the Jacksonian frontier, Carroll Smith-Rosenberg observes that Crockett is credited with killing and eating every sort of wild animal. This includes, in at least one tale of cannibalism, killing two Indians, "smashing number one into Injun gravy with my foot, spreading it on number two and made a dinner for me and my dog. It was superlicious." [58] The eating of taboo food endows Crockett, who could claim to be half-man, half-alligator, with preternatural power: "I'm a horse . . . I can walk like an ox, run like a fox, swim like an eel, yell like an Indian, fight like a devil, and spout like an earthquake, make love like a mad bull, and swallow a nigger whole without choking if you butter his head and pin his ears back." [59]

While the eating of "wild" animals and "wild" people might endow the young frontiersman with savage strength, the Chinese are identified with eating dogs and cats, animals that are domesticated but not raised for food. The consumption of dogs and cats is the most common image of Chinese foodways; typical of these images are these stanzas from Luke Schoolcraft's "Heathen Chinee."

> Lady she am vellie good, make plenty chow chow
> She live way up top side house,
> Take a little pussy cat and a little bow bow
> Boil em in a pot of stew wit a little mouse
> Hi! hi! hi!
>
> Some say pig meat make good chow chow
> Too much largie, no muchie small
> Up sky, down sky, down come chow chow
> Down come a pussy cat, bow bow and all
> Hi! hi! hi! [60]

The Chinese are also identified as eating mice and rats, animals considered filthy and disease-carrying and therefore dangerous and polluting. In the last stanza of Billy Rice's "Chinese Ball," the visitor recounts an imagined Chinese supper.

> For supper we had red-eyed cats
> And boot-legs stuffed with fleas.
> We had fish boiled in castor oil,
> Fried clams and elephant knees,
> We had sauer-kraut and pickled meuse,
> And oysters on the half-shell.
> We had Japanese tea in the key of G,
> Which made us feel quite well.[61]

A third focus of minstrel attention was the braided plait of hair or queue worn by Chinese men. The length and manner in which hair is cut and groomed has been a central marker of gender, age, and class in many cultures. In Judeo-Christian culture, hair has been symbolically identified with sexual power since at least Samson and Delilah. Since the establishment of the Qing dynasty in 1644, Han Chinese men were required to shave their foreheads and wear their hair in a braided plait as a sign of fealty to their Manchu conquerors. Failure to wear the queue was a sign of rebellion and punishable by death. In California, however, the queue presented a cultural anomaly and a source of ambiguity. In an age when middle-class white men had shorn their hair, and among so-called civilized people only women wore their hair long (although Native American men also often wore their hair long and in a braids), the Chinese males' practice of wearing their hair long and in a braid was perceived as sexually and racially ambiguous, and therefore dangerous.

The Chinaman's queue thus became a principal target for the victimization of the Chinese by every bigot, old and young. Bret Harte reported in a letter to the *Springfield Republican* on March 30, 1867,

> Even legislation only tolerated [the Chinese], and while they were busy in developing the resources of the state, taxed them roundly for the gracious privilege. Regularly every year they were driven out of the mining camps, except when the enlightened Caucasian found it more convenient to rob them—a proceeding which the old statutes in regard to the inadmissibility of their evidence in the courts rendered quite safe and honorable. They furnished innocent amusement to the honest miner, when gambling, horse racing or debauchery palled on his civilized taste, and their Chinese tails, particularly when tied together, cut off or pulled out, were more enjoyable than the Arabian nights entertainments. Nature seemed to have furnished them with that peculiar appendage for the benefit of the Anglo-Saxon.[62]

Assaulting the Chinaman and cutting off his queue was by no means an activity limited to the street thug or rowdy. Charles DeLong, who became a prominent lawyer and Democratic Party leader, had also taken Chinese queues as he began his California professional career as a collector of the Foreign Miner's tax. The law imposing this tax, which was largely aimed at driving the Chinese from the mining districts, provided for deputized tax collectors who would be paid a percentage of the revenue they had collected. As a result, Chinese miners would often be taxed two or three times over or simply robbed by freebooting tax collectors. On numerous occasions, tax collectors were reported to have murdered Chinese miners in the course of collecting their taxes. In a nonchalant journal entry dated October 23, 1855, DeLong wrote, "Started with Dick Wade and Bob Moulthrop collecting : supper at Hesse's Crossing went down the river in the night collected all the way had a great time, Chinamen tails cut off." [63]

The cutting of the Chinaman's pigtail allowed white men in the mid- and late nineteenth century to reenact, at least at a symbolic level, an earlier savage eighteenth-century American ritual—scalping.[64] Indeed, the cutting of queues in conjunction with the collection of taxes is reminiscent of the taking of Indian scalps for bounty, a popular practice among English colonists on the old frontier. The taking of "scalps" enabled white workingmen to relive an imagined earlier pre-industrial past. It enabled them to reenact their economic anxiety and social frustration in the symbolic castration and disempowerment of a potentially dangerous pollutant. While the display of cut-off queues was not a common public practice, the similarity between scalp-taking and the taking of the queue is not limited to the level of the symbolic. Hundreds of Chinamen were murdered before, during, or after their queues were removed.

The nemesis of John Chinaman was most likely to be a white man in search of foreign miners' taxes or simple loot. Just as the taking of Indian scalps by their colonial forebears was lost to historical amnesia and laid at the doorstep of the savage red man, the practice of cutting off the Chinaman's queue was an opportunity to bring the specter of the "savage" Indian back into the narrative of race relations. In a narrative that confronts the Chinese immigrant, the Native American is not characterized as an obstacle to European settlement or progress, but rather is welcomed as the tormentor of an equally superfluous presence in the social structure. "Big Long John" by the minstrel songwriter Luke Schoolcraft illustrates this relationship.

> Big Long John was a Chinaman,
> and he lived in the land of the free. . . .

He wore a long tail from the top of his head
Which hung way down to his heels. . . .
He went to San Francisco for Chinee gal to see,
Feeling tired, he laid down to rest,
Beneath the shade of huckleberry tree,
He feeling very warm soon fell asleep,
And he laid his head on a plank,
Along came an Indian with his big tomahawk.
And chopped off a piece of his scalp

Now when he awoke, he felt so bad
That he hollered with all his might,
Put his hand to his head and it made him so sick,
That he died that very night.
He was found the next day a bout 12 midnight
By the captain of a Hong Kong crew;
He wrote to his sweetheart, Chum, Chum, Foo
That he died from loss of his queue.[65]

The queue may have been the most public target of the attack on the Chinaman, but it was not the cause of his victimization. In fact, there was little that the Chinaman did to occasion such an assault on his person, and there was little the Chinese could do to deter such attacks. The presence of the Chinese, as anomalous, ambiguous, and hence representative of a dangerous pollution, was itself sufficient to require punishment. Although physical attacks, robbery, and murder were a frequent occurrence, the mode of punishment most celebrated in the song was the cuckolding of the Chinese.

Typical of this theme is Nick Gardner's song "Hong Kong," wherein John Chinaman laments that he has lost his "lillie gal" to minstrelsy's archetypal white working-class hero, Mose. John Chinaman settles in Chinaman Lane and is a friend of Mose, with whom he sells gin.

Me stopee long me lillee gal nicee
Wellee happee Chinaman, me no care,
Me smokee, smokee, lillie gal talkee,
Chinaman and lillee gal wellee jollee pair.

When John Chinaman goes for a walk he returns to find Mose has seduced his girl.

Me catchee white manee lillee gal talkee
Kiss-kiss lillee gal, give her lots of smack.

In the chorus, John Chinaman's transgression of eating taboo canine flesh is directly tied to losing his "lillee gal" to the whitee man.

Me likee bow wow, wellee goodee chow-chow,
me likee lillee gal, she likee me
Me fetchee Hong-Kong, whitee man comee long,
Takee lillee gal from a poor Chinee.[66]

Although Hinton Rowan Helper launched scurrilous denigrations of Latin Americans, Mexicans, and Negroes who had settled in California ,and particularly vicious attacks on California Indians, he regarded these "lesser" peoples as dying out. Their presence was less threatening to him than the entry of the Chinese into the social body of California. Helper's abolitionist magnum opus, *The Impending Crisis of the South,* is driven by an obsessive fear of "miscegenation" between black and white. His *Land of Gold* is similarly obsessed with the presence of the Chinese as a deterrent to the immigration of respectable white women and thus a barrier to "normal" family development. No direct evidence links Helper's anxiety about Chinese immigration and interracial amalgamation to the fact that the family home in which he grew up was only one county distant from the farms on which Chang and Eng were raising their families. Nevertheless, Hinton Helper was ten years old when the twins settled in nearby Wilkes County, and the widespread attention paid to the marriage and later fatherhood of the twins in both the local and national press is not likely to have escaped Helper's notice. We might well imagine that the young Hinton Helper, in addition to sharing the salacious but almost universal fascination with the imagined sexual practice of the twins and their wives, resented the fact that the Siamese twins were land owners of substance and slaveholders to boot, while Helper's own family found itself in reduced financial circumstances on its small farm as the result of his father's early death.

In *Land of Gold,* Helper finds everything about the Chinese disturbing and objectionable. Their mere appearance and their habit of dress is "uncouth" and offensive.

[John Chinaman's] feet enclosed in rude wooden shoes, his legs bare, his breeches loosely flapping against his knees, his skirtless, long-sleeved, big-bodied pea-jacket, hanging in large folds around his waist, his broad-brimmed chapeau rocking carelessly on his head, and his cue [sic] suspended and gently sweeping about his back! I can compare him to nothing so appropriately as to a tadpole walking upon stilts.[67]

The arrival in California of Chinese women "among [whom] good morals are unknown, [and who] have no regard whatever for chastity or virtue," was no solace to Helper, for whom only the presence of true (white) womanhood could provide the moral nurturing required by a new republic of virtue in California. Indeed, the fashion among Chinese women of wearing trousered suits of cotton or silk caused Helper to become confused about the gender difference between Chinese immigrants. "The only apparent difference is, that they are of smaller stature and have smoother features." [68] Nevertheless, lest his audience become curious about Chinese women as objects of desire, Helper is quick to report that "Chinese women are not generally neat in their outward habit. Those who are from the extreme Northern parts of the Chinese empire, are the ugliest and most rugged featured human beings I ever saw." [69]

For Helper, the "national habits and traits of the Chinese character . . . are strikingly anomalous and distinct from those of all other nations." In Helper's view, the totality of this cultural difference defined the Chinese and positioned them as a dangerous pollutant in the already precarious moral order of gold-rush California. Pollution required containment of the Chinese in a racialized body. Helper describes the Chinese body thus:

> There is a marked identity about their features, person, manners, and costume, so unmistakable that it betrays their nationality in a moment. So stereotyped are even the features and form of this singular people, that we cannot fail in their identity in the rudest cut that pretends to represent them. [70]

Yellowface minstrelsy also contained and displayed the racialized Chinese body. To the extent that the moral ambiguities and anomalies signified by the Chinese body posed a danger of moral contamination, the yellowface minstrel provided the sanctioned space through which to view the unknowable. Writing about actual Chinese Californians, Hinton Helper summarized the yellowface difference: "The similarity of their garb, features, physical proportions and deportment is so great that one Chinaman looks almost exactly like another, but very unlike any body else." [71]

"Yellowskins Get Out!"

Put's song "National Miner," sung to the air of the blackface minstrel song "Massa's in de Cold Cold Ground," painted the hardworking American miner in the California gold fields as a victim of alien interlopers, "Those who had fought at Palo Alto, were driven off by nations they had tanned." Put exaggerated the number of Chinese in the mines to make them equal to the total number of people in the entire state.

> Here we're working like a swarm of bees,
> Scarcely making enough to live,
> And two hundred thousand Chinese
> Are taking home the gold we ought to have. [72]

For Hinton Helper and others, the perceived failure to adopt American costume and foodways and to engage in trade with white Californians was a sign of Chinese arrogance, parasitic nature, and intention to exploit California's resources so that the Chinese could return home wealthy men.

"John Chinaman," a song published in the *California Songster* in 1855, the same year Helper's *Land of Gold* appeared, simply represented the white Californian as disappointed by Chinese aloofness and as victimized by Chinese greed.

> I thought you'd open wide your ports,
> And let our merchants in,
> To barter for their crapes and teas,
> Their wares of wood and tin.
>
> I thought you'd cut your queue off, John,
> And don a Yankee coat.
> And a collar high you'd raise, John,
> Around your dusky throat.
>
> Imagined that the truth, John,
> You'd speak when under oath,
> But I find you'll lie and steal too—
> Yes, John, you're up to both.
>
> I thought of rats and puppies, John,
> You'd eaten your last fill,
> But on such slimy pot-pies,
> John, I'm told you dinner still.
>
> Oh, John, I've been deceived in you
> And all your thieving clan,
> For our gold is all you're after, John,
> To get it as you can.[73]

But in making these complaints, Helper and his ilk by no means conceded that the Chinese showed a superior degree of industriousness or intellect. Failure or refusal to adapt to American customs proved to Helper and his ilk the inherent moral and intellectual weakness of the Chinese.

[The Chinese] have neither the strength of body nor the power of mind to cope with us in the common affairs of life; and as it seems to be a universal law that the stronger shall rule the weaker, it will be required of them, ere long, to do one of two things, namely—either to succumb, to serve us, or to quit the country.[74]

Central to the image of California as God's free soil was the vision of California as a space in which free labor might be created anew. Indeed, the exclusion of racial slavery from California made it possible to imagine the "resurrection" of an exclusively white Mechanic's Republic in which artisan labor might flourish. For many of its white "sons of toil," making California into God's free soil meant not only keeping the state free of slavery but also keeping California free of nonwhites. However, the Californian *Herrenvolk* republic would not be built on the wage labor of a multiracial proletariat but on the artisan labor of free white republicans. Free Labor ideology rested on the Jacksonian conviction that most laborers could achieve ownership of capital and escape permanent "wage slavery," becoming "free" to participate in civic life.[75] Free labor therefore resided only in those who could become eligible for civic participation, white men.

The idea of a white republic, free from both slavery and racial difference, was hardly new in the 1840s. Jefferson had warned that slavery would destroy republicanism, by leading whites to become tyrannical and blacks to become alienated and enraged. Jefferson's view was that whites' "natural" superiority made it impossible for the two races to live side by side in equality and would result in white domination. Comparing the problem of slavery to holding a "wolf by its ears," Jefferson concluded that slavery could only be eradicated in conjunction with a plan to eject Africans, once emancipated, from the republic.[76]

New England—the region in which Free Soil and Free Labor ideology was strongest—was also the arena for the ideology and practice of creating a white republic. Legislation and constitutional interpretation had provided for the gradual emancipation of African slaves in the New England states beginning around 1780. Over the course of the next several decades, New Englanders erased virtually all historical memory of the region's history as a slaveholding society and through disenfranchisement, "warning out," and not infrequent mob violence against black neighborhoods and places where the races intermingled attempted to eliminate Africans' physical presence as well. In the 1820s, many of the abolitionist movement's leading luminaries, including Harriet Beecher Stowe and even William Lloyd Garrison, favored colonization as the answer to the problem that the presence of free people of color presented for the republic. (Only later would Garrison break with the colonizationist position in favor of integration.) During the 1840s and -50s, colonization was widely popular, as evidenced by the burgeoning membership of the American Colonization Society, which sought to relocate freed Blacks to Africa. Ralph Waldo Emerson, a champion of abolition, revealed his expectation of an exclusively white republic when he asserted that "soon the negro will only be seen in museums, like the Dodo." Emerson envisioned a renewed republic free of slavery and of blacks, an extension of New England "from Canada to the Gulf and to the Pacific." [77]

In 1848, even as the gold rush had begun, *The Californian,* one of two papers published in San Francisco at the time, unequivocally stated its Free Soil position against slavery and its commitment to a white California.

> We desire only a white population in California; even the Indians among us, as far as we have seen, are more of a nuisance than a benefit to the country; we would like to get rid of them. . . . In conclusion, we dearly love the Union, but declare our positive preference for an independent condition of California to the establishment of any degree of slavery, or even the importation of free blacks.[78]

The editorialist for the *California Star,* the *Californian*'s Republican counterpart, echoed that opinion:

> Though slavery could not be generally introduced, . . . its recognition would blast the prospects of the country. It would make it disreputable for the white man to labor for his bread, and it would thus drive off to other homes the only class of emigrants California wishes to see; the sober and industrious middle class of society.[79]

The idea of California entering the Union as a land free of slavery was a broadly popular one, not only among Free Soilers outside the territory but among white settlers in California. At its 1849 constitutional convention in preparation for its petition to statehood, the unanimous assembly passed without debate the provision that "Neither slavery, nor involuntary servitude, unless for the punishment of crimes, shall ever be tolerated in this State."

While Free Soil was widely supported, race matters were hotly contested. The same Monterey convention that unanimously ratified the antislavery provision fragmented over the rights of free persons of color to settle in California. McCarver, the representative of Sacramento, a district in which 200 of the fewer than 1,000 African Americans in California resided, proposed to create legislation that would prohibit free black settlement as well as bringing slaves into California in order to free them there.[80]

At the convention, Representative Wozencraft, who had immigrated to California from Louisiana, argued that for democracy to thrive "the low, vicious and depraved" must be excluded.[81] Representative Tefft, a settler from New York, argued that the labor of people of color, "negros, peons of Mexico, or any class of that kind," regardless of its legal status, degraded white labor.[82] Taken together, the arguments of Wozencraft and Tefft laid out the ideology of *Herrenvolk* California as a nostalgic reading of Jeffersonian notions of an egalitarian republic based upon natural law. Wozencraft identified equilibrium as the state of nature in which "happy unity" can be produced by acting in accordance with natural law. The laws of nature dictate a "harmonious whole" in which each member is "on a level with the mass" and "able to perform his appropriate duty." "Incongruities in the structure," slavery and industrial capitalism, have "fettered society elsewhere"; the construction of California is the opportunity to start anew. In order to restore this state of nature, however, as Tefft argued, "negroes, peons of Mexico, or any class of that kind" who might constitute "discordant particles" or the "low, vicious and depraved" must be excluded lest "incongruities in the structure" emerge.

Over two days of debate, the arguments put forward at the convention in favor of the excluding of free persons of color from California can be grouped into five broad positions: the racial inferiority of persons of color made assimilation on the grounds of equality impossible; their exploitation would result in social inequalities: their presence would degrade white labor and discourage "more desirable classes" of immigrants; they constituted a vicious and disorderly element; and, as a result, the expenses of governing and supporting them would increase the tax burden.[83] The McCarver Amendment was narrowly adopted even though it met strong opposition on the political grounds that its adoption into the territory's constitution would alienate Free Soil and Abolitionist members of Congress whose support for California statehood was critical. Although the McCarver Amendment was rescinded soon after legal and political challenges, the status of blacks in Free Soil California remained a politically salient issue through the 1850s.

Although the debate over race in California was first framed in terms of Negro slavery and (white) free labor, and Negro slavery and its abolition dominated national politics, *Herrenvolk* republicanism in California continued to be shaped by immigration. In California, the terms of the racial debate shifted to the "Chinese Problem." By the end of the 1850s, the 4,000 black residents of the state seemed a lesser threat, to the apostles of a white Mechanics' Republic, than the 47,000 Chinese residents of California.

The threat of the Chinese as anomalous free persons of color coincided with a crisis in the gold fields. In the mid-1850s, the production process in the California gold fields began to be transformed by the introduction of capital-intensive hydraulic mining and soon put tremendous pressure on the independent miners, the small producers who stood at the heart of *Herrenvolk* republicanism.[84] On the one hand, *Herrenvolk* republicanism was useless as an ideological weapon with which the workingman could resist the accumulation of capital and technology and the rise of a capitalist class; on the other, its appeal to race offered a powerful rationale for whites who failed as small producers.

Although the Chinese primarily worked tailings (i.e., abandoned claims) in small groups of two or three with simple "long tom" placer frames, the fact that they could survive, even thrive, on a small margins of profit caused resentment among white miners.[85]

The crude ditty "Get Out Yellowskins!," one of the few genuine "folk songs" surviving from the gold rush oral tradition, delivers a straightforward message and an unmistakable threat of violence. Unlike its popular music counterpart, however, it lacks any of the aesthetic pathos through which to construct a nostalgic imaginary of California.

> The Yellow-skins here in these hills
> Now know how it appears
> To have their gold by others stole
> As we have suffered for years.
>
> Get out, Yellowskins, get out!
> Get out, Yellowskins get out!
> We'll do it again if you don't go,
> Get out, Yellow-skins, get out![86]

As early as 1851, well before the end of surface mining, white miners on the Yuba River passed a resolution to prohibit Chinese from mining in the district. In the previous year, the state legislature had required a license fee from all who were not native-born American citizens or who had not acquired citizenship through the Treaty of Guadalupe Hidalgo. While the tax was initially aimed at all foreign miners, in 1853 a second act provided for the translation of the act into Chinese and its widespread publication. Amendments to the act in 1854 and 1855 exempted naturalized citizens and those who had declared their intention to apply for citizenship. The first naturalization act, passed in 1790, had established that only "free white persons" were eligible for naturalization; the assumption that the category of "free white persons" did not include persons from China is suggested by the introduction into the California legislature in 1855 of a bill titled "An Act to Discourage the Immigration to This State of Persons Who Cannot Become Citizens." Few Chinese in the 1850s appear to have challenged that requirement for citizenship.[87]

In 1854, the California Supreme Court threw out the murder conviction of George Hall on the grounds that it depended on the testimony of two Chinese witnesses. The California Civil Practice Act stipulated "that no Indian or Negro shall be allowed to testify as a witness in any action in which a white person is a party." Chief Justice Murray argued that such terms as Negro and Indian were generic in nature, and when broadly construed should include Chinese.[88] Justice Murray concluded, "The same rule that would admit them to testify, would admit them to all the equal rights of citizenship, and we might soon see them at the polls, in the jury box, upon the bench and in our legislative halls." In California, for the next decade and a half, until a year after the passage of the Federal Civil Rights Bill in 1868, a Chinaman had no rights that a white man was bound to respect.

In 1855, Hinton Helper's bitter critique of California as a cesspool of motley races, while more virulent and desperate than others, was well within the logic of a restorationist white republic. Indeed, Hinton Helper's generalized statement of white supremacy, while it brought up to date the racial hierarchies in America, replicated the racial logic of Thomas Jefferson.

> No inferior race of men can exist in these United States without becoming subordinate to the will of the Anglo-Americans, or foregoing many of the necessities and comforts of life. They must either be our equals or our dependents. It is so with the negroes in the South; it is so with the Irish in the North; it was so with the Indians in New England; and it will be so with the Chinese in California. . . . Certain it is, that the greater the diversity of colors and qualities of men, the greater will be the strife and conflict of feeling. One party will gain the ascendancy, and dominate over the other. Our population was already too heterogeneous before the Chinese came; but now another adventitious ingredient has been added; and I should not wonder at all, if the copper of the Pacific yet becomes as great a subject of discord and dissension as the ebony of the Atlantic.[89]

In the 1870s, California's fragmented working class coalesced around the demand to remove the Chinese from the white Mechanics' Republic by barring them from entering the country and by driving them from the workplace. The great majority of those who harangued, sang, marched, and rioted against the Chinese in the 1870s were new to California. While their anti-Chinese movement scapegoated Chinese Californians for immediate economic problems, it could draw on a dense set of symbols already in play in the ideological imagination of the state.

California as God's Free Soil envisioned a restored republic of virtue, free of the "fetters" of both slavery and people of color, whose very presence as natural inferiors would lead to the "degradation" of white labor.

God's Free Soil did not have space for the Chinese, whose presence disrupted the mission into the wilderness. The fact of John Chinaman's arrival from the East, his language, food, dress and labor, his very body polluted the Eden that California represented. The victim of this fall from grace was the white miner, the lost hero seeking to restore his identity as an independent producer.

"The Days of '49," a song published by E. Zimmer in 1876, lamented the late pioneers of the gold rush days. Its narrator, one Tom More, is a "relic of by-gone days" who like the "miner" in "California As It Was and Is," "often grieve[s] and pine[s]/For the days of old, the days of gold, The days of forty nine" Old Tom More mourns the loss of camaraderie of heroic miners, "rough . . . But staunch and brave, and true as steel, like hunters from the west." The death by misadventure of these colorful quintessential "American" figures had left Tom More a lonesome figure. But far worse than the disappearance of the heroic California miner was the arrival of the racial Others. The last stanza mourns the "loss" of the white republic.

> Since that time how things have changed In this land of liberty,
> Darkies didn't vote nor plead in court, Nor rule this country,
> But the Chinese question, the worst of all In those days did not shine,
> For the country was right and the boys all white,
> In the days of '49.[90]

The Coolie and the Making of the White Working Class

Coolie—1. By some considered to be originally Tamil, and
identical with the word kuli 'hire, payment for occasional
menial work "... [a] hireling, labourer, man who does odd
jobs.... A variant of Kuli or Koli, name of a numerous
aboriginal tribe of Gujarat, formerly noted as robbers, but now
settling down as respectable labourers and cultivators....
2. a. The name given by Europeans in India and China to a
native hired labourer or burden-carrier; also used in other
countries where these men are employed as cheap labourers.

The Oxford English Dictionary

n November 1885, *The Wasp,* an illustrated weekly, published
a lithograph titled "The Consequences of Coolieism," bear-
ing a detailed caption.[1] The picture, together with its caption,
densely encapsulates the racialization of proletarian labor
through the creation of the category of coolie labor. Coolie
labor is identified as cheap Chinese labor, while its opposite,
Free Labor, is identified with the white workingman's family.
In the *Wasp*'s view, the problem of "coolieism" is not narrowly economic but extends to every member of the workingman's family. The caption calls for the old animosities between Saxon (English) and Celt (Irish) to be put aside in
favor of the common cause of a "white" struggle in opposition to Chinese labor.

51

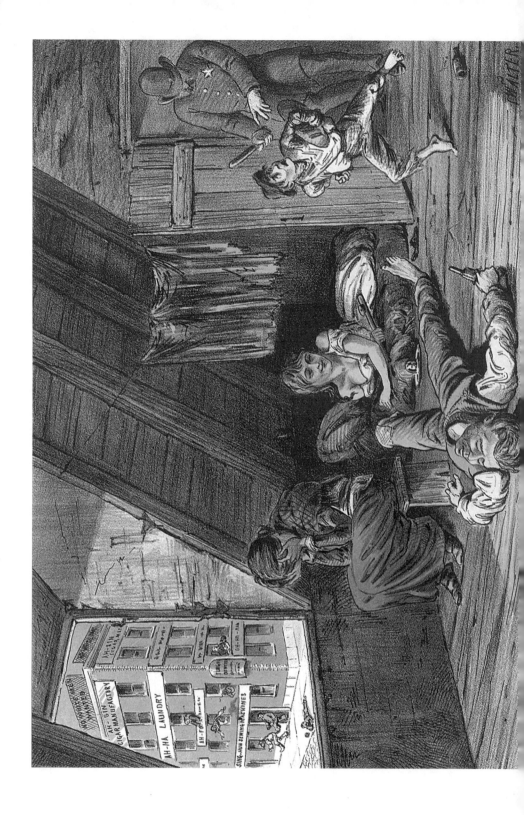

This chapter examines the consequences of the mid-nineteenth-century American idea of coolieism. The racialized construction of a category of proletarianized common labor as "coolie labor" preserved Free Labor as an ideological refuge, if not an economic reality, for the white workingman. The racialized category of coolie labor enabled the working-class movement to articulate its goals not around the issue of proletarianization but around the demand for the restoration of craft privileges and the family wage. It enabled the largely European immigrant working class of the mid-nineteenth century to coalesce as a white working class and articulate its demands as a defense of the white American family.

Herrenvolk Republicanism and the Boundaries of Whiteness

The ethnic stratification of the labor market and the racialization of class struggle resulted from the massive wave of immigration to America between 1840 and 1870, the emancipation of southern slaves in the wake of the Civil War, and the homogenization of industrial labor, which began in earnest in the 1870s. These three socioeconomic processes reconfigured the categories of race and ethnicity in the 1870s and 1880s. Central to this reconfiguration of race was the emergence of a labor movement that defined the American working class in racial as well as economic terms. David Roediger describes white working-class resistance to the abolition of chattel slavery as *Herrenvolk* Republicanism.

> Subordinate groups, notably hirelings, still existed among whites. . . .
> Rather than leveling, there was a simple pushing down on the vulnerable bottom strata of society; even when there was little to be gained, except psychologically, from such a push. Since republicanism encouraged fear of plots between those above and those below against the independent producers, perhaps we should speak of a *Herrenvolk* republicanism, which read

---

"But it is not alone in the field of labor that the evils of the Asiatic interloper are felt. He is the ruin of the household. . . .The wreck of the Workingman's family is graphically depicted. The leering immodest attitude of the daughter of the house shows the damning influence of the opium pipe; the father, driven from employment, despairingly seeks relief in a suicide's death, leaving his widow destitute, famished and despondent; the son, driven to stealing bread for himself and mother, finds himself a felon in the clutches of the law; while nearby a huge manufactory may be seen the cause of all the evil in the fact that Chinese are driving the white men from employment, hurling them from the windows and kicking them out of the doors. Surely such a spectacle must stir the blood in the veins of either Saxon or Celt."
"Consequences of Coolieism" [*The Wasp*, 7 November 1885, p. 16]
(permission of the Beinecke Library, Yale University)

African-Americans out of the ranks of the producers and then proved more able to concentrate its fire downward on to the dependent and Black than upward against the rich and powerful.[2]

The white working class looked quite different in the late 1870s, when the organized anti-Chinese movement was reaching its apex, than the way it looked in the 1850s, when Chinese had begun to immigrate to California in large numbers. The nineteenth-century transition to industrial capitalism, the socioeconomic and cultural changes that were a part of the industrial revolution, can be divided into two overlapping periods. The first, roughly between 1790 and 1850, has been called a period of initial proletarianization, or after Marx and others, "primitive accumulation"; small farmers, artisans, and independent producers of all sorts were brought into an expanding market economy and factory production. "Prices" set by craftsmen gave way to "wages" set by employers.[3]

By the 1860s, however, this initial process of proletarianization had begun to decay as a structure of accumulation that could sustain economic growth.[4] Although the factory system had brought thousands into the productive process as wage workers, master craftsmen still controlled the conditions, patterns, and internal hierarchy within most plants. They continued to exercise traditional prerogatives over hiring assistants, process, and the pace of work. Artisans and independent small producers still represented a large proportion of the economy. Even within the factory sector of the economy, production fluctuated and returns to productive capital investment remained unpredictable. These problems persisted despite the experiments with innovations in both technology and management systems that capitalists had begun in the late 1840s.[5]

By the 1870s, capitalists were attempting to rationalize and reduce the cost of production, ushering a second phase of accumulation. The long-term decline in economic activity brought about by the erosion of the first phase and the secular decline of the business cycle produced the devastating depression of 1873. As it deepened and extended into the crisis of the 1870s and 1880s, "virtually all manufacturers were forced to explore new efficiencies";[6] their strategies to the introduce mechanization and reduce skilled work were aimed at cutting costs and increasing controls on production.

Gordon, Edwards, and Reich have described the erosion of internal hierarchies based on the widely differing levels of skill and the traditions of craft production during these decades as the "homogenization" of labor. They point out that by the beginning of the twentieth century, industrial production would take place in ever larger, impersonal factories under the direction of professional managers and the supervision of foremen whose loyalty was to management.[7] During this period of exploration for new efficiencies, manufacturers introduced new technologies and labor drive systems, such as internal contracting and, most significantly, drew on new sources of factory labor—women, children, and immigrants.

Immigrant labor was introduced along with new machines and new systems of supervision into factory production. Indeed, mechanization, reducing the need for skilled work, often opened shop doors to immigrant workers with a minimum of training or apprenticeship. In the 1850s, the use of immigrant labor in American industry soared, representing fully half of all factory workers in the country. Their distribution was uneven. Particular ethnic groups tended to coalesce in certain industries, as a result of both discriminatory hiring practices and the traditional skill mixes and settlement patterns of these groups. For example, native born Anglo-Saxon men maintained their privileged position in such industries as iron-molding, furniture making, and mule spinning (i.e., ropemaking), where craft guilds still dominated, while in the textile and clothing factories, for example, immigrant women and children replaced native-born women. In shoemaking, immigrant men, particularly Irish and French-Canadian Catholics, entered the shoe factories of western Massachusetts, displacing Yankee Protestant women. Occupations were also divided along gender lines.

As mechanization threatened to reduce factory work to the lowest common denominator of unskilled labor and craft guilds resisted by striking, manufacturers turned to immigrants as a reserve army of labor. The use of Irish and Italian as well as Chinese immigrants as strikebreakers became commonplace in the 1870s. In the Buckingham Boot Company strike in San Francisco in 1869, the Sampson Shoe Company strike in North Adams, Mass., in 1870, and the Passaic, N.J., laundry strike of 1875—three widely publicized labor disputes in which Chinese immigrants were used as strikebreakers—the initial labor disputes came about with the introduction of new mechanization and the resultant "deskilling" of production.

In both San Francisco and North Adams, the shoemakers' trade guild, the Order of Saint Crispin, organized resistance to the introduction of the MacKay stitching machine. By attaching the shoe's upper to its sole, heretofore a craft skill, the MacKay stitcher made possible hugely expanded production. More important for the Crispins, the machine promised to replace the highly paid and privileged master craftsmen of the soling rooms, the craftsmen who controlled the pace of production. The very ability to train workers quickly to operate the Mackay stitcher, even recruits as foreign to the ancient craft of shoemaking as the Chinese appeared to be, gave capitalists a threat far more powerful than simply using the Chinese as replacements.

The transformation of labor between 1850, when *Herrenvolk* republicanism first shaped a white workingman's ideology around a nostalgic vision of a white republic, and the 1870s, when mechanization and immigration were in full bloom, shaped quite different attitudes among those who found themselves in the working class. In the 1850s, the principally American-born migrants who fled the Eastern seaboard to California in the face of proletarianization sought desperately to reconstruct a pre-capitalist social order on the Free Labor of small producers. By 1870 such a vision was problematic. As factory production boomed and the internal structure of the industrial workplace became progressively less stratified, the small-producer ethic, which was the basis of Free Labor ideology, was stretched to its ideological limits. Even as ever more skilled workers became machine tenders working in ever larger factories, Free Labor maintained a craft consciousness based on a nostalgic reconstruction of the pre-capitalist workplace and home. In the face of the homogenization of industrial labor, this new working class sought to preserve or reconstruct the privileges and prerogatives of skilled craftwork and to establish the right to a white "family wage," which might provide a means to escape permanent proletarian status. However, as Roediger has pointed out, a commitment to the nostalgic vision of *Herrenvolk* republicanism limited the capacity of the working-class movement to incorporate the demands of its most proletarianized workers.[8] *Herrenvolk* republicanism defined the working-class movement in terms of its craft elite and simultaneously addressed the desire of European immigrant workers (who by 1870 made up a majority of industrial labor) to be included as part of an ethnically diverse working class racially defined as white.

The Racialization of Common Labor

The most proletarianized of workers, common laborers had long earned a daily subsistence wage by selling their brute strength—digging, lifting, and hauling. Labor historian David Montgomery observes that the physical nature of common labor has remained much the same over the centuries.

> The men who wielded shovels and pushed wheelbarrows on twentieth-century construction projects bore an uncanny resemblance to those who had dug canals and erected fortifications two hundred years earlier. Their work gangs were totally male, as those not constituted of slaves or serfs had long been in western Europe and North America. They had shoveled be-

tween sixteen and nineteen tons per day when they were studied by Sebastienne Vauban in seventeenth-century France, by early Victorian contractors of English navies, and by Frederick Winslow Taylor at the dawn of the twentieth century. They exchanged simple physical force for a daily wage, whose level changed only gradually over the course of the nineteenth century.[9]

Although the nature and pace of common labor remained remarkably consistent over time, the place of origin of day laborers changed dramatically over the course of the nineteenth century. Gangs of Irish, Chinese, and other immigrant men had built the great infrastructure of the American industrial revolution: its dams, canals, and of course railroads. Montgomery notes that far from a throwback to earlier stages of development, common laborers were employed in the most advanced sectors of the economy, "their largest employers included the most highly capitalized industries: railroads, steel, chemicals, mining and metal fabricating."[10]

Laborers' wages rose more rapidly than manufacturing wages during the late 1850s and the inflationary boom of the 1860s. Railroads in mid-century always struggled to attract sufficient numbers of track layers at prevailing wages for unskilled labor. Although wages even for common laborers in the United States attracted immigrants from Europe and Asia, the gap between common labor and manufacturing or other kinds of wage labor widened both in economic and cultural terms.

The cultural and moral status of common labor has long been problematic. Common labor has often been a morally suspect category. Common day laborers, often unmarried, migratory, and poor, were traditionally viewed as a dangerous class. Furthermore, as the wage gap between common labor, particularly sweated or heavy labor, and other forms of work widened, menial and heavy tasks became identified with racially subordinated peoples. Such heavy work at subsistence wage was deemed suitable for freed blacks and Chinese or morally degraded "white trash." In some construction projects in the South, such as the Augusta Canal in Georgia, Irish and Chinese immigrant day laborers were employed as a cheaper and more expendable work force than enslaved Africans, whose skilled labor could bring in greater returns in cotton production. In such cases, white common laborers were sometimes called "white niggers" and the work "white slavery."[11] In the post–Civil War decades, the problematic pre-abolition metaphors of "white slavery" and "wage slavery" gave way to "Nigger work" and "coolie work."

The moral and racial status of common labor was underscored by its economic status at the lowest end of the labor market. After 1870, all wages dropped sharply, especially during the depression of 1873–78.

The gap between the average wage in manufacturing and the laborer's wage widened appreciably after the depression of the 1870s. Although wages in the manufacturing sector climbed again in the 1880s, the wages of unskilled workers never regained their 1870 levels before for the end of the century.

The Workingman vs. the Proletarian

The entry of Chinese workers into the labor market provided white workers the opportunity to explicitly identify the categories of wage slavery and Free Labor in racial terms. There is little to support the common nineteenth-century claim that the Chinese arrived in the United States as "unfree" labor, similar to the thousands of Chinese who were transported as contract labor to Cuba and Peru or the chattel enslavement of Africans in the South. The Chinese who immigrated to the United States as laborers arrived, in fact, as free labor in both the legal and the economic sense. However, once here, Chinese workers became intensely proletarianized and racially excluded "coolies." The designation of hireling labor as "coolie labor," like its analog "nigger work," racialized the meaning of common labor.

In 1856, Elihu Burritt, widely celebrated as the "Learned Blacksmith," published a pamphlet in which he commented extensively on a plan being discussed among Southern slaveholders to replace their African slaves with Chinese wage labor. Burritt, a self-taught ironmonger, who became prominent as a humanitarian reformer and antislavery advocate, was the epitome of the self-educated and morally upright model republican workingman, the pinnacle of Free Labor.[12]

Aware of the steady stream of Chinese to the Americas, both to the United States as proletarian labor and to the West Indies as indentured labor, Burritt recognized that as replacements for enslaved Africans, the Chinese would be wage workers. In fact, it was precisely their proletarianized status as "free" labor that, the planters and Burritt agreed, offered profitability to the plantation owners. Burritt wrote:

> Doubtless all the Southern planters, who have considered this suggestion have concluded that these Chinese laborers must not be literally bought and sold and flogged as slaves; that they must be paid after a certain rate for their toil; that they be allowed a considerable scope and verge of liberty.
>
> What earthly advantage could accrue to the Southern States from the change of races on their soil? . . . There surely can be but one advantage anticipated from such a substitution, and that must be predicated on the positive admission that Chinese labor would be more profitable, because it would be comparatively *free,* that, among other conditions, it would all

be hired labor, and hired of those alone whose own sinews were to perform the work. That consequently all the capital invested in the labor bestowed on one years crop would be the wages of the men employed to plant and gather it.[13]

Although Chinese labor might be free in its proletarianized sense (i.e., free to sell one's labor), Chinese labor was not Free Labor in the republican sense, because it had been decided that the Chinese were not capable of transcending their status as wage labor to become independent producers (notwithstanding the widespread existence of Chinese laundry operators, shopkeepers, masons, carpenters, tailors, etc.), and therefore participants in civic life. Such a status was reserved for free white men. Burritt saw both Africans and Asians as naturally suited for sweated labor and heavy work. He writes:

> Now, then, why not at once put them [African Americans] at least in the very condition in which it is proposed by some Southern economists to introduce the Chinese? On what possible ground can you apprehend that it would be unsafe to give the men and women born on your plantations that degree of freedom which you would accord to those idolatrous foreigners from Asia? Would you prefer Chinese labor because it would be free and easily obtained on hire? Then free the human sinews that you have bought, and which you hold as property, an you will have the best, most natural, faithful and trusty laborers the world can yield you.
>
> If the Southern planters and farmers had the range of all races and populations of the globe, they would not find one more suited to their sun and soil than the three millions of African blood who now cultivate their fields, and serve them in every capacity of industry. The raw material of their labor is the best the world can furnish them. It is the *natural, native, acclimated* labor of the South, fitted to bear the heat and burden of Southern sun and agriculture; to live and thrive where white men would droop and die. Search the earth over and you will not find for the South labor more docile, or laborers, male and female, more capable of endurance, or more susceptible of warm and faithful attachment to their employers. Then why change them for an equal number of copper-colored pagans from China?[14] [Emphasis added.]

Such sweated labor, had it been performed by whites, would have been called white slavery. Indeed, although he ignores the implication, Burritt waxes enthusiastic on the suitability of Africans to be transformed from chattel slaves into wage slaves in the South.

The Chinese worker in the United States was not more completely proletarianized than his European counterpart because of secret contracts or special indebtedness, as many enemies of Chinese immigration charged. Many immigrants from Europe traveled to America on similar systems of credit. The chief vulnerability of the Chinese immigrant was that he or she enjoyed few protections of American law. As the Supreme Court of California had done in *The People v. George Hall* in 1854, a similar decision in *People v. Brady* removed the Chinese from the protection of law in California until 1873, when the California legislature repealed all laws prohibiting Chinese from testifying in court. Before 1870, naturalization practices differed widely from state to state, so that California could rigidly refuse naturalization to Chinese residents while Massachusetts routinely granted citizenship to Chinese from the 1850s onward. In amending the Naturalization Act with the Page Act in 1870, however, the U.S. Congress explicitedly welcomed persons of African nativity or descent to naturalized citizenship but closed the door to "persons born in the Chinese empire." [15]

Furthermore, both custom and economics dictated that only the relatively prosperous could bring wives from China to settle in the United States. After the Page Act, a series of laws made the immigration of Chinese women virtually impossible, rendering Chinese marriage and family formation in the United States extremely difficult. Because the great majority of Chinese men who immigrated as workers arrived without families and had few opportunities to marry in the United States (many were married prior to their immigration or on trips to their familiar villages), they had little access to the advantages a family in this country might offer: pooling work and savings, or buffering against the worst exploitative and demoralizing effects of proletarianization.

Even while Free Labor ideology had held that wage work was a temporary station on the way to independent small producer status, the homogenization of labor in the 1870s made permanent proletarianization a reality for thousands. The ethnic segregation of occupations brought about by immigration and the end of chattel slavery supplied a set of new racial meanings to the idea of proletarianized work. The usefully ambiguous metaphor of white or wage slavery could no longer be sustained in the absence of black chattel slavery. White workers could no longer take up the anti-abolitionist banner in defense of white privilege. Slave status was no longer available as a morally justified rationale for the exclusion of African Americans from the industrial labor force. Exclusion of blacks from ranks of industrial labor could only be done on the grounds of brute racial difference.

The designation of Chinese proletarianized labor as coolie labor enabled the ideologists of Free Labor to evade the question of wage slavery, *née* white slavery. The myth of the Chinese coolie laborer allowed white American workers, both native-born and immigrant, to racialize a stratum of wage work equated with wage slavery while reserving for whites a semi-artisan status within the wage labor system. Free Labor ideology held out the hope that proletarianization, the descent into wage labor, might only be a temporary result of hard times. Proletarian status was only permanent for Others defined as racially degraded and unfit for Free Labor. Separated by boundaries of race from black chattel slavery (later nigger work) and Chinese proletariat labor (coolie labor), the white workingman of the 1850s and -60s was assured by the ideology of Free Labor that his downward mobility might be only temporary and that the permanent racial status of whiteness might provide a new center for an imagined organic community.

The anxiety brought about by the absence of slavery as a racially defined category of labor only heightened when cultural differences of language, religion, and folkways exploded on the factory floor or in city life. Although differences attributed to national origin had not yet collapsed into the term "ethnicity," at this moment they were accorded a different status from race, and the distinction between culture and "race" became critically important. In the post-emancipation reconfiguration of an industrial working class, white workers responded by invoking whiteness as a broadly inclusive racial category, able to encompass broad cultural or "ethnic" differences.

Constructing The Coolie

By the 1870s in California and elsewhere, Chinese workers frequently replaced another group of laborers whose cultural and racial status was itself ambiguous and fluid—the Irish. Throughout the second half of the nineteenth century, the Irish and the Chinese maintained an antagonistic relationship. Chinese immigrant workers were often cited by commentators on the state of labor relations as superior replacements for Irish workers, who were seen as undisciplined, ill-tempered, and recalcitrant. In turn, Irish labor leaders were among the most prominent in the anti-Chinese movement. In California especially, trade union leaders, Democratic politicians, and California Workingman's Party demagogues vied in forging a working-class consciousness around a rhetoric of anti-monopoly and white supremacy.

In March of 1876, hoping to influence the California state constitutional convention, *The Marin Journal* printed the following broadside in the form of a resolve against the Chinese residents of California. The broadside summed up several charges that had been leveled against the Chinese presence in California "on behalf of the workingmen of the state and their families."

That he is a slave, reduced to the lowest terms of beggarly economy, and is no fit competitor for an American freeman.

That he herds in scores, in small dens, where a white man and wife could hardly breathe, and has none of the wants of a civilized white man.

That he has neither wife nor child, nor expects to have any.

That his sister is a prostitute from instinct, religion, education, and interest, and degrading to all around her.

That American men, women and children cannot be what free people should be, and compete with such degraded creatures in the labor market.

That wherever they are numerous, as in San Francisco, by a secret machinery of their own, they defy the law, keep up the manners and customs of China, and utterly disregard all the laws of health, decency and morality.

That they are driving the white population from the state, reducing laboring men to despair, laboring women to prostitution, and boys and girls to hoodlums and convicts.

That the health, wealth, prosperity and happiness of our State demand their expulsion from our shores.[16]

In the course of the 1876 the state's numerous anti-coolie clubs had united in the Anti-Chinese Union, whose members had pledged not to employ Chinese, not to purchase goods from those who did, and not to sustain Chinese or the employers of Chinese. By the following year, the Anti-Chinese Union would be overshadowed by the more radical Workingman's Party of California. This group, under the leadership of Denis Kearney, a charismatic but unprincipled Irish American politician, rallied a white working class around anti-Chinese and anti-monopoly banners.[17] In that year, the song "Twelve Hundred More" was one of scores written and sung that excoriated the Chinese in California. Its lyrics repeat the charges against the Chinese that had been published in the *Marin Journal* and that were being repeated in sandlots all over California.

> O workingmen dear, and did you hear
> The news that's goin' round?
> Another China Steamer
> Has landed here in town.
> Today I read the papers
> And it grieved my heart full sore
> To see upon that title page
> O Just "Twelve Hundred More!"
>
> O, California's coming down,
> As you can plainly see:
> They are hiring all the Chinamen
> And discharging you and me;
> But strife will be in every town

Throughout the Pacific Shore
And the cry of old and young shall be,
"O, damn 'Twelve Hundred More!'"

They run their steamer in at night
Upon our lovely bay,
If 'twas free and honest trade,
They'd land it in the day.
They come here by the hundreds—
The country is overrun.
And go to work at any price—
By them the labor's done.

If you took a workman in the street
And look him in the face,
You'll see signs of sorrow there—
O damn this long tailed race
And men today are languishing
Upon a prison floor,
Because they've been supplanted by
This vile "Twelve Hundred More."

Twelve hundred honest laboring men
Thrown out of work today
By the land of the Chinamen
In San Francisco Bay
Twelve hundred pure and virtuous girls
In the papers I have read,
Must barter way their virtue
To get a crust of bread.

This state of things can never last
In this, our golden land
For soon you'll hear the avenging cry,
"Drive out the Chinaman!"
And then we'll have the stirring times
We had in days of yore,
And the devil take those dirty words,
They call "Twelve Hundred More!" [18]

It is notable that "Twelve Hundred More" is sung to the tune of "O Mother Dear," an Irish nationalist song whose lyrics begin,

Oh Mother Dear and did you hear
The news that's goin' round.
The Shamrock is forbid by law
To grow on Irish ground. [19]

Transformed from a popular Irish nationalist tune into an anti-Chinese song, "Twelve Hundred More" links Irish nationalism to the construction of a racially exclusive white American nationalism. Its assertion that the arrival of Chinese will put men out of work and throw innocent girls into prostitution prefigures by almost a decade the racial claims in *The Wasp*'s "The Consequences of Cooliesm" and the Rock Springs massacre, a peak in anti-Chinese violence.

Chinese coal miners, brought by the Union Pacific Railroad to Rock Springs, Wyo., in the early 1870s shortly after the completion of the transcontinental railroad, had been working in the area for a decade before the arrival of white miners, many of whom were recently arrived Cornish and Welsh immigrants and members of the militantly anti-Chinese Knights of Labor.[20] While there may well have been tension between the 200 whites and 600 Chinese miners, the two groups had worked in the same mines for several years without major incident until a dispute over which group had the right to work a rich "room" in the mine. On the afternoon and early evening of June 4, 1885, an armed mob of 200 white miners attacked the Chinese section of Rock Springs, setting fire to houses and shooting down the Chinese miners as they fled from the burning neighborhood.[21] By evening, twenty-nine Chinese miners lay dead, fifteen were wounded, and all of the 600 Chinese residents of Rock Springs had been driven from their homes, most of which had been put to the torch. Once order was restored by federal troops, a trial acquitted all the whites accused of murder on the grounds that no individual killers could be identified.

The Rock Springs Massacre occurred three years after the Chinese Exclusion Act, which barred all but a handful of Chinese teachers, clergy, and merchants from entering the country. Rock Springs was the most notorious of many acts of violence against Chinese immigrants in the decades of the 1870s and 1880s, but hundreds of Chinese were driven from their homes in small towns and cities up and down the West Coast, and an untold number were murdered.[22]

"Eight Hours a Day Good for White, All the Same Good for Chinamen!"

On June 24, 1867, more than 8,000 Chinese railroad builders on Central Pacific's roadbed in the high Sierras walked off their jobs. Their slogan was "Eight hours a day good for white, all the same good for Chinamen!"

Charles Crocker, the managing director of the railroad, later wrote that, to a man, all 8,000 Chinese "staid in their camps; that is they would walk around, but not a word was said, nothing was done; no violence was perpetrated along the whole line." [23] The Chinese workers demanded pay and working conditions equal to those of their white co-workers, a wage of $40 to $45 a month, and an eight-hour workday. The strike collapsed after a week, after Crocker cut off food to the Chinese camps and took "other such coercive measures." [24] While the strike itself failed to win the full equal treatment that the Chinese workers sought, it prompted the Central Pacific to increase their pay from $30 to $35 a month without board (it paid its white laborers $35 dollars a month, with board that was worth between 70¢ and $1 a day).

Despite the powerful and sustained efforts of Chinese to establish solidarity with white workers, the white workers remained convinced that the Chinese must be expelled because they were a naturally subservient people who could neither participate with white workers in any sort of common working-class consciousness nor be organized effectively into a common resistance movement.

Although major newspapers on both coasts reported the massive strike, unprecedented in its size in the United States, neither the leadership of the growing American labor movement nor its rank and file showed any interest in it whatsoever. The labor movement, dominated by skilled crafts guilds, still hewed closely to the argument that Chinese common laborers (in this case mainly ex-miners who had been driven off their claims in the earlier years of the decade before being recruited to the backbreaking work of carving a railroad through the Sierras) were incapable of organizing as workingmen. A decade later, the great 1867 strike on the Central Pacific had been forgotten or ignored by the racist labor agitation of the anti-Chinese clubs and the California Workingman's Party.

The 1867 strike was by no means an isolated episode of Chinese (or other Asian) labor acting on its own behalf in nineteenth-century America. In 1870, some 250 Chinese workers who had been recruited to work on the Houston and Texas Central Railroad filed suit against the railroad for breach of contract when the railroad failed to live up to its promises. Hundreds of Chinese who had been brought in to build the Alabama and Chattanooga Railroad were among the workers who seized the company's cars and equipment when that company went bankrupt in an attempt to enforce their demands for back wages. Between 1869 and 1871, some 600 Chinese had been recruited to work on sugar and cotton plantations in Arkansas, Louisiana, and Mississippi. Chinese plantation labor disappointed the plantation owners who were used to, and had been led to expect, a compliant labor force. Chinese plantation crews demanded strict adherence to their contracts and would not yield to arbitrary work rules. Mistreatment of Chinese workers by overseers was often met by mass protest, work stoppages and, on occasion, violence. Few Chinese renewed their contracts, and Chinese work in the post–Civil War plantation economy was short-lived.[25]

In 1870, Calvin Sampson brought a crew of seventy-five Chinese workers to North Adams, Mass., to replace striking Irish and French-Canadian workers in the soling room of his shoe factory. This use of Chinese as strikebreakers in the highly industrialized Northeast gave the "Chinese question" national notoriety. Yet even here, Chinese workers were not the ideal, docile labor force the employers had hoped for. Initially, Northern manufacturers saw the introduction of Chinese labor as an ideal strategy by which to undermine the growing strength of the Order of St. Crispins. However, the North Adams experiment only partially succeeded. Although the introduction of Chinese workers did result in breaking the Crispins' strike at Sampson's shoe factory, the Chinese workers proved less than submissive. In 1873, as the contracts of his first group of Chinese workers were running out, Sampson brought a second crew of Chinese workers to North Adams. Within a few months, forty-three of them were summarily dismissed after rioting and attempting to murder their Chinese foreman, who had tried to hold their pay in escrow. The foreman escaped with his life, but Sampson was forced to pay his workers directly.[26] In the same year, Chinese workers were also brought to Belleville, N.J., to replace striking female Irish workers in the Passaic Steam Laundry plant. Within a year, however, the frustrated owner reported that the Chinese workers were themselves engaging in strikes and that many had left the plant. By 1885, all the Chinese workers at the Passaic Steam Laundry had been dismissed.[27]

A strike by a "large force" of Chinese hop pickers in Kern County, Calif., in 1884 was described in a report to the new national organization, the Knights of Labor, as "militant" and a positive indication that the Chinese could be successfully organized.[28] Three years later, Chinese assemblies of the Knights of Labor were organized in New York by District 49. These assemblies were disbanded on the order of Terrence Powderly, the national leader of the Knights. Powderly had gone on record as not only opposing Chinese labor but also declaring that Chinese and Japanese were unfit to reside in the United States. Powderley would later become the scourge of Chinese immigrants as the first U.S. Commissioner of Immigration.[29] Despite the powerful and sustained efforts of Chinese to establish solidarity with white workers, the white workers remained convinced that the Chinese must be expelled because they were a naturally subservient people who could neither participate with white workers in any sort of common working-class consciousness nor be organized effectively into a common resistance movement. The accusations that the Chinese were a degraded and servile labor force, incapable of class consciousness or unwilling to organize as workingmen, camouflaged the racial ideology of the labor movement.

John Chinaman and Paddy

More than other groups, Irish workers perceived themselves directly threatened by the Chinese in California of the 1870s. Driven out of mining, railroad building, and agriculture, Chinese in California often displaced Irish immigrant workers in manufacturing, laundering, and domestic occupations. As Chinese entered the manufacturing labor market, employers directly and often favorably compared them to Irish immigrant workers. To some extent they could be viewed as a nineteenth-century "model minority," and Irish resentment of the Chinese is understandable. As a people whose own racial identity remained in flux in their transition from British colonialism to American republicanism, the Irish resisted any popular form of association or conflation with Chinese identity. Much as working-class Irish immigrants on the east coast had agitated against the abolition of black slavery and had labored hard to draw a clear color line between the Irish working class and free African Americans in the 1850s and -60s, so Irish immigrant labor politicians led the anti-Chinese movement as a crusade for a white working class.

Prior to 1840, more than a million and a half Irish immigrants had arrived in the United States and gained a tenuous foothold in workplaces. They were by no means welcomed by longer-established groups of workers. The widespread employment of Irish immigrant workers in Northern factories displaced American-born women and children. The acceptance of earlier groups of immigrants to America had assumed that they would be "amalgamated" into American Protestant culture, but the Irish brought Roman Catholicism into Protestant communities. After 1848, many regarded the massive immigration of deeply impoverished Irish fleeing the starvation of the Great Famine as a Roman Catholic challenge to an American republicanism deeply grounded in Protestantism. By the 1850s, the secretive American Party, popularly known as the Know-Nothings, led a political movement to counteract what many old stock Protestants saw as Roman Catholic subversion of Protestant republican values and institutions (for example by establishing Catholic schools). Expressing the fear that the large blocs of immigrant votes would be mobilized to support Mother Church as dictated by the Pope rather than by republican ideals, the nativists called for restricted Irish immigration and more stringent voting requirements. In addition to religion, nativists also criticized the unruly behavior of the "wild Irish"—a reputedly hard-drinking and fighting people—and rampant political corruption among Irish in U.S cities. Thus the nativist position charged the Irish with both excessive moral allegience to the Church and insufficient moral control over their behavior, showing the logical inconsistency of ethnocentric and racist arguments.

In the popular press, many a political cartoonist portrayed the stereotyped Irish Mike or Paddy as ape-like, with hideous low brow and jutting lower jaw. Such simian images of the Irish immigrant were as commonplace as similar subhuman images of the Chinese and the African American, and challenged the racial status of the Irish as white. They followed the style of British caricaturists, who adhered to the Darwinist position of Anglo-Saxon racial superiority over the Celt, but while this evolutionist argument was powerful in Britain, it had limited appeal in the United States.[30] Radical Republican critics of the "Celtic Race," such as Thomas Nast (in his early period), despite the savagery of many of their drawings, were constrained by their sympathy for abolition and for Chinese immigrants to limit their criticism of the Irish to an attack on popery, drunkenness, and political corruption, and avoided picturing the Irish as subhuman.

So intense was the bias against the Irish in the Northeast that when Chinese were brought to North Adams, the local newspapers, echoing the attitudes of the Protestant elite, directly compared the two immigrant groups, often favoring the Chinese. In 1868 *The Berkshire Eagle* asked, "Will Massachusetts have to become Chinese, to avoid becoming Hibernian?"[31]

Bret Harte reported from San Francisco to the *Springfield [Mass.] Republican* on the 1867 attacks by whites on the Chinese in that city. Though he did not put all the blame the Irish for the violence against the Chinese, Harte, a supporter of Chinese rights, made the invidious comparison of the two groups as economic rivals.

> This supercilious ignoring of [Chinese] rights by the Americans and better class of European residents, encouraged and fostered the blind hatred and active malice of our Celtic citizens, who from the first regarded them with a jealousy and malevolence equal only to their intolerance of the Negro. Convinced from the beginning of the superiority of freckles, red hair, and a brickdusty epidermis, over the smooth, shining India ink washed faces of their Chinese rivals, they at once put the Mongolians on the level of the African and abused them on theological grounds.
>
> There is no doubt that the Chinese are gradually deposing the Irish from their old, recognized positions in the ranks of labor. The Chinese not

only fill their places, they fill them more acceptably . As servants they are quick-witted, patient, obedient, and faithful, the old prerogatives of Bridget and Norah in the domestic circle are seriously threatened by the advent of these quiet, clean and orderly male chambermaids and cooks.[32]

With such reports as Harte's on the qualities of the Chinese as workers and the successful use of Chinese in the Buckingham shoe strike in San Francisco (where Chinese were used as replacements in conjunction with the introduction of the MacKay stitcher), it should not be surprising to find *Hide and Leather,* a publication of the shoe manufacturers' association, enthusiastic about the potential of the Chinese.

It is a pretty thing for the American workingmen who boast of their freedom! Of their country, and a large number of whom are themselves, like the Chinese emigrants, from other lands to stop the tide of emigration. . . . We should like to know where the Irish Crispins would have found themselves if they had not this country to come to. . . . We should like to know where this country would have been if the first Congress had prevented immigration?[33]

When seventy Chinese arrived in North Adams the next year to replace striking Irish and French Canadian Crispins at Calvin Sampson's factory, the *North Adams Transcript* reported that "they looked neat, smart and intelligent and had a merry twinkle with their eyes." The Chinese, the paper reported, "Marched from the cars two by two, perfectly peaceable and cleanly in appearance, and in a delightful contrast in these parts to the Celtic population who vociferously abused Mr. Sampson." [34]

In 1875, when seventy-five new Chinese workers were brought to North Adams to replace workers whose contracts had run their course, the *Berkshire Eagle* editorialized:

What are the objections to the Asiatics coming among us as laborers in any field? It can't be color, for they are as white as many of the Germans that come over, more so that the French and Spanish, and less swarthy than a majority of Southern brethren. . . . It should not be the "odor" for they come from the land of flowers and spices and can't emit worse perfume than the emigrants from the Isle of Erin or many of the citizens of this model republic. The only tangible objections are that they may usurp places of labor of the existing working classes, and that they are heathens. We think the last objection is disposed of in the hint above thrown out, that the very object Christendom aims at—the conversion of the heathen—is much more likely to be obtained by their coming into Christian communities than by sending to them. But the fact is, this outcry doesn't come from the Americans, so much as from the natives of other countries, who having got a fast hold are now clamorous to keep other people out, who are just as much entitled to the inning as they.[35]

If the Chinese came off better than the Irish in these comparisons, why did they not flourish? How did the Irish find a place in American society while the Chinese did not?

Patsy's Whiteness

In order to find a place within the category of the people defined in *Herrenvolk* republican terms as a white working class, the Irish simultaneously had to escape the status of the permanent proletariat and, in the face of considerable social discrimination, to consolidate their racial status as white.

Unlike the Chinese—who were effectively disenfranchised, prohibited from testifying against whites in California courts, prohibited from naturalization, and finally excluded from immigration—the Irish had the status of "free white persons." Regardless of the ethnic or cultural opprobrium they encountered, they were eligible for naturalization and enjoyed access to the legal and political systems. Their concentration in large numbers in urban centers and their eligibility to vote as naturalized citizens gave the Irish an almost immediate foothold in American politics at the local level. Irish ethnic political organization stretched from the union local and the volunteer fire company through city hall, and ran deeply through the Democratic party and the union movement.

Irish political leaders were thus well situated to mobilize working-class support for the Irish claim to a white racial identity that could contain significant cultural and religious differences. They did so by leading white working-class resistance to both the abolition of black slavery in the 1860s and Chinese proletarian labor in the 1870s.[36] As if in direct response to the newspapers and journals that reflected the Anglo-Protestant bourgeoisie's favorable view of the Chinese, the popular songs of Denis Kearney's Workingman's Party and other unions attacked the Chinese as a threat to the white workingman and his family. By focusing on the white family, these songs constructed the problem of proletarianized labor as a question of race and simultaneously identified Irish labor leaders as the champions of the white workingman.

The song "John Chinaman" was published in 1869 in the *Workingman's Advocate* and revived in 1877 by the Workingman's Party of California. Like the song "Twelve Hundred More," also published in 1877, "John Chinaman" invokes the *Herrenvolk* Republican vision of the white workingman's family threatened from above by "nobles" and from below by "slaves." For the Irish immigrant workingman, the difference between enslaved Africans and proletarianized Chinese labor is negligible: "one set of men of late we've freed," the song says, but "another takes his place." The claims of the white mechanic and his family in this song are not justified by the distinction between enslaved labor and proletarian labor, but between white and nonwhite.

> Let the mechanic pack his traps,
> And ready make to flit;
> He cannot live on rats and mice,
> And so he needs must quit,
> Then, while he can with babes and wife,
> Let him in peace retire,
> Lest in the shadowed future near
> His children curse their sire.

> At full cost of bloody war,
> we've garnered in a race,
> One set of men of late we've freed,
> Another takes his place.
> Come friends, we'll have to leave this land
> To nobles and to slaves
> For, if John Chinaman comes in,
> For us—there's only graves.[37]

Among the songs praising Kearney as the leader of the white working-man, "Denis Kearney, The White Working Man's Hero" displays a range of Irish names and places Kearney squarely in the context of Irish immigration and explicitly links Irishness and whiteness in a war against the Chinese.

> You have heard of Moriarty, Mulcahey and Malone,
> Also of McNamara, O'Malley and Muldoon;
> But I will sing of Kearney, an anti-Chinaman,
> He's down upon Mongolians, and all their dirty clan.

> So give three cheers for Kearney,
> For he's a solid man;
> He'll raise a grand big army
> and drive out the Chinaman.

Kearney's well-known anti-Chinese posture enabled him to rally a working class defined by ethnically inclusive but racially exclusive whiteness, not only against the Chinese but against capitalists as well.

> Last week we held a meeting, down forenest [sic] the City Hall
> The bold undaunted Kearney was first to get the call.
> Said he, my fellow laborers, if you'll be lead by me
> We'll make Capital respect us
> and drive out the cursed Chinee.

In the final stanza, Kearney, the Irish immigrant politician, stands as hero to labor, racially defined in terms of the "white workingman."

> Now goodnight, my fellow-laborers, I have to go away,
> I'd like to stop and talk to you, but believe me I can't stay
> So join me in a the chorus now, and let your motto be,
> God Bless the poor white workingman
> and the devil take the Chinee.[38]

John Chinaman Marries

The illustration of "The Consequences of Coolieism" in *The Wasp* made the white working-class family the victim of the "invasion" of Chinese immigrant labor. The conception that the Chinese threatened the (white) workingman's family in the economic sphere coincided with the actual emergence of Chinese within the household sphere itself. In 1890 *Harper's* reported on the rare event of a Chinese wedding on New York's Mott Street, the heart of the city's Chinese quarter. It illustrated the event with a lithograph.

Most prominent in the picture is a family whose members are not a part of the wedding but merely casual spectators. This family, which takes center stage, consists of five people; a white woman dressed in working-class style with cotton cap and aproned skirt, holding a baby in her arms, stands in the company of a Chinese man, dressed in a Chinese-style collarless jacket and trousers and wearing his queue tucked under an American-style felt hat; two slightly older children, a boy dressed in garb similar to the father's and a girl dressed much like the mother, play on the curb.

The permanent presence of the Chinese settler brought with it a threat of marriage and family formation by Chinese men and white women. This possibility was especially threatening to a nascent working class in the process of defining and defending its privileges in racial terms as white. The fear that the Chinese might become a permanent feature of California society had motivated white settlers in 1854 to bar Chinese settlers from testifying in court and in 1868 from becoming citizens. The Page Act made it almost impossible for Chinese men to bring wives to the United States. Nonetheless, critics of the Chinese often charged Chinese immigrants with stripping the United States of its resources and Americans of their hard-earned cash while having no intention of settling in the United States.

From the beginning of Chinese immigration to America, many Chinese did arrive with, or soon adopted, the intention of establishing a permanent place in America. Sucheng Chan estimates that just over a

"A Wedding in the Chinese Quarter—Mott Street, New York" [*Harper's Weekly*, 22 November 1890, pp. 908–909]
(Permission Brown University Library)

third of nineteenth-century Chinese immigrants did eventually return to China.[39] Although this was a greater return rate than that of either Irish immigrants who fled the Great Famine of Ireland or Jews fleeing murderous pogroms in Russia, it was approximately the same as, or substantially smaller than, the return migration rates for many other immigrant groups from Europe during the same period.[40]

In addition, throughout the mid- and late nineteenth century, thousands of Chinese immigrants litigated civil cases in state and federal courts to fight discriminatory laws that limited their ability to secure a permanent livelihood in America. Hundreds of these cases concerned their rights to establish businesses and to freely engage in trade.[41] In the celebrated case of *Yick Wo v. Hopkins,* the U.S. Supreme Court substantially defined the concept of due process and extended the aegis of the constitution from citizens to all persons residing in the United States. It is worth noting that the owner of the Yick Wo laundry, who we know only by the name of his business establishment, had resided and operated his laundry in San Francisco for more than twenty years before he was arrested in 1884 for operating his business without the license that the city fathers had that year required, but then denied, to all Chinese applicants.

Marriage and the establishment of households also indicated the intention on the part of many Chinese to settle permanently in America. Despite the Chinese imperial prohibition on emigration and the social taboos on the emigration of women, and the expense of transportation, many of the merchants who arrived in California in the 1840s and 1850s brought their wives and families with them. For Chinese immigrants, establishing a permanent place in America did not preclude the maintenance of ties to the old homeplace in China. For at least two centuries before Chinese settlement in California, Chinese had settled in Southeast Asia. Among Chinese in that region, it was not uncommon for permanent residences, households, and businesses to be established both in the new homeland and in China and for Chinese to travel between homes, businesses, and families. For Chinese immigrants to the United States, distance, expense, and, later, restrictive immigration laws made circular travel between the United States and China, difficult, dear, and risky. Though they might remain linked in many ways with China, the Chinese were here to stay.

Permanent settlement implied that a Chinese man who might not be able to bring a wife from China might marry or reside with a non-Chinese woman in America. In Southeast Asia, the Pacific, and other destinations of Chinese immigration, it was not uncommon for Chinese men to establish families with local women. In Cuba and Peru they married Cuban and Peruvian women. In Hawaii it was common for Chinese immigrant men to marry and form families with Native Hawaiian women. In the post–Civil War South, Chinese men, originally imported as plantation labor, married both African-American and white women. In the West, although little statistical evidence is available, reports of Chinese-Indian marriage were not uncommon.[42]

Chinese immigrant men also married white women. This seems to have been a more common occurrence on the East Coast than on the West, for a number of reasons. Although Chinese merchants and working-class Chinese, primarily sailors and laborers who had left plantations in the West Indies, had begun to settle in New York as early as the late 1830s, their numbers were vastly smaller than the Chinese population of California; just under 150 Chinese residents of New York's "Chinatown" were counted in the 1880 census. The small size of the Chinese population was less likely to provoke hostility. Furthermore, as historian Jack Kuo Wei Tchen has argued, the southern tip of Manhattan, where the Chinese settled, was a harbor with a constant flow of immigrant groups.[43] Indeed, Chinese-Chinese households in New York were so rare that in 1875 *Frank Leslie's Illustrated Weekly* reported on the first such marriage in the city. The article went on to report that most of the Chinese residents of New York had married white women.

Because more women survived the Irish famine than men, and because the marriage prospects for Irish immigrant women, (at least for finding a suitable Irish man) were not good, many of the white women who married Chinese men were Irish. Tchen reports that at least one quarter of all Chinese men who lived in New York between 1820 and 1870 were married to, or lived with, Irish women.[44] In 1882 Charles MacCabe, Jr., in *New York by Sunlight and Gaslight,* reported that in fact the "great majority" of the seventy or so Chinese families in the city were interracial, involving Chinese men and Irish women.[45]

New York was not the only location in which Chinese men married white women, nor were Irish immigrant women the only white women they married. In the South, Chinese workers leaving the plantations after their contracts were over married white women as well as black. In Massachusetts at least eighty Chinese immigrant men, mostly laundrymen, married white, mostly Irish immigrant, women. In North Adams, where Chinese workers had been brought in to break the largely Irish St. Crispin's strike at Calvin Samson's shoe factory, several of the Chinese workers stayed and married local Anglo-Protestant women. In San Francisco (even though the social taboo on marriage between Chinese men and white women was more rigidly enforced in California), Chinese-white intermarriage took place. A 1870 report declaring San Francisco's Chinese quarter a public health threat professed outrage at the discovery of a dozen such interracial couples living together in that quarter of the city.

The marriage of Chinese immigrant men to Irish immigrant women, while not significant in a demographic sense, occurred with sufficient frequency to present itself as an imagined threat to working-class whites whose class status was precarious and to immigrants whose amalgamation into whiteness was not yet complete. Intermarriage disrupted the narrative of the Irish as the champion of the exclusively white working-class family and represented a crisis in the amalgamation of European immigrants into the "white workingman's family" that was the popular representation of the people. While nativists attacked the Irish immigrants on religious and moral grounds, their physical amalgamation with the Anglo-Saxon Protestant majority was still at least a legal possibility despite substantial social barriers. Intermarriage between racialized groups, between whites and blacks or between the Chinese and Irish, for example, threatened to blur the emerging but still somewhat unclear distinction between amalgamable ethnicity and excluded race.

The terms "amalgamation" and "miscegenation" have a related political history. In the nineteenth century, amalgamation was used to describe both interethnic and interracial marriage and was a somewhat neutral term that implied the absorption of the Other into the People. (Later, in the 1920s, the Supreme Court would define as white only those groups who were "readily amalgamated" into American society.)

As early as the 1830s, the critics of abolition would accuse abolitionists of being "amalgamationists," implying that interracial marriage was part of the abolitionist agenda. The proslavery attack notwithstanding, the term "amalgamation" retained its more ambiguous field of meanings. It should therefore be no surprise that the neologism "miscegenation" was invented in 1863 by two Irish immigrant anti-abolitionists who published a fake abolitionist tract purporting to plan forced intermarriage between Irish and blacks.[46] They purposely coined the term "miscegenation" to express, in negative, pseudoscientific terms, the unacceptable nature of sexual relations between races. Its entry into the lexicon of race enabled the older and more neutral term "amalgamation" to stand for marriage relations among different ethnic groups deemed white.

A number of popular songs on the minstrel circuit referred to unacceptable Chinese-Irish marriages. One tells the story of such a relationship through the voice of one "Hay Sing, Come from China," and its refrain suggests his desire for a permanent bond.

> Me got a an Irish girl, she well nicee.
> Me makee her some day my wife.
> We have a nice time, go back China
> Eat much plenty rats and mice.[47]

Typical of the songs referring to love relationships between Chinese men and white women, the song ends with Hay Sing's Irish girl being stolen by a "Melican" man. Recounting the story of their life together in a house on Bottle Alley, drinking and selling gin, Hay Sing is jailed for opium smoking, while his Irish girl finds the company of a white man.

A second song, "The Marriage of John Chinaman," printed in *Conner's Irish Songbook* in 1868, also employs the theme of the Irish wife cuckolding and eventually abandoning her Chinese husband. "The Marriage of John Chinaman" tells of a Chinaman who has "saved a lot of gold and who seeks a wife." The song expresses the strong popular opprobrium attached to these relationships and denigrates the white women who associated with Chinese men; the only girl who will come out with this man is one Cock-eyed Fan.

> To look at her, t'was hard to say
> Exactly where her beauty lay:
> Her complexion was a dirty brown,
> and she lately came from famed Hangtown
> Small pox had left big traces there,
> She'd a snub nose and carroty hair;
> But finding fault was not his plan,
> she was just the cheese for the Chinaman.

The wedding sacrament itself is profaned because of John Chinaman's inability to speak proper English, and the marriage is doomed by the inability of the Chinaman to either satisfy or control Cock-eyed Fan.

> They went to Church and John with pride,
> surveyed his fat and blooming bride
> He'd have talked finely if he could,
> but he kept on saying "velly good"
> At length, quite lushy, home she'd reel,
> and for a row she then would peel;
> to play her pranks she then began,
> and she walked into the Chinaman.
>
> She put poor John in quite a fright
> for often she'd stay out all night;
> and in the morning home she'd come,
> smelling delightfully of rum.

> She then repudiated rice,
> and swore such grub would not suffice;
> at length from him clean off she ran
> and she left her faithful Chinaman.

The abandonment of her Chinese husband enables Cock-eyed Fan to return to the white community, and even to garner some modicum of notoriety and grudging admiration for having "bamboozled the Chinaman." Nevertheless, the fact that the "old folks know her go," i.e., her past, and that small boys can openly taunt her in the streets, makes it clear that her relationship with John Chinaman has marked her indelibly as racially and sexually degraded.

> And after doing John so brown,
> She toddled back to her native town;
> but the old folk there know her go
> and her doings down in Francisco
> and now whenever she goes out,
> the little boys behind her shout:
> Twig her Bill, that's Cock-eyed Fan,
> The girl that bamboozled the Chinaman! [48]

Miscegenation as Farce: Paddy Turns White

In 1900, T. S. Denison, a prolific writer and publisher of plays, skits, and popular fiction, published *Patsy O'Wang, an Irish Farce With a Chinese Mix-Up,* a three-act play "suitable for production by schools, civic and amateur theater groups." [49] The farce turns on the remarkable transformation that Patsy O'Wang is able to make. Patsy O'Wang, also known as Chin Sum, has "a slight flaw in his pedigree": he is the offspring of an Irish father and a Chinese mother. He is freak, a person with a schizophrenic racial persona. As the play's notes explain, "Whiskey, the drink of his father, transforms him into a true Irishman, while strong tea, the beverage of his mother, has the power of restoring fully his Chinese character." [50]

Patsy O'Wang is a comedy of class, ethnicity, and race. An array of social types are satirized: Dr. Fluke, who runs a "modern sanitarium," and Mr. Boyles, his hypochondriac patient, represent both the newly professionalized medical profession and the middle-class obsession with therapeutic regimes. Mrs. Fluke is old-fashioned and fearful of the exotic, while their friend Miss Simper runs a Chinese Sunday school and represents the female social reformer. Mike and Nora, both Irish immigrants, constitute the domestic staff. The stage instructions emphasize their ethnic and class differences: Mike and Norah are instructed to speak in a thick brogue, while Patsy is instructed to speak in standard "gentleman's" English; but while in yellowface, as Chin Sum, he is to speak in a ersatz pidgin. The stage instructions admit the following:

> No instruction can be given here concerning the Chinese part except that the timbre and tones of the Chinese voice are very peculiar and can be learned only by listening to Chinamen. The Chinese dialect as written here (and elsewhere in America) is at best but a poor imitation, but good enough to be funny, which is the only object in view.[51]

Chin Sum is hired as a cook by Dr. Fluke, who has "tried everything but the Chinese—Irish Swede, German , French, African, Yankee— that's so as we haven't any Hindoos yet or Cannibal Islanders." [52] Middle-class enthusiasm for domestic labor from diverse and "exotic" sources is underscored with the arrival of Miss Simper, a pillar of moral reform, who announces that she is in "a dreadful hurry. The African Argonauts meet at eleven and I preside. . . . At four p.m., The Mongolian Mediators have a meeting, and at eight is the debate in which we shall answer the Cannibal Calumniators." When Miss Simper declares "My heart bleeds for the millions of Asia who sit in outer darkness," Fluke responds that Chin Sum "will be a capital acquisition to your mission school, so intelligent, so docile, so affectionate, so—, so—."

On meeting Chin Sum, Miss Simper extends this litany of middle-class celebration of the Chinese domestic by describing him as "charming! and childlike!" The shallow naiveté of this sentiment is not lost on Chin Sum who, feigning not to have understood, asks with a grin, "All same like big man-shile?"

The Irish domestics are, on the other hand, not at all happy to see a Chinese join the household staff. Mike says "its an outrage, that's the whole blessed truth. To think of a blackguard haythen cookin' for dacint people," and swears to refuse to eat Chin Sum's cooking.

The Chinese Chin Sum's transformation into the Irish Patsy O'Wang occurs in the course of the chaos that results when Chin Sum takes over Mike's job operating the modern machinery of the clinic. In the ensuing melee, Chin Sum comes upon and drinks from a bottle of brandy. The spirits release the "spirit of Hibernia" in Chin Sum, and he is suddenly transformed into Patsy O'Wang.

Dr. Fluke attempts to transform Patsy O'Wang back into Chin Sum by feeding him great quantities of tea, measuring progress by how obedient he perceives Patsy to be. Patsy siphons off the tea and declares that he has always been and is determined to remain "Irish forever." Disappointed, Dr. Fluke declares, "I hired you for a Chinaman. A bargain is a bargain." Patsy reveals his true ambition for himself as a new Irish American. "Keep your place," Patsy tells Mike, "I can do better. I'm in America now, the land of opportunities. I'm going into politics. Me ambition is to be an alderman and die beloved and respected by all." [53] The play ends with a song, the first stanza of which tells of Chin Sum/Patsy's origins:

> Me father was a Hooligan, me mother was Chinay
> And I was born in Hong Kong town ten thousand miles away
> Me father was a soldier in the tenth artilleree,
> He took me to the barracks there in Hong Kong by the sea.
> Me Christian name was Patsy and O'Wang me name Chinay
> An' while they took all the toddy I drank nothing but green tay.
> One day I brewed the punch meself an then I tried the same:
> Hooray! It touched a vital spot: it lit the Irish flame. [54]

Patsy O'Wang plays on the competing stereotypes of the Chinese and Irish working-class common in the late nineteenth century while it satirizes a newly prominent middle-class stratum of professionals and social reformers. When Mike, the Irish hired hand, threatens to refuse meals cooked by Chin Sum and asserts that "O'im all right as long as free lunches at the local tavern hold out," the threat serves to underscore Mike's reputed ethnic weakness for strong drink. Nora makes this explicit by reminding him that getting drunk one more time risks dismissal. In contrast, Chin Sum is described repeatedly as obedient, docile, and childlike by his middle-class employers and their missionary friend. Mike's working-class status is underscored by the clear pretension of his repeated claims to be in the medical profession when he is only a hired hand. When he is in his Irish persona, Patsy O'Wang's "gentlemanly" English underscores the thick brogue in the speech of Mike and Nora and suggests that class might be more malleable than race and that Mike and Nora would do well to learn American English.

In the schizophrenic mixed-race Chin Sum/Patsy O'Wang, the "wild" Irish and the "docile" Chinese together represent the duality of working-class nature as simultaneously fearsome and childlike, in need of both training and discipline. Irish wildness is controlled and reformed by the presence of the Chinese. Once his true Irish nature is unleashed by liquor, Patsy becomes potentially dangerous. Nevertheless, the plot must end with Patsy choosing his Irish whiteness, however tainted it may be by ethnic stereotype, because it alone offers a path into America. However divided by class, accent, and religon the Irish might be, whiteness confers upon them the freedom to create a unified ethnic identity as Irish-Americans and use it as the vehicle for political power and economic mobility. Although Chin Sum may be preferable as an obedient, docile, and childlike domestic servant, as a Chinese barred from naturalization in 1870 and from entering the country since 1882 he has no hope of becoming "amalgamated " with the People or, like Patsy, free to run for alderman.

Miscegenation as Tragedy: The Chinese Go Mad

In 1898, two years before Denison's *Patsy O'Wang* played the racial and class history of the Chinese and the Irish as farce, Louis Beck, in his detailed journalistic account, *New York's Chinatown,* offered another, darker story of Chinese-Irish relations.[55] In Beck's account of Quimbo Appo and his son George, the racial and class violence that is densely encoded in *The Wasp*'s "Consequences of Coolieism" is refracted through the lens of the Chinese-Irish family. The extent to which Appo's story is meant to be a parable about Chinese-white relations is suggested by the fact that Beck begins and ends his narrative of New York's Chinese community with the twin stories of Quimbo Appo, the Chinese father, and George Appo, the Chinese-Irish son.

According to Beck's account, Quimbo Appo (Lee Ah Bow) was among the first Chinese to settle in New York, arriving from California in the early 1850s. Quimbo Appo is, at first, successful in New York, making a small fortune as a tea merchant. He then marries Catherine Fitzpatrick, like himself an immigrant, and, according to Beck, on July 4, 1856, their son George is born. In Beck's book, when sober, Quimbo Appo is the epitome of charm and civility, but when he touches liquor he, like Denison's farcical character Patsy O'Wang, undergoes a transformation. Unlike the farcical Patsy O'Wang, Quimbo Appo becomes irrational, paranoid, and savage. In 1859 Quimbo Appo is convicted of the manslaughter of his landlady, whom he had beaten to death in a drunken rage. During his first stay in prison, Quimbo Appo appears to be a model prisoner and is pardoned after four years. In the meantime, his wife Catherine has died in an accident at sea, and his son George has been abandoned to the mean streets of New York's infamous Five Points District (soon to become Chinatown). Eight years later, Quimbo Appo is convicted of assault and sent to Sing Sing prison. After several years in Sing Sing and Auburn Prison, Quimbo Appo, "the first" Chinese to settle in New York, is sent to a Matteawan asylum for the criminally insane where, for the last thirty years of his life, he labors under the delusion that he is back in China.

George Appo, the American born Chinese-Irish son of Mr. and Mrs. Quimbo Appo, is Beck's dark version of Patsy O'Wang. Like the son of the white working-class family pictured in "The Consequences of Coolieism," half-Chinese George Appo is driven to a life of crime. But unlike the son of the white workingman's family, it is not support of his destitute and despondent widowed mother that leads George Appo into the criminal life. At an early age George Appo is abandoned by his criminally insane father and orphaned by the death of his mother. Beck describes George as intelligent, well spoken, and a youth who would have been handsome but for a scar across his face, the result of an early knife fight. For Beck, George Appo's life of crime from an early age is symbolic of the emergence of a "new hybrid brood," a dangerous "half-breed" population in the immigrant city. Unlike Patsy O'Wang's farcical ability to shift from one racial identity to another, George Appo's "hybrid" status does not offer a choice between white and Chinese. Despite his intelligence and beauty, his half-breed racial status makes him a permanent outcast and dooms him to a life of criminality. Of the terrible product of "miscegenation," Beck concludes, "In all fairness, such a man is better dead." [56]

The story of Quimbo Appo and his son George is a tale of madness and death that inveighs against miscegenation, the unacceptable alternative to coolieism. Harper's picture of the "Consequences of Coolieism" sought to mobilize Saxon and Celt, Anglo-American and Irish immigrant in defense of the white family. The construction of coolieism was an attempt to insulate the white working-class family from the worst consequences of proletarianization by defining the lowest stratum of menial work as fit only for the coolie or the nigger, and preserving the ideal of artisan labor, with its hope for upward mobility, for the white workingman and his family. As a racial ideology of labor articulated around the trope of the beleaguered White workingman's family, coolieism had to define the Chinese immigrant as a racial Other unfit for white work or white wives.

3

The Third Sex

The Pacific Railroad Complete

n June 1869, *Harper's Weekly* published a lithograph with the title "Pacific Railroad Complete."[1] The illustration shows a Chinese man, mustachioed, with a thickly braided queue hanging beneath a skull cap, dressed in a baggy Chinese tunic and trousers, standing arm in arm with a white woman dressed in middle-class fashion with a fancy hat and bustled dress. The couple are posed in front of the "church of St. Confucious." [sic] With its caption celebrating the geographic consolidation of the nation, the picture of the wedding of East and West is an ironic visual representation of the complicated anxieties that nineteenth-century Americans had about the changing nature of nation and their families.

The lithograph suggests that the transcontinental railroad ironically "completes" the geographic consolidation of the nation, but in doing so opens up a new set of class, gender, and racial contradictions. It offers a vision of the completed nation as a family, but one that is disturbingly biracial. The West can now be represented by the Chinese man, while the East is represented by the white woman. Their marriage not only is interracial but appears to cross class boundaries as well. The white woman, wearing middle-class attire, represents both the Victorian familial culture and the autonomous female public sphere emerging in the nation's cities; the mustachioed Chinaman represents the new racial and sexual possibilities and threats inherent in the incorporation of the "frontier" into the nation.

In the decades following the Civil War and the completion

83

PACIFIC RAILROAD COMPLETE.

"The Pacific Railroad Complete" [*Harpers Weekly*, 12 June 1869, p. 384]
(Permission Brown University Library)

of the transcontinental railroad, the family became the principal background against which the ideology of citizenship was debated. At the same time that women renewed their demands for the vote and other rights of citizenship, the nation was faced with the question of citizenship rights for nonwhites. In 1869, Charles Sumner, whose Radical Republican faction in Massachusetts supported both the demand for woman suffrage and the enfranchisement of blacks, urged Congress to eliminate the single word "white" from the naturalization law of 1790. Although Congress amended the statute to allow the naturalization of persons of African nativity or descent, it was unwilling to abandon the principle of a racial qualification for citizenship. Specifically, Congress acceded to the wishes of the Western delegates who opposed immigration from Asia. Even in Massachusetts, where radical egalitarianism was strongest, efforts to give women the vote failed consistently in the early 1870s. As Dale Baum observes, woman suffrage and the "Chinese Question" were the two issues that defined the limits of Radical Republicanism in this most radical of states.[2]

Kathryn Kish Sklar notes that in the middle three decades of the nineteenth century, white middle-class American women had already constructed vital and autonomous political institutions.[3] Middle-class white women constructed a moral authority that challenged male political authority and were able to define their own gender-specific goals outside the formal political system. As historian Peggy Pascoe has shown, particularly in the decades after the Civil War, this moral authority rested on the power of middle-class white women to speak for the needs of women of other races and classes while bolstering the supremacy of middle-class values and institutions, especially with regard to family life.[4] As the white Victorian bourgeois family took its place as the social norm, the relations of desire with the Oriental (male or female) offered an alternative (albeit a tabooed one) to the social order represented by the racially exclusive, presumptively heterosexual, nuclear family. Against an emergent heterosexual and dimorphic order, Oriental sexuality was constructed as ambiguous, inscrutable, and hermaphroditic; the Oriental (male or female) was constructed as a "third sex"—Marjorie Garber's term for a gender of imagined sexual possibility.[5]

The dynamics of sexuality, gender, class, and race that shaped the Victorian family were driven by changes in the capitalist order. Sexuality, like race, is a socially constructed category of power, formed by the social and political relations of a given culture at a given moment. Sexuality does the political work of defining and regulating desire as well as the body, determining whose bodies and what body parts are eroticized; what activities are sexual and with whom; under what conditions those activities are acceptable; what privileges, rewards, and punishments accompany sexual behavior; and how the erotic may be distinguished from the non-erotic. Articulated by systems of race and class, with the logics of national identity, and with the organization of gender, sexuality is organized to produce and reproduce the social relations of production.[6]

Nowhere was the capitalist transformation in mid- and late nineteenth-century America so powerfully felt as within the family. Structures and meanings of kinship changed as extended households shrank into nuclear families. Gender roles were redefined as women and men both left (or were forced from) hearth, farm, and workshop to go into the factory. By 1870, cities populated by a new working class, by free people of color, and by immigrants created new possibilities for encounters across class, racial, and sexual boundaries unimaginable a decade or two earlier.

In the middle decades of the nineteenth century, the transformation of the pre-capitalist household into the nuclear family established polarized middle-class gender roles and sexual behavior in what social historians have called the Cult of Domesticity.[7] The triumph of the bourgeois family transformed American culture from a male-dominated homosocial culture represented by the frontier to a heterosexual culture represented by the Victorian family.[8]

Stephanie Coontz has argued that the cult of domesticity emerged as an ideology whose purpose was to contain the deepening contradictions between the new urban life and older ideals of community, family, and social order. The urban revolution of the 1830s and 1840s had brought about an explosion of new sexual possibilities. In the cities now burgeoning with immigrants, free people of color, professional men, and dandies, factory girls and working-class boys, no longer under the watchful eyes of parents and village, entered into new social relations in the factory, dormitory, and boardinghouse, on the boulevard and boardwalk.[9]

In Coontz's view, for the emergent middle class of the nineteenth century, the private nuclear family with the True Woman as its moral center was imagined to provide a haven from the alienation and anomie of the new competitive and chaotic public life.[10] This construct granted women a monopoly of morality, sensibility, and nurture within the feminine mystique of True Womanhood, while in fact freeing men from such ethical burdens in the public sphere. Home was, however, only a temporary haven, a space in which men might restore their mental and emotional strength before returning to battle in the marketplace. The skills and techniques of crafts and farming handed down from father to son were supplanted by the inculcation of values needed to negotiate and survive in the marketplace. The discipline of the home, with mother at its center, was expected to reinforce and encourage the development of the competitive values needed to succeed within the new capitalist order.

The Geography of Sex

As the imaginary "frontier" of American culture, a space where male fantasies of sexual, gender, racial, and class aggression and transgression might find expression, the West neatly reversed the reality of the Eastern city.[11] At the far edge of the pastoral farm homestead with its links to the communal village, the frontier was conceived of as savage, devoid both of comforting and constraining civilization and of the actually existing capitalist relations of the burgeoning cities. The symbolic emptiness of the West allowed young men to flee both the civilizing disciplines of their families and ruthless capitalism and to recreate themselves not as victims but as vanguard.

The cult of the Western masculine hero, first embodied in the figure of Davy Crockett, valorized untamed savagery in the young single male in service to an onward march of civilization. The frontier provided ground for an anti-familial narrative that reconfigured alienation and isolation as independence and self-sufficiency. It was on the frontier that loneliness could be hammered and honed into the "savage" skill of competitive individualism that was required for survival and success in the capitalist city.

Carroll Smith-Rosenberg notes that the mythic frontier in which Crockett could freely actualize himself and his historical mission was imagined as largely without women, particularly without mothers.[12] Literary critic Eve Sedgewick observes that it is precisely on the register of the homosocial that the boundaries between the heterosexual and the homosexual are contested. The homosocial can thus be understood as the liminal range of alternatives between heterosexual and homosexual oppositions. The Western imagery is often described as homosocial—that is to say, dominated by same-sex relations (like male bonding) that have no sexual component. Yet, as Sedgewick argues, although the homosocial is constituted by that which is not sexual and is distinguished from the homosexual, it does not exist independently of the erotic, but rather is deeply infused with desire.[13] To describe the West as homosocial is not to deny its sexuality. The land itself was feminized in the metaphor of the virgin land, and the westward movement was imagined in terms of masculine penetration and conquest.[14] In Western frontier imagery, whether the Davy Crockett narratives or the songs of the California gold rush, the land may have been a woman, but it was a place where boys could be boys.

Imagined as a space where desires that crossed class, racial, and sexual borders were unfettered, the West's freedom from the familial rendered it vulnerable to the homophobic accusation. That is, the Western homo-sociality engendered and restrained the transgressive impulse; it also sometimes transformed longing into aggression. By the 1870s, as the number of westering women increased, the male-dominated homosocial culture of the West began to be displaced by the Victorian Cult of Do-mesticity. Domesticity established an increasingly binary and naturalized code of gender and sexuality in an attempt to restore order to sexual behavior. The doctrine of True Womanhood overturned the Protestant republican view that women's sexuality was a natural source of evil. Vic-torian moralists regarded sexual passion in women as unnatural, deviant, and a marker of degraded lower-class status. Chastity and moral order formed the ideal in which Victorian middle-class women were to fulfill the true nature of their sex. The unbridled sexual energy of men, cele-brated in the myth of the Western hero, was to be sublimated to the psychic demands of the marketplace or brought into the service of class reproduction within the privatized family. Sexuality was harnessed to reproduction; the pleasure of the erotic, especially the autoerotic and homoerotic, was to be strictly suppressed.

The cult of domesticity, only partially successful as an ideology of sexual repression, succeeded in constructing the bourgeois family as a private sphere of chastity and piety. On the other hand, a public sphere of sexualized activity also flourished. Prostitution in various forms, from the informal exchange of sexual favors for gifts and meals to the ex-change of cash, grew to be commonplace in mid-century American cit-ies.[15] In his 1858 study of prostitution in New York, the social reformer William Sanger found that fully one quarter of his male respondents had visited prostitutes.[16]

In the transition from the male-dominated homosocial world of gold rush California to the settled domestic Victorian discipline of California of the 1870s, the Chinese represented a third sex—an alternative or imagined sexuality that was potentially subversive and disruptive to the emergent heterosexual orthodoxy. The Oriental in America could be imagined as an erotic threat to domestic tranquillity for two related rea-sons. First, during the later decades of the nineteenth century, more than 10,000 Chinese women were brought, for the most part forcibly, to the United States as prostitutes. The Chinese prostitute embodied the avail-able and mute but proletarianized sexuality that mirrored the exoticized female long displayed in the Western literary tradition of Orientalism. If not contained by race, this image of female sexuality, uninhibited albeit coerced, threatened to undermine the image of the passionless True Woman as the moral center of the chaste and obedient social order. Second, thousands of Chinese immigrant men, displaced from earlier employment in manufacturing, agriculture, or mining, entered the new middle-class family as household servants. This entry into the domestic sphere not only displaced female labor (more often than not, female Irish immigrant workers) but, by opening up possibilities for relations of intimacy and desire across race and class, also threatened to disrupt the patriarchal hierarchy of the family.

The Silenced Presence of Chinese Women

During the middle and later decades of the nineteenth century, thousands of Chinese and later Japanese women were brought to the United States, often under brutally coercive conditions, to labor as prostitutes. In the 1870s and '80s, the figure of the Chinese or Japanese prostitute as a conduit of disease and social decay was sensationalized in newspaper accounts, magazine articles, and official inquiries into the social hygiene of the new cities of the West. Renewing fears of moral and racial pollution, "Chinese" prostitution became a significant political issue in California and a major weapon of those supporting the prohibition of Chinese (and later other Asian) immigration to the United States. The first act limiting Chinese immigration was the Page Act of 1870, which ostensibly prohibited "Chinese, Japanese, and Mongolian women" from being brought to or entering the United States to "engage in immoral or licentious activities." The Page Act, on the presumption of bad character and immoral purpose, required all Chinese women who wished to come to the United States to submit to lengthy and humiliating interrogations of their character prior to being issued a visa in China. The Page Act effectively closed off the immigration of Chinese wives of immigrants already in the United States. But it did little to stop the illegal trade in women, which was protected by corrupt officials on both sides of the Pacific.

The perception of Chinese prostitution as a widespread threat to the nation's moral and physical well-being was greatly exaggerated. At the peak of Chinese prostitution in the late 1870s, Lucie Cheng reports, some 900 Chinese women in San Francisco worked as prostitutes.[17] The number of Chinese (or other Asian) women who worked as prostitutes other than on the West Coast, however, was quite small. Although New York's Chinatown gained notoriety for prostitution, opium smoking, and gambling, the social reformers Helen Campbell and Thomas Knox reported that only three of the prostitutes in the quarter were Chinese, while the overwhelming number of prostitutes who worked there were white.[18] Anne Butler found that only three of the several hundred prostitutes working in Denver in 1875 were classified as "Oriental."[19]

Nevertheless, the image of the Chinese prostitute as a source of pollution was considered a matter of urgent concern. Chinese prostitutes were said to constitute a particular threat to the physical and moral development of young white boys. In San Francisco, a Public Health Committee investigating conditions in Chinatown in 1870 professed shock that boys as young as ten could afford and did regularly use the services of the lowest level of Chinese prostitutes.[20] In a popular environment in which theories of national culture were freely combined with theories of germs and social hygiene, it was asserted by some public health authorities that Chinese prostitutes were the racially special carriers of more virulent and deadly strains of venereal disease. The general public tended to ignore the reality and focus on the sensational accounts that fueled the perception of a social crisis.

While highly visible as a symbol in the popular discourse of urban social crisis, the Chinese woman is an almost invisible and absolutely voiceless figure in nineteenth-century popular entertainment. Unlike the figure of "John Chinaman" about whom much is sung, the figure of "China Mary," as Chinese women were often called, is virtually absent in popular songs. One looks in vain for the Chinese prostitute as the subject of some of the several hundred lewd or bawdy songs documented from the period. Perhaps the songs in which she appeared have vanished; more likely they did not exist. Apart from a handful of short stories in *The Overland Monthly* and the *Californian,* in which the Chinese woman appears as the passive object of competition among Chinese men, there is little trace of Chinese women in nineteenth-century popular entertainment.

The Chinese prostitute could not be made a subject of popular entertainment in the nineteenth century because such publicity would unveil the complex homosocial exchange between Chinese men and white men that made possible the profitable exchange of Chinese women's bodies as a commodity. In China, Chinese girls could be bought from their often destitute parents for as little as $40 and resold to brothels in San Francisco for as much as $2500. The huge profits involved in this illegal but low-risk trade created a web of exchange between Chinese merchants, brothel owners, and tong members on the one hand and white sea captains, immigration officials, policemen, and politicians on the other. The exchange was not limited to the merely economic, but extended to a shared sexual desire for the bodies of Chinese women. This exchange of commodity and desire created a homosocial bond that was both forbidden and unspeakable.

When the Chinese woman was portrayed at all, she was portrayed as victimized, passive, and silent. The Chinese woman in California, whether a prostitute or the wife of a merchant, was invariably represented in short stories and magazines, such as *The Overland Monthly,* or in travelers' descriptions of Chinese life in California as a silent and isolated figure. The voicelessness of the Chinese woman in American popular culture served the purposes not only of her exploiters but also of her would-be rescuers. Abolitionist Lydia Maria Child, in an early "national culture" survey of the world's women, painted a picture of Chinese women as having an "unknowing visage" and being inherently passive and mute.[21] Victorian moral reformers, such as the Presbyterian missionary Donaldina Cameron, who freed many a Chinese prostitute from sexual bondage (whose Chinese nickname was fittingly "Lo Mo" or Old Mother), saw her charges as victims without agency, whose only hope was that of being saved by their white missionary mother and perhaps eventually marrying a Chinese Christian convert.[22] For the social purity reformers, the image of the mute Chinese woman bound to sexual enslavement, which no doubt accurately described many but not all Chinese prostitutes in nineteenth-century America, served as synecdoche for all prostitutes, indeed for all women whose passionless True Womanhood was at the mercy of predatory male sexuality. The voicelessness of the Chinese woman seemed to confirm the claim to the passionless true nature of womanhood in general.

Fictions of Domesticity

Two short stories, "The Haunted Valley" by Ambrose Bierce and "Poor Ah Toy" by Mary Mote, which tell the story of desire between whites and Chinese, and its tragic consequences, exemplify the ways in which the discourse of desire was overdetermined by race, sex, and class in the transition from the homosocial frontier to the heterosexual family. Although "The Haunted Valley" is a classic Gothic tale and "Poor Ah Toy" is a domestic fiction, both stories address the boundaries of race, class, and gender that divided Chinese and whites in late nineteenth century California.

The stories were published twelve years apart.[23] *The Overland Monthly,* which began publishing in San Francisco in 1868 with Bret Harte as its first editor, was considered the premier literary magazine of the West. Although Harte's work did not appear in the magazine, fiction by Ambrose Bierce, Gertrude Atherton, Jack London, and Frank Norris, among other notable Western writers, did.[24] Its editorship, its literary content, and the fact that it was a monthly publication suggest that *The Overland Monthly* was aimed principally at a middle-class audience.

The *Overland Monthly* paid extraordinary attention to the presence of the Chinese in California; of the eighty-two pieces of short fiction that the magazine published throughout its history, sixty-nine involved Chinese characters.[25] Ranging from fantasies of a Chinese invasion of the United States to sympathetic accounts of Chinese victimization at the hands of white racists, these stories reflect a contradictory and highly ambiguous view of the Chinese presence in California. The editorial ambivalence and generally sympathetic tone of many of the stories further suggest that the magazine sold to a middle-class readership less hostile to the Chinese than was the white working class.[26]

"The Haunted Valley"

"The Haunted Valley," the first piece of short fiction that Ambrose Bierce published (in March 1870), shows that Bierce, like his editor Harte, was politically sympathetic to the Chinese. Bierce's journalism criticized in acid prose those he saw as oppressors of the Chinese, in particular Denis Kearney and the Workingman's Party of California.[27] Bierce's intense skepticism regarding ideology was both a result of his experience in the Civil War and his interest in the epistemological work of Charles Pierce, an American philosopher interested in linguistics and the indeterminacy of language. "The Haunted Valley" foreshadows many of the themes of the uncertain and the unknowable that would become the hallmarks of Bierce's better-known fiction.[28]

"The Haunted Valley" is a gothic tale of murder and transracial desire that turns on a sexual masquerade.[29] (I use the term transracial, as opposed to interracial, here to indicate that the reader is given no indication that the desire is reciprocated.) The narrator, a young journalist recently arrived in California from the East, can easily stand in for the middle-class reader of *The Overland Monthly* and, as a naif, can interrogate the story at its various levels. Revealed through a series of interviews, the story revolves around two murders, one that has occurred before it opens and one that occurs during the course of the story.

"The Haunted Valley" begins with the journalist's interview with "Whiskey" Jo Dunfer, an old-timer who is known for his hatred of the Chinese and his love of strong drink. He is reputed to have murdered his Chinese cook and hireling, Ah Wee, some years earlier. Dunfer is willing to tell his story to the young Eastern reporter as a way of explaining to the newcomer the "nub of the [Chinese] problem." The reason Dunfer gives for killing Ah Wee is that Ah Wee "put on airs" and refused to chop down the trees on the site of a new cabin in the manner in which Dunfer had instructed. This shallow rationale for homicide, absurd on the face of it, was one that had been accepted with full faith and credit by the local jury, which had acquitted Dunfer of any wrongdoing. The interview comes to an abrupt end as Dunfer recoils in terror when he sees "an eye black as coal" looking at him through a knothole in the barroom wall.

On his way back to the city, the young reporter comes across Ah Wee's neatly kept and flower-decorated grave, and discovers that the story is perhaps more complicated than Dunfer has let on. The gravestone reads:

Ah Wee—Chinaman
  Aig unnone. Wikt last Wisky Jo.
  This monument is ewrekted bi the saim to keep is memmery
  grean. An liqusize a wornin to Slestials notter take on ayres
  like Wites. Dammum! She was a good eg.[30]

When the young reporter returns to the Haunted Valley, it is Jo Dunfer who has died. On his weed covered grave a crudely carved sign simply says, "Jo Dunfer, Done For." [31]

In a subsequent interview Dunfer's other hired hand, "a little cuss named Gopher" (as Whiskey Jo called him), tells another story. In his version, Ah Wee was a woman. Gopher had fallen in love with Ah Wee and had rescued her from prostitution but had subsequently lost her to Dunfer in a card game. Gopher had followed Dunfer and Ah Wee to the valley so that he could be near her. After some time, Dunfer had himself fallen in love with Ah Wee. As Gopher recounts the story, Dunfer killed Ah Wee by accident when he came across Gopher and Ah Wee in what he had thought was a sexual embrace. Immediately after striking the fatal blow with his ax, Dunfer had discovered, to his horror, that the embrace had actually been an innocent attempt by Gopher to brush a wasp away from the face of the sleeping Ah Wee.

Although he had not contradicted Dunfer's preposterous story to the jury, Gopher admits to having poisoned Dunfer to avenge Ah Wee's death. After this now complicated tale is told, however, the reporter elicits the admission that Gopher has himself gone mad.

This is no simple ghost tale. In the middle of the story, the reader is led to Ah Wee's flower-decorated gravestone with its inexplicable inscription, "with its meagre but sufficient identification of the deceased; the impudent candor of confession; the brutal anathema, the ludicrous change of sex and sentiment." The inscription is an invitation to revisit the story offered by Whiskey Jo in his cups. When Dunfer says at the beginning of the interview, "You young Easterners are a mile and a half too good for this country, and you don't catch on to our play," and asserts that his story will explain the "nub of the [Chinese] problem," the derisive comment should be a warning to us that to accept, on faith,

Dunfer's glib rationale for murder is to naively recapitulate the racism of the jury.

The triangle of desire between Dunfer, Gopher, and Ah Wee turns on the racialized and sexualized relations of capital. In direct competition for Ah Wee, the object of desire, are Dunfer and Gofer. The primitive pun on their respective surnames parallels the stage of primitive accumulation of capital that their relationship represents. For Whiskey Jo Dunfer, the petty capitalist, the economic structure of primitive accumulation and its homosocial culture that allow him to control both Gopher and Ah Wee are ideal. For Dunfer, the "nub of the problem" comes with the introduction of bourgeois familial society, represented here by religion and politics. It is the church (here Bierce is forecasting his lifelong feud with what he called "organized hypocrisy"[32]) that introduces taboo into the homosocial idyll. Nostalgically, Dunfer recounts that he had hired Ah Wee in the days before the onset of politics and religion, when he "had no nice discriminating sense of my duty as a free W'ite citizen; so I got this pagan as kind of a cook and turned off a Mexican woman." Dunfer claims that it is when "I got religion over at the Hill and they talked of running me for the legislature, it was given for me to see the light"—that is, the error of his racial transgression. Despite the pressure to dismiss his Ah Wee, he resists. "If I made him sling his kit and mosey, somebody else'd take him and mightn't treat him well," Dunfer asserts, revealing some concern for the well-being of his Chinese hireling.[33]

Dunfer's view of the "nub of the problem" has some historical merit. In the 1850s and 1860s, California was still a largely male terrain. Until the arrival of large numbers of white women from the East Coast in the mid-1870s, the gender ratio in California was twelve men to one woman. Between 1860 and 1882, thousands of Chinese workers who had been dismissed as railroad builders and driven from the mines and farms took up independent employment in service industries as launderers, tailors, and restaurateurs, or worked for wages as domestics and cooks.

While the study of the anti-Chinese movement in California generally has emphasized its economic rationales, Ralph Mann's study of the anti-Chinese movement in Nevada City and Grass Valley demonstrates that it was the arrival of white women and the establishment of families that precipitated the movement in those two gold-mining communities. The establishment of family life reconstructed bachelor life in the mining towns around a new more hierarchical social and moral order. Many of the services that Chinese immigrant men had provided, such as laundering and cooking, were now performed by families, or by white women who provided services to bachelor populations to supplement their family incomes. Other, heretofore welcomed services provided by the Chinese, such as gambling, prostitution, and opium smoking, were declared morally unacceptable and provided justification for the control, segregation, and finally removal of the Chinese residents of these communities.[34]

Dunfer's rhetorical and somewhat cynical questions—"What was I to do? What'd any good Christian do, especially one new to the business?"—make it clear that racial transgression in the realm of employment is framed as a moral transgression.[35] The regime of the bourgeois nuclear family, reproductive and heterosexual, extends its reach by defining the boundaries between acceptable nonsexual homosociality and deviant same-sex relations. In this case, the accusation against Dunfer and Ah Wee is overtly a charge of economic racial transgression, the employment of a Chinese. In light of Dunfer's affection for Ah Wee, however, the effect of the accusation is homophobic panic. Ah Wee's masquerade as a man is no longer necessary and sufficient to protect the relationship. Ah Wee must "take on ayres like Wites" if the relationship is to survive.

This intervention of the bourgeois family into the homosocial frontier explains Bierce's insistent description of the valley not in pastoral terms but as a "twisted and blasted heath, a unnaturally foreboding place." It also explains his suggestive choice of the word "hermaphrodite" to describe Dunfer's dwelling.[36] The overtly racial and covertly sexual dilemma also explains Dunfer's effort to build a new cabin far back in the woods as an attempt to reconstruct a pastoral utopia in the face of heterosexual and racial discipline.

Gopher, the hired man, is described as misshapen and deformed, while Dunfer, the petty capitalist, is described as looking like he had not worked for some time, and as a prodigious consumer of tobacco and drink. Gopher's body is deformed both by his economic exploitation and by his frustrated desire for Ah Wee. The erotic rivalry between Dunfer and Gopher is intense but, given their class relations, one-sided. It ends only in the death of Dunfer and can be measured by the terse bitterness of the crude grave marker that Gopher has made for his erstwhile master. Bierce uses the figure of Gopher to represent working-class frustration, both at capitalist affection for and exploitation of the Chinese and with its own desire for the Chinese. Gopher has won and lost Ah Wee. He does not object to Dunfer's glib rationalization of Ah Wee's homicide in the public record, for to do so would also reveal his own secret desire for Ah Wee. Instead, he waits to poison Dunfer.

As a racially subordinate object of desire, Ah Wee has neither voice nor agency while alive. Even Ah Wee's physical description is limited to Dunfer's exclamation that "Ah Wee had face like a day in June, and big black eyes—I guess maybe they were the damn'dest eyes in this neck o' woods." Only Ah Wee's eyes are physical markers of difference. The only other thing that sets Ah Wee apart is a distinctive style in chopping down trees—chopping around the base of the tree, whereas Dunfer chops across. Whether this difference in woodsmanship is symbolic of other unspoken differences in sexual behavior, one can only speculate. On his return trip the young reporter does note, however, that the tree stumps, however differently cut, seem all to have rotted away in the same manner. This discovery reveals the superficiality of Whiskey Jo's courtroom rationale for homicide. The "nub" of the question is obviously elsewhere.

Ah Wee's masquerade as a man works to protect the interracial couple as long as it is assumed that the homosocial relations that sustain it are not erotic. However, the introduction of the bourgeois family with its heterosexual orthodoxy brings with it the threat of the homophobic accusation, and the sexual masquerade becomes as threatening as the exposure of racial transgression. Thus the threat of the Chinese servant as an ambivalent sexual object reasserts itself.

Although Ah Wee's sexual identity is what Dunfer and Gopher must both keep secret so as not to reveal their (racially and/or sexually) transgressive desires, it is race and not sex that determines Ah Wee's fate. Ah Wee's death is a warning to other Chinese not to "put on ayres as White" after all. It is race that asserts itself in determining the value and outcome of this relationship. While "The Haunted Valley" does not secure the sexuality of Ah Wee or Dunfer or Gopher, the gender triangle does secure racial difference. The story finally turns on the establishment by bourgeois society of an immutable difference between Ah Wee's Chineseness and Dunfer's and Gopher's Whiteness. Ah Wee's permanent status as the subordinate object of desire is determined by race. Ah Wee is "won," after all, in a poker game. On the face of it, Ah Wee's race, not her sex, is the principal social marker of difference and transgression. It is Ah Wee's Chineseness to which the people upon the Hill object. It is this racial object in the first instance which makes necessary Ah Wee's sexual masquerade. As it turns out, the question of Ah Wee's sex is made moot by the jury's unquestioning acceptance of Jo Dunfer's silly plea; the public value of Ah Wee's life is measured only by Ah Wee's race.

It is only in death that Ah Wee's presence is felt through the supernatural power of the evil eye. Mary Douglas reminds us that those who represent the danger of pollution are often endowed with magical powers, especially the power to cast evil spells.[37] It is Ah Wee's eyes, the very same eroticized body parts that Dunfer exclaims are the "damnd'est eyes around," the physical markers of race that have "incapacitated his servant for good service," which, in death, become Ah Wee's instruments of terror. After Dunfer's scream of fear, the young reporter "saw that the knot-hole in the wall had indeed become a human eye—a full, black eye, that glared into my own with an entire lack of expression more awful than the most devilish glitter." [38] In this moment, sexualized and racialized difference is reified in the persistence of the sign of the Oriental body—the inscrutable eye.

"Poor Ah Toy"

By contrast to the unknowable gothic of "A Haunted Valley," Mary Mote's "Poor Ah Toy" seems at first glance to offer a didactic and straightforward cautionary tale about the potentially disastrous consequences of miscommunication between white mistresses and Chinese servants. Historian Glenna Matthews notes that the "servant problem" dominated the pages of women's magazines between the 1870s and the First World War. Matthews writes that in the mid-nineteenth century, the "help" of neighboring farm girls who were, more often than not, considered part of the family was displaced by immigrant (often Irish) "servants" whose cultural, linguistic, religious, and class differences were pronounced. "No one was going to call "Bridget," as she was frequently so personified, a republican independent dependent. She was Catholic, poorly educated, and highly vulnerable." [39] For thousands of middle-class white families, finding a substitute for Bridget meant turning to a male Chinese servant.

"Poor Ah Toy" tells the sad story of the relation between a young white middle-class matron, Fanny Siddons, and her Chinese servant, Ah Toy. Fanny Siddons arrives in California shortly after the end of the Civil War to take over the household duties of her deceased sister-in-law, who has left Robert Siddons a widower with two young children. Finding the Irish female housekeeper unsuitable and trying a series of imperfect Chinese servants, Fanny is sent Ah Toy, the young cook and houseboy of a close family friend.

Ah Toy proves to be an excellent domestic servant in every respect, a quick learner and a patient worker under Fanny's tutelage. For some time, domestic order and tranquillity are restored, and Ah Toy becomes a member of the household. When he falls ill after news of the death of his mother, Fanny cares for him as a child, much the way that she had for an old Negro slave in her father's home in Virginia. Ah Toy is entrusted with the care of the family and, in Robert Siddons' absence, is invited to join the family at the hearth.

This idyll of reconstructed family begins to unravel with the arrival of Captain Ward, a suitor to Fanny. Ah Toy becomes immediately jealous of Captain Ward. After Ward and Fanny are engaged, Ah Toy angrily confronts Captain Ward and is dismissed by Fanny for his insolence. In the kitchen after his dismissal, overcome by frustrated passion, Ah Toy attempts to kiss Fanny's hand and to profess his love for her.

Fanny recoils in horror, saying that her brother would kill Ah Toy if he found out what Ah Toy had done. Shaken, Fanny tells Ah Toy that he must leave at once. She hires another Chinese servant, one Gong Wah, who proves to be an incompetent. Nevertheless, Fanny is distracted and can no longer sustain an interest in the household's management.

A dramatic change for the better in the condition of the household makes Fanny suspicious of Ah Toy's renewed presence. She believes she hears him singing and she thinks she feels someone touching her cheeks at night. She sends her brother on a fruitless search for Ah Toy that seems to reveal only the extent to which Fanny has been driven to distraction by her emotional entanglement with Ah Toy.

The next morning, however, Gong Wah finds Ah Toy's body in the barn. Ah Toy has hanged himself and left a note stating that he cannot bear to be apart from Miss Fanny and that he desires to be buried on the farm so as to be with her forever. This extraordinary request is granted. Fanny goes on to marry Captain Ward, but returns often to visit the grave of Ah Toy.

"Poor Ah Toy" is at one level a domestic fiction that reiterates the taboo on interclass and interracial intimacy. Like Charles Nordhoff, Mary Mote serves up a warning to female employers of Chinese household servants.[40] They should not succumb to their own image of the Chinese as childlike. They should be careful not to let their own "natural" kindness be mistaken for affection. Finally they should be careful not to allow servants to assume positions within the private realm of the family as surrogate family members.

"Poor Ah Toy" reverses the power relations of social history: the least socially powerful, the spinster homemaker and the Chinese servant, are the principal agents of the story. The most socially powerful, Robert Siddons, Fanny's older widowed brother, and Captain Louis Ward, a former Union officer, are given little agency in this story. In the rivalry between Ward and Ah Toy for the affections of Fanny, there is nothing equal in the social contest between the white gentleman and the Chinese houseboy. Ward has to do nothing to gain the adoration of Fanny, while there is seemingly nothing that Ah Toy can do to gain her affection. Nevertheless, at the psychological level, Ah Toy's transgressive display of affection, his departure, and his death all have a deep effect on Fanny, the unattainable object of his desire.

Fanny and Ah Toy are economic orphans of the post-Civil War economy. Fanny is like many a young woman from a genteel former slaveholding family, for whom factory work is unsuitable and marriage to the ap-

propriate gentleman difficult. One of Fanny's few options, apart from teaching, for making her own living and enabling her to retain her class status is to establish herself as the surrogate mother of her widowed brother's family. Ah Toy, like thousands of other Chinese immigrant men displaced from mining, railroad building, or farm work in the 1860s and 1870s, enters the white middle-class household as cook, houseboy, and laundryman. In entering into domestic labor either as household servants or independent service providers, such as laundrymen or tailors, Chinese men avoided competition with white men but competed directly with women, particularly immigrant Irish women.

Indeed, Fanny's first act in establishing her rule as a True Woman in command of the household is to replace the "slatternly" Irish housekeeper, "who had aspired to become the mistress of the situation." The housekeeper leaves muttering that Miss Siddons was only fit to be served by "them nasty Chinamen, for no dacint woman would stand the likes of her domineerin' ways." Ah Toy's arrival relieves Fanny of "the hundred petty details to be attended to in paying sacrifices to the exacting Moloch of neat housewifery" which, "in addition to the watchful observance of the children, were on the shoulders of the conscientious and diligent girl." [41]

While it saved True Womanhood from the physical demands of the secular cult of cleanliness, the entry of men into the domestic sphere threatened to unsettle the gendered division of labor, putting men in domestic roles such as cleaning and cooking and assigning supervisory and management roles to women. The creation of the domestic male required a place for an alternative masculinity. This alternative masculinity, opposed to True Womanhood by gender and class and to the Western Hero by race and class, could be contained by racial taboo and facilitated by the assumption that the Chinese male immigrant, bereft of family in the United States, would eventually return to China. Thus a critical turn is taken when Ah Toy is orphaned by the death of his mother in China. Her death takes away the reason for his future return to China; he declares his permanent residence in the United States: "Me no go to my Chiny-place, me allee time stay here." Ah Toy's orphan status makes him available to assume a permanent position within the domestic sphere of the Siddons household, transforming him from sojourner to permanent alien. It also make him available as both a surrogate child to Fanny and an alternative head of household.

This surrogacy is made manifest when Ah Toy falls ill and "Fanny wait[s] on him with the womanly tenderness her mother had shown to a favorite slave." This is a clear warning that Fanny's behavior is anachronistic, better suited to the extended pre-capitalist household under the

rules of slavery. The same act in the "modern" bourgeois family has been given a different meaning and has different consequences.

The construction of Ah Toy as a surrogate child accomplishes several things. It symbolically shifts him from an object of exchange, a commodity, into an imagined family member. The reader recalls that Ah Toy had been "given" to Fanny by a friend of the Siddons. His arrival had been accompanied by a note:

> Now that you have undertaken the charge I am not willing that all the sacrifices shall be yours; and therefore tender to you my own private and particular factotum, Ah Toy, hoping that he will lighten your burdens as he has mine. He is cleanly, honest, faithful, but lest you disbelieve in my paragon, I must own that he is unduly sensitive and has been somewhat spoiled.[42]

Ah Toy's childlike, "feminine" qualities can be safely contained, indeed inventoried and deployed in the service of the household. Initially, Ah Toy is described as "tall, youthful, comely, jauntily dressed. With a bow, this Mongolian exquisite presented a delicately tinted, faintly perfumed billet."[43] Ah Toy's fastidiousness and sensitivity distinguish him from earlier household servants. "Evidently Ah Toy was of another ilk, and as complement to his exceptional tidiness, his bedroom was hung with cheerful paper, a dozen flaming lithographs were bestowed to adorn the walls, and a bright colored matting laid upon the floor."[44]

Since Ah Toy's labor has restored "comfort and order" to the "storm-tossed" Siddons household, attention to his sensitivity is a small price to pay. When Robert Siddons attempts to admonish Ah Toy, Fanny is quick to remind her brother that Ah Toy is "the very center of our domestic economy."[45] Here Ah Toy's role in restoring the domestic economy is seen as part of a pastoral restoration; his dual role as servant and surrogate child recapitulates the role of bonded servant or apprentice in the pre-capitalist extended household. In actuality, his role as waged servant brings the entering wedge of capitalism into the bourgeois household itself.

As a surrogate child, Ah Toy can enter into the intimate sphere of the family. After a short time, Robert Siddons leaves the family in Ah Toy's trusted and skilled hands while he travels on business. Ah Toy is able to claim a space within the family sphere.

> Ah Toy, solitary in the kitchen one rainy evening, donned his best silk blouse and, tapping at the door, timidly begged leave to join the little circle. As the dog and cat were outstretched in lazy content on the rug, it seemed hard to deny the one lone servant admission to the hearth; so he was welcomed to a humble seat corner, where he shared the mirth and good cheer in a deferential way: popping corn, cracking nuts, and making ingenious little toys for the children.[46]

In crossing to the hearth, Ah Toy is crossing the internal boundaries of race and class. Despite his trusted position as temporary guardian of the household, his permission to enter the domestic sphere of the hearth relies on his status as a surrogate child. He is not, and he is conscious of the fact he is not, the surrogate master. "Henceforth, in Mr. Siddons's absence, he often joined the group, never presuming to do so when the master presided."[47]

Finally, Ah Toy's status as a surrogate child makes possible, and at the same time, unresolvable, the erotic tension between himself and Fanny. Establishing a surrogate mother/child relation between Fanny and Ah Toy establishes an alternative vehicle for intimacy that conforms to Victorian codes of gender and desire and thus was extremely familiar to the Victorian woman.

In the ideology of domesticity, the constrained relationship between disciplined husband and passionless wife was paralleled in importance only by the intimacy between mother and her male child. G. M. Goshagian has demonstrated the central role that an obsession with imagined incest between mother and son played in the domestic ideology of the Victorians.[48] The male child/mother relationship established a vehicle for intimacy and simultaneously raised an incest taboo to suppress or contain passion.

It is the confrontation between this third, alternative gender, figured as the male child, and the Western hero that is at the heart of the relations of desire among Ah Toy, Louis Ward, and Fanny Siddons. "Poor Ah Toy" directly compares this version of Orientalized sexuality with Western masculinity. Fanny describes Louis Ward, a former Union officer whom she admires despite his former status as an enemy, as "a real Yankee, but a gentleman, intelligent, accomplished, agreeable." On his arrival at the Siddons's door, Ward is described as dark and handsome, in sharp contrast to the more elaborate and feminized description of Ah Toy on his arrival. In keeping with Victorian conventions of gender and sexuality, which assigned emotional sensitivity, if not sexual passion, to the female, Ah Toy is rendered as vastly more sensitive and emotionally complex than either Robert Siddons the brother, or Louis Ward the suitor, who are depicted as civil and restrained. In emotional terms Ah Toy is much more closely aligned to Fanny.

Ward's arrival is marked by a bold assertion of his masculinity: "Fanny's smile of welcome was more eloquent than speech, for Captain Ward took both her hands and boldly kissed her lips."[49] It is when Ah Toy presumes to assert his own sense of racial equality and to act in the same way that the incest taboo asserts itself. Refusing a large tip for the favor of walking twelve miles to deliver the very telegram that will bring Ward to the Siddons home, Ah Toy asserts a claim to class status. "I no

T-a-r-t-a-r. I allee same gentleman." [50] Later, frustrated by the evident permanent presence of Ward, Ah Toy attempts to use his indispensability to the domestic economy to oust his perceived rival for Fanny's affections from the position as honored guest. When Ah Toy angrily confronts Ward, Fanny rebukes and dismisses him; moments later in the kitchen, a space that Ah Toy shares with Fanny, he makes the following advance.

> The yellow features of the spectator grew ashen with suppressed feeling, his black eyes glittered with a strange light, as he caught her hand and pressed the jeweled fingers to his lips, in imitation of a salute he had seen when the captain fancied himself and Fanny unobserved. [51]

Fanny recoils in horror and shameful knowledge. Ah Toy's kiss has pierced the veil that has marked their relationship. The single gesture of desire violates the surrogate child/mother relationship and breaks the incest taboo, exposing the seams of race, class, and sexuality that suture their relationship.

That Ah Toy has broken the incest taboo between mother and surrogate child is made clear from Fanny's immediate verbal response to his kiss. Her first words are, "you are a bad man." [52] This is the first and only time Ah Toy is referred to as an adult. Fanny's further response is to internalize the incest violation, blaming herself as mother for the failure to successfully tutor the child: "She darted from the room, white, cold, heart-sick, to throw herself on her bed in an agony of shame and apprehension, sobbing to herself: I am to blame, I am to blame." [53]

This transgression is cathartic and transformative. Although Ah Toy has been driven from the household, his presence continues to be felt. Although Ah Toy's successor proves incompetent, the once fastidious Fanny is distracted from her duties as superintendent of the household. "Fanny bore herself to Gong Wah with an icy hauteur that astonished Robert. She kept entirely aloof from the kitchen, and refused to correct his short comings." [54]

It is Ah Toy's racially and sexually transgressive kiss, and not her engagement to Ward, that transforms Fanny from a girl into a woman. This transformation is beset with pain, since it flows not from an orderly transition from girlish innocence to True Womanhood but from exposed desire, both Ah Toy's and her own. After Ah Toy's exile, Fanny is described as being full of "womanly shame and remorseful anxiety." Desire, guilt, and remorse have transformed Fanny. She has become

> a changeling, for the frank, sunny girl had been displaced by an irritable, absent-minded, and dejected woman—a metamorphosis that dumbfounded the men to whom she was dear, she grew wan, careworn, and

strangely nervous. The truth was that she was harassed by vague fore-
bodings and by constant self-reproach.[55]

The search for Ah Toy on the Siddons ranch reveals the depth of her
mixed feeling for him. "The pitiable condition of the wretched creature
and his presence in the valley filled her with apprehension that drove
her half wild." When her "eager quest" for Ah Toy turns up no sign of
him, she admits that "I have thought about that wretched boy till I am
almost insane."

Ah Toy's suicide is his final gesture of resistance. He hangs himself in
a manner that underscores his status as a racially defined subordinate,
the racial status that makes his desire for his white mistress impossible.
Ah Toy kills himself by the very sign of his difference: "He had managed
to suspend himself with the long and thick cue which had been the object of his pride."[56]

Ah Toy leaves a note stating that, unlike many Chinamen who die in
America, he does not want his remains to be sent back to an ancestral
home in China but wants instead to be buried on the Siddons ranch.
Gong Wah translates and paraphrases the note to Fanny: "He no wantee
bones go back Chiney, he wantee puttee in glound here, so he allee time
see Miss Fanny."[57]

Gravestones mark the presence of people on the landscape. In both
"The Haunted Valley" and "Poor Ah Toy," the headstones of Chinese
immigrants signify their status as permanent resident aliens in America.
Both headstones are inscribed with epitaphs that, reflecting the ambivalence of their authors toward their subjects, are layered in meaning. Both
mark the racial parameters that simultaneously created and constrained
new possibilities for relations of desire, conflating the sexual with race,
class, and gender formations. The crude warning on Ah Wee's gravestone to "Celestials" not to be "putting on airs" underscores Ah Wee's
subordinate and vulnerable status as a racial Other. The warning against
"putting on airs" of presumptive racial equality is ironic, in the face of
the "airs" of sexual identity that Ah Wee is supposed to have put on in
collaboration with Dunfer and Gopher. Just below the warning, the "revealing" comment "She was a good egg," attests to that ambiguity of
transracial (and more ambiguously, homosexual) desire that shaped the
relationship between Ah Wee, Dunfer, and Gopher in the transition between the homosocial world of the gold rush and the heterosexual world
of Victorian California. On the second headstone, the simple inscription
"Poor Ah Toy" both recognizes Ah Toy's subordinate class status dictated
by his race and, at the same time, is an oblique expression of sympathy
for his desires. In his suicide note, Ah Toy stakes two claims, both unat-

tainable for the Chinaman in life: The first is on the heart of Fanny Siddons, the second is for a place in America. The first is achieved simply by interment, the second by the memorial. "Fanny Siddons never returned to the spot; but Mrs. Louis Ward came more than once to see an humble grave whose headstone bore the brief inscription, 'Poor Ah Toy.'"[58]

Displacing Women, Destabilizing Gender

The presence of the Chinese male disrupts the fragile balances between sexes within the household, both in the realm of sexuality and in the realm of labor. On the one hand, the Oriental domestic could be made the site of homoerotic and/or multiracial alternatives to the emergent heterosexual and monoracial orthodoxy of Victorian America. At the same time, the employment of the male Chinese servant to do "woman's work" destabilized the gendered nature of labor.

In 1868, the song "Irish Widdy Woman," meant to be sung in Irish brogue, castigated Chinese laundryman for having "ruint th' thrade."

> For I kin wash an' iron a shirt,
> An' I kin starch a collar as stiff
> As any Chineseman, I'm sure;
> But ther dhirty, pigtail haythens,
> An' ther prices they are paid
> Have brought me to the state you see—
> They've entirely ruint th' th'rade.[59]

Boycotts of industrial and agricultural employers of Chinese led Chinese to seek employment in the home or to open small businesses in industries most identified with "woman's work." In both "The Haunted Valley" and "Poor Ah Toy," the Chinese immigrant enters and displaces a non-Chinese woman (in the first case, Mexican, and in the second, Irish).

In 1910 the State of Montana attempted to drive the Chinese out of the laundry business by requiring the purchase of a ten-dollar license to operate a laundry. The law exempted steam laundries and laundries operated by women. Quong Wing, a Chinese male laundry operator, sued for the return of his ten dollars. Arguing the case before the US Supreme Court, Quong Wing's attorney did not claim that the intent of law was racial discrimination, which it was, but rather that the law discriminated against Quong Wing as a man. Seeking to preserve a separate (and protected) female sphere and the gendered nature of work, Justice Oliver Wendell Holmes responded:

Hand laundry work is a widespread occupation of Chinamen in this country; while on the other hand, it is so rare to see men of our race engaged in it that many of us would be unable to say that they had ever observed the case. . . .

If Montana deems it advisable to put a lighter burden upon women than upon men with regard to employment that *our people commonly regard* as more appropriate for the former, the Fourteenth amendment does not interfere by creating a fictitious equality where there is a real difference.[60] (Emphasis added.)

The presence of Chinese men in the sphere of domestic labor, once naturalized as "woman's work," required a new formulation of the separate spheres. Although Justice Holmes did not empower the Fourteenth Amendment to create "fictitious equality," the "real difference" between sexes could no longer be taken for granted, but now had to be recognized as a social construction, defined by the "common regard."[61]

Inner Dikes and Barred Zones

A t the end of the nineteenth century, Theodore Roosevelt wrote to his friend, the diplomat Spring Rice, "Together . . . the two branches of the Anglo-Saxon race . . . could whip the world."[1] Roosevelt joined Alfred Thayer Mahan, the apostle of American naval power, in calling for a program of vigorous military preparedness and an "Anglo-Saxon" alliance of English-speaking peoples.[2] Roosevelt and Mahan shared a concern about competition from Germany, Russia, and Japan for concessions and spheres of influence in China and Korea and an anxiety about a revanchist challenge to the white domination of Asia. In 1905, this anxiety over a "Yellow Peril" assumed the status of a nightmare after Japan's stunning military victory over Russia.[3]

While a formal British-American alliance never materialized, the spirit of Anglo-Saxonism expressed by Roosevelt shaped the racial discourse of the first two decades of the new century. Between the time that Roosevelt rode off to liberate the Cubans and the passage of the Immigration Act of 1923, Cuba, the Philippines, Hawaii, and Puerto Rico were all brought under the American eagle. The American transformation from republic to (comparatively small) empire created anxieties about new immigration and "racial suicide." These anxieties were voiced in debates over nationality, naturalization, and family in which the Oriental was consolidated as the Yellow Peril.[4]

The construction of the Yellow Peril was paralleled by a consolidation of whiteness. Roosevelt's call for an Anglo-Saxon alliance prompted columnist Finley Peter Dunne's trenchant observer of American life, Mr. Dooley, to observe to his pal Hinnissy:

106

An Anglo-Saxon . . . is a German that's forgot who was his parents. . . . Mack is an Anglo-Saxon. His folks come fr'm th' County Armagh, an' their nay-tional Anglo-Saxon hymn is 'O'Donnell Aboo.' Teddy Rosenfelt is another Anglo-Saxon. An' I'm an Anglo-Saxon. . . . Th' name iv Dooley has been th' proudest Anglo-Saxon name in th' County Roscommon f'r many years. Schwartzmeister is an Anglo-Saxon, but he doesn't know it, an' won't till some wan tells him. Pether Bowbeen down be th' Frinch church is formin' th' Circle Francaize Anglo-Saxon club, an' me ol' frind Domingo . . . will march at th' head iv th' Dago Anglo-Saxons whin th' time comes. There ar-re twinty thousan' Rooshian Jews at a quarther a vote in th' Sivinth Ward; an', ar-rmed with raghooks, they'd be a tur-r-ble thing f'r anny inimy iv th' Anglo-Saxon 'lieance to face. Th' Bohemians an' Pole Anglo-Saxons may be a little slow in wakin' up to what th' pa-apers calls our common hurtage, but ye may be sure they'll be all r-right whin they're called on.[5]

As Dooley observed, the Anglo-Saxon "race" had become a big tent, under which immigrants from many nations might be gathered, so long as they shared the "common hurtage." How exactly the "common hur-tage" might be defined was never clear. The Naturalization Act of 1790 offered U.S. citizenship to immigrants if they had resided in the United States for five years, had declared their intent to become American citi-zens two years prior to applying for naturalization, and were "free white persons."[6] The 1790 act was inclusive with regard to cultural difference (it allowed Catholics and Jews, German and French immigrants to be-come citizens), but it was exclusive with regard to race (only "free white persons" could be naturalized).

The category "free white persons" appeared clear enough when contrasted to enslaved Africans or indentured Europeans. However, it seemed less obvious when it came to Asians. George Washington, for example, had expressed surprise to discover that Chinese were not "white."[7] In practice, the naturalization of Asian immigrants was incon-sistent across the country. In the 1850s and 1860s, Chinese immigrants were denied citizenship by California courts, but courts in Massachusetts naturalized Chinese applicants. In the early decades of the twentieth century, courts in Oregon and Washington granted citizenship to Sikh and Muslim applicants from India, while California courts approved the naturalization petitions of Filipinos. Similar petitions were denied in New York, Pennsylvania, and Massachusetts.[8]

By 1870, the abolition of slavery and the passage of the Fourteenth Amendment prompted the amendment of the "free white persons" stip-ulation of the naturalization statute. Charles Sumner, the old Radi-cal Republican from Massachusetts, called for the simple removal of the single word "white" removed from the naturalization statute, thereby opening citizenship to all regardless of race. However, the law was amended to specifically include only "persons of African nativity and descent." Furthermore, the 1870 legislation expressly prohibited Chinese immigrants, "subjects of the Celestial Empire," from gaining citizenship through naturalization.[9] In 1882, Chinese workers were barred from entering the United States.

Although the Immigration and Naturalization Act of 1870 explicitly denied Chinese immigrants the right to become naturalized citizens, it did not define the term "free white person." Other Asian immigrants continued to settle in the United States. Between 1885 and 1908, more than 150,000 Japanese immigrants came to the United States. After the United States conquered the Philippines at the turn of the century, 26,000 Filipinos immigrated. Almost 6,000 Korean immigrants and just over 5,000 immigrants from the Indian subcontinent arrived in America in the first two decades of the twentieth century. Hundreds of these Asian immigrants, not barred as Chinese, would apply to be naturalized Americans and challenge the notion of the "free white person" in an effort to share Dooley's "common hurtage."

All of these Asian immigrants met widespread and well organized hostility; anti-Japanese, anti-"Hindoo" and anti-Filipino political movements, violence, and discriminatory legislation followed in the tradition of the anti-Chinese movement.[10] Although hostility toward the Japanese, Korean, Filipino, and Indian immigrants was concentrated on the west coast, local agitation led to state and federal legislation aimed at curbing "Oriental" immigration and prohibiting "Orientals" from becoming naturalized citizens. At the federal level, the Gentlemen's Agreement of 1907 insisted that Japan "voluntarily" agree to stop issuing visas to Japanese laborers seeking to come to the United States. As part of the Immigration Act of 1917, Congress created the "Asiatic Barred Zone," which prohibited the immigration of any person whose ancestry could be traced to the Asian continent or Pacific Islands. In 1922, Congress passed the Cable Act, which stipulated that a female American citizen who married a foreign national would lose her citizenship. In 1924, the exceptions for immigrants from Japan were eliminated, and Japanese immigration was brought to a halt.[11]

It was not only a fear of the Yellow Peril but also a thirst for overseas markets and its passion for coaling stations that had led the United States to seize dominion over Puerto Rico, Cuba, Hawaii, Guam, Samoa, and the Philippines. Notwithstanding its rapid acquisition of a mid-sized empire at the turn of the century, the United States was deeply divided on the issue of direct colonial rule over overseas possessions.[12] President McKinley himself professed ambivalence about the annexation of the Philippines. In an interview with Protestant ministers who had come to express their concerns about the brutal war to suppress Filipino independence, the deeply religious McKinley offered this account of his epiphany about "The White Man's Burden":

> The truth is I didn't want the Philippines and when they came to us as a gift from the gods, I did not know what to do about them. . . . I thought first we would take only Manila: then Luzon: then other islands, perhaps also. . . . One night late it came to me this way. . . . One, that we could not give them back to Spain—that would be cowardly and dishonorable; two, that we could not turn them over to France or Germany—our commercial rivals in the Orient—that would be bad business and discreditable; three, that we could not leave them to themselves—they were unfit for self-government— and they would soon have anarchy and misrule over there worse than Spain's was; and four, that there was nothing left for us to do but to take them all and by God's grace do the very best we could do by them, as our fellowmen for whom Christ also died. And then I went to bed, and to sleep and slept soundly.[13]

The anti-imperialist movement marshaled a wide array of arguments against colonial expansion. Some argued that an American imperium was antithetical to its republican tradition and values. Others cited a popular revulsion against the brutality of the Philippine war, and a sympathy for national independence movements. However, many of its most prominent participants opposed the annexation of Hawaii and later the Philippines on the grounds that it would result in the arrival of millions of yellow and brown immigrants.

The steel magnate Andrew Carnegie saw the potential addition of Asian subjects to the polity as a threat to national unity and asked, "Is the Republic to remain one homogeneous whole, one united people, or to become a scattered and disjointed aggregate of widely separated and alien races?"[14] Historian C. Vann Woodward has noted that

> The doctrine of Anglo-Saxon superiority. . . . which justified and rationalized American imperialism in the Philippines, Hawaii, and Cuba differed in no essentials from the race theories by which [anti-imperialist] Senator Benjamin R. Tillman of South Carolina or Senator James K. Vardaman of Mississippi justified white supremacy in the South.[15]

Both imperialists and anti-imperialists shared the view that the threat from the East represented a peril to the nation; they differed on its proximity.

David Starr Jordan, the founding president of Stanford University, held that democratic institutions had been uniquely developed by Anglo-Saxons and could only exist where Anglo-Saxons thrived. Anglo-Saxons, in particular the Anglo-Saxon family, Jordan asserted, could not thrive in the tropics, hence democratic values and institutions could not take root there, nor were those born under such conditions likely to become assimilable citizens. "Colonial Aggrandizement is not national expansion; slaves are not men. Wherever degenerate, dependent or alien races are within our borders to-day, they are not part of the United States. They constitute a social problem; a menace to peace and welfare."[16]

Jordan warned that the race problem was an even greater problem for the United States than the threat of foreign armies. He compared the potential "social problem" presented by the attempt to incorporate millions of yellow- and brown-skinned peoples into America to the "social problem" presented by the freed African American. Jordan feared the annexation of the Philippines would expand the "race problem" in the United States, since he believed that because of their tropical environment Filipinos were naturally unsuited to democratic institutions and hence to economic and social development. Jordan asserted, "The race problems of the tropics are perennial and insoluble, for free institutions cannot exist where free men cannot live."[17]

Quoting "The White Man's Burden," Kipling's sardonic ode to the American annexation of the Philippines, on the floor of the Senate, Senator "Pitchfork" Ben Tillman, the Georgia populist who had led the crusade to disenfranchise blacks and to establish Jim Crow segregation in the South, also invoked the so-called Negro Problem in warning against the racial problems implicit in the imperialist adventure.[18]

> We [Southerners] understand and realize what it is to have two races side by side that can not mix or mingle without deterioration and injury to both and the ultimate destruction of the civilization of the higher. We of the South have borne this white man's burden of a colored race in our midst since their emancipation and before.
>
> It was a burden upon our manhood and our ideas of liberty before they were emancipated. It is still a burden, although they have been granted the franchise. It clings to us like the shirt of Nessus. . . . Why do we as a people want to incorporate into our citizenship ten millions more of different or of differing races, three or four of them?[19]

More explicitly, Samuel Gompers, who as president of the Cigar Makers Union and president of the American Federation of Labor had waged a successful war against Chinese immigration and who was in the midst of mobilizing the organized labor movement against Japanese immigration, asked rhetorically,

> If the Philippines are annexed what is to prevent the Chinese, the Negritos and the Malays coming to our country? How can we prevent the Chinese coolies from going to the Philippines and from there swarm into the

United States and engulf our people and our civilization? If these new islands are to become ours, it will be either under the form of Territories
or States. Can we hope to close the flood-gates of immigration from the
hordes of Chinese and the semi-savage races coming from what will then
be part of our own country?[20]

The same narrative that linked the racial peril at home to the one
abroad could be found in the popular culture as well as in the elite debates over America's imperial adventures. A one-act skit, *The King of the
Philippine Islands,* is an example of the popularity of this theme.[21] Sub-
titled "a ludicrous afterpiece," *The King of the Philippine Islands* was written for the vaudeville and amateur stage by Frank Dumont, a veteran of
the blackface minstrel stage. In the classic Jim Crow style, the skit features Willie Danger, a "colored cook" who, through cowardice and stu-
pidity, brings about an attack by Filipino rebels on an encampment of
American soldiers. But Danger, like his model Zip Coon, survives and
finally outwits his captors. Willie Danger is portrayed as an abject coward
who survives out of blind luck and a willingness to claim that he is "half
Filipino." Danger then outwits the "savage natives" by offering them
"citizenship" in a sham republic of which he has declared himself president. Just before he is to be cooked and eaten by the Filipino "savages,"
Willie in desperation announces,

> Now that you're free as Cuba, and you have reciprocity and beet sugar men
> with you, it is just that we should rule the Philippines and we will! (Natives
> cheers) . . . These islands are the only free and independent spots on the
> globe. (cheers) [J. P.] Morgan owns everything on the sea—[Mark] Hanna
> owns the land. But we've got this and were going to hold it! (cheers).[22]

The Filipinos follow Danger until he greedily takes all of the island's
spoils for himself. The farce ends when Danger is blown up, although he
appears again waving an American flag while white American soldiers
round up the native insurgents.

In this sketch, it is the emancipated black Willie, and not the Filipinos,
who is the real danger to the republic. The Spanish American War was
the occasion for white veterans from both the Union and the Confed-
eracy to reconcile around a military call for national unity.[23] In the first
instance, the portrayal of Willie as a coward serves to erase from public
memory the actual courage of black American troops in the Spanish
American War, much as their service in the Civil War had been effaced.
Willie is fit only to be a cook; when assigned to guard some prisoners, he
immediately becomes a groveling coward, as a result of which the American camp is overrun by Filipino insurgents. This is a thinly disguised play

on reconstruction. Willie is only fit for servitude; once enfranchised he leads to ruin.

Reversing the account of atrocities that took place in the brutal suppression of the Filipino independence struggle, the White American troops are shot from cannons.[24] The portrayal of the Filipinos as savages and, when they threaten to cook and eat Willie Danger, as cannibals corroborate David Starr Jordan's contention that the native of the tropic lacks the capacity to participate in democracy. Finally, the image of the two colored peoples coming together to form an ersatz republic underscores the need for a policy that ensures white supremacy.

The identification of imperialist policy abroad specifically with the "Negro problem" at home was by no means coincidental. Walter Benn Michaels argues that the non-racialist argument against imperialism as a violation of constitutional limitations on federal power and an erosion of the republican tradition went hand in hand with the racist claim that empire would open the floodgates to undesirable nonwhite immigrants. Southern anti-imperialists saw Reconstruction as nonconstitutional and a form of imperialism. The notion of constitutional limits on federal power abroad bolstered Southern arguments for the limited federal power in the enforcement of Reconstruction at home.[25] Benn Michaels points out that Thomas Dixon, whose novel *The Clansman* (1905) became the film *The Birth of A Nation,* characterized the South under Reconstruction as an "African" empire. Benn Michaels writes, "For Progressives like Dixon, however, citizenship in the "new nation," produced out of resistance to an "African" empire, became essentially racial; the legitimacy of the state (its identity as nation rather than empire) was guaranteed by its whiteness." [26]

The King of the Philippine Islands also served the agenda of progressive reform. Willie Danger's pronouncement of his rule over the Philippines is a blackface mimicry of McKinley's justification of American conquest, and his "presidency" satirizes the corruption scandals of the McKinley administration. Willie Danger's first act is to pardon "all persons found guilty of postal frauds and other trivial matters." He celebrates the tycoons Mark Hanna and J. P. Morgan and warns his new citizens "not to expect too much—you've got your freedom! You will vote as you are told to, or you won't get any patronage." The natives later throw out Danger, crying, "we've been buncoed again." [27]

The satire of William McKinley speaks to the concerns of the powerful progressive reform movement that had emerged in the last decades of the nineteenth century in the face of capitalist industrialization and the failure of party politics to address the progressives' desire for more responsive government. The movement, building on the autonomous female public sphere that had arisen in mid-century, mobilized thousands of middle-class women and fostered the maturation of their political culture in the years between 1900 and 1920.[28]

Female reformers saw a need for reconstructing the home as a sphere apart from the office or factory. Eileen Boris observes that "progressives attempted to mitigate the impact of capitalist industrialization by consciously or unconsciously stabilizing the social order, in which reconstructing the family was a central component."[29]

Although disenfranchised in all but a few states, and excluded from the male domain of party politics, women mobilized support for the protection of women and children through social legislation and court action. By the turn of the century, the state actively protected the reconstruction of the family in an effort to preserve gender-based obligations; in separating home from polity and economy, the state ratified not only existing power relations within families but also the relationship of different family members to the state.[30]

This newfound concern on the part of the state for the reconstruction of the family was not unrelated to the question of race and empire. The influx of immigration, not only from Asia but also from Central and Southern Europe, had given rise to anxieties among the still predominantly "old stock" Anglo-Saxon middle class about "racial suicide." Alisa Klaus notes that Theodore Roosevelt linked the nation's military and economic vigor with the strength of the family and likened motherhood to military service.[31] When the Supreme Court upheld legislation establishing a minimum wage for women in 1911, it did so on the basis that the compelling national interest was the survival of the common heritage. "As healthy mothers are essential to vigorous offspring, the physical well-being of a woman becomes an object of public interest and care in order to preserve the strength and vigor of the race."[32]

Fu Manchu: Consolidating the Oriental

The threat to the white race was not from Willie Danger's "cannibals"; the Filipino nationalist movement was crushed with brute ferocity. The Yellow Peril came in the form of immigrants who resided in the Chinatowns of the white world. This Yellow Peril was given a face and a body in Dr. Fu Manchu, the fiendish mastermind created in the novels of Sax Rohmer.

> Imagine a person tall, lean and feline, high shouldered, with a brow like Shakespeare, and a face like Satan, a close shaven skull and long magnetic eyes of true cat green. Invest him with all the cruel cunning of an entire

> eastern race, accumulated in one giant intellect, with all the resources . . .
> of a wealthy government. . . . Imagine that awful being, and you have a
> mental picture of Dr. Fu Manchu, the yellow peril incarnate in one man.[33]

Although Fu Manchu resided in London's Chinatown, he served "Eastern dynasts" who sought to bring the world under the rule of an "Asiatic Empress." The tales of Fu Manchu harnessed the great tradition of Orientalism to the purposes of Yellow Peril hysteria. The pulp fiction villain was created by Arthur Sarsfield Ward who, as Sax Rohmer, wrote thirteen novels, four short stories, and a novelette about his machinations. The first three novels, *The Insidious Dr. Fu Manchu* (1913), *The Return of Fu Manchu* (1916), and *The Hand of Fu Manchu* (1917), set the pattern for the whole series. The novels enjoyed massive popularity in the United States. Fu Manchu was the first universally recognized Oriental and became the archetype of villainy. After a hiatus of fourteen years, Sax Rohmer moved to the United States and resumed the Fu Manchu series in 1931. His last Fu Manchu tale was published in 1959. In the forty years that spanned Fu Manchu's career in evil, millions read the books, listened to stories about him on the radio, watched him on film and television, and followed his crimes in the comics.[34]

Orientalism, like other theories of domination and difference, relies heavily on establishing authority over the Other through knowledge of and access to the Other's language, history, and culture as a privilege of the colonial agent. The power of knowledge lies in the authority to define the colonized subject and determine its fate. Edward Said writes that "to have such knowledge of such a thing is to dominate 'it', to have authority over 'it.' . . . Since we know it and it exists in a sense as we know it." [35]

In the Fu Manchu stories, Rohmer simultaneously deployed Orientalist authority and reduced the Orientalist tradition of humanistic scholarship and textual authority to a simple racial struggle between the evil Fu Manchu, bent on nationalist revenge, and his Anglo-Saxon nemesis, the ex-colonial agent and Asia expert, Nayland Smith. Just as Kaiser Wilhelm insisted that the struggle between Christendom and the Orient was a "fight to the knife" for racial survival, the "Asiatic" threat that Rohmer's Fu Manchu represents is explicitly the threat of racial annihilation. Nayland Smith makes clear to Dr. Petrie, his sidekick and chronicler, that "the swamping of the white world by Yellow hordes might well be the price of our failure." [36]

The following passage from *The Hand of Fu Manchu,* in which Nayland Smith reveals the secret Oriental plot to rule the world, contains all the elements of the Orientalist paradigm.

You will perhaps remind me . . . of the lowly place held by women in the East. I can cite notable exceptions, ancient and modern. In fact, a moment's consideration will reveal many advantages in the creation by a hypothetical body of Eastern dynast-makers not of an emperor but of an Empress. Finally there is a persistent tradition throughout the Far East that such a woman will one day rule over the known peoples. I was assured some years ago, by a very learned pundit, that a princess of incalculably ancient lineage, residing in some secret monastery in Tartary or Tibet, was to be the future empress of the world.[37]

First, Smith sounds the alarm, introducing the latest and most "shocking" Asiatic problem. The threat from the East is not the open challenge of military might but the threat of subversion. As the chief agent of domination by an Oriental "empress of incalculably ancient lineage," Fu Manchu threatens not only international political stability but also "natural" gender categories that are the pillars of Western civilization and of the white race itself. In carefully balancing received wisdom about the Orient ("the lowly place of women in East") with obvious fantasy ("a secret monastery in Tartary or Tibet . . . assured by an ancient pundit"), Rohmer establishes his Anglo-Saxon hero, Nayland Smith, as an Orientalist authority with appropriate references to logical analysis and a command over both "fact and fantasy" about the Ancient East. "Much of this is legendary," Smith informs Petrie, "some of it mere superstition, but . . . *part of it is true.*[38]

As the shift from Fu Manchu's Chineseness to "Tartary or Tibet" and "the East" suggests, Rohmer's Orientalism collapses national histories into an ahistorical cultural category of Oriental Otherness. Although Fu Manchu is presented as Chinese and the headquarters of his evil empire is located in London's Limehouse Chinatown, his Chineseness is only a marker of his generalized Oriental alienness. Chinatown, long familiar to American readers as a den of vice and moral corruption, is less distinctively Chinese than Oriental. Here, Sax Rohmer describes a "den" in Chinatown that is a hideout for Fu Manchu and his many minions.

These divans were occupied by a motley company of Turks, Egyptians, Greeks, and others, and I noted two Chinese. Most of them smoked cigarettes, and some were drinking. . . . A girl was performing a sinuous dance . . . accompanied by a young Negro woman upon a guitar.[39]

As Smith explains to an awed Petrie, the place is "sort of a combined *Wekaleh* and place of entertainment for a certain class of Oriental residents in or visiting London." In this passage, Nayland Smith exercises his power as the Asia expert to define the Orient. In doing so, he simultaneously constructs the Orient and establishes authority over his audience.

Throughout the Fu Manchu stories, distinctions among Asian nationalities and cultures are collapsed. Chinamen skulk about in Chinatowns. Reference is continuously made to the underworld of the British empire inhabited by dacoits (Indian bandits), thugees (murderous devotees of the cult of Kali, the Hindu deity of destruction), Lascars (originally a term for Indian soldiers which was extended to include sailors on merchant vessels and laborers and servants), and the "Burmese" death via the suitably exotic "Zayat-kiss." The authority of Nayland Smith, the archetypal area studies expert, comes from his ability to recognize the evidence of a myriad of different Asian criminal elements and to track them back to Fu Manchu, the fount of Oriental evil. Smith's ability to reveal and explain this hidden spectacle to the reader through Petrie establishes his bona fides as an Asia expert and is ultimately the source of Smith's power to thwart Fu Manchu's stratagems.

In an age of beleaguered Victorian masculinity, with its obsession about racial suicide induced by anxieties about over-consumption, over-civilization, and the loss of martial spirit, virility, and authenticity, the "fight to the knife" for racial survival served as a masculine tonic, another opportunity for regeneration through violence.[40] The racial struggle is marked on the bodies of the two contestants. Fu Manchu, cruel of lip and long of fingernail, the agent of the ultimate female domination, is invariably described physically in feline and androgynous terms; Nayland Smith, like Owen Wister's Virginian, is the imaginary archetype of the Anglo-Saxon hero: gaunt, tanned, weathered, a figure evolved from Sir Walter Scott's novels of romantic knighthood.[41] Fu Manchu's power to incite the fevered imagination lies in his ambiguous sexuality, which combines a masochistic vulnerability marked as feminine and a sadistic aggressiveness marked as masculine. Fu Manchu is the archetype of the sado-masochistic Asian male character in American popular culture narratives of the twentieth century. His sexual attractiveness (and his popularity) springs from this simultaneous heterosexuality and homoeroticism. The sexual ambiguity is reflected in the ambiguity of Fu Manchu's racial and cultural background. His Chinese racial identification is decentered by the fact that much is made of his scientific Western education and his sophistication. Fu Manchu is the very definition of the alien, an agent of a distant threat who resides amongst us. He represents the cosmopolitan world of Empire. Yet this cosmopolitanism masks his evil intent, which, Nayland Smith warns, "is to 'pave the way' . . . for nothing less than a colossal Yellow Empire. That dream is what millions of Europeans and Americans term 'the Yellow Peril!' "[42]

The construction of the Oriental has always made sexuality a contested terrain. The Orient, Edward Said reminds us, is constructed as a feminized object of desire. At the heart of Fu Manchu's underworld lies Rohmer's Orientalist sexual fantasy, domination by the Orientalized woman.

> [The would be Empress of the world] always remains young and beautiful by means of a continuous series of reincarnations; also she thus conserves the collated wisdom of many ages. In short she is the archetype of Lamaism. The real secret of Lama celibacy is the existence of this immaculate ruler, of whom the Grand Lama is merely a high priest. She has as attendants, maidens of good family, selected for their personal charms, and rendered dumb in order that they may never report what they see and hear. "Her body slaves are not only mute, but blind; for it is death to look upon her beauty unveiled." [43]

Having momentarily lost himself in this sexualized Orientalist reverie, Nayland Smith quickly recovers his position of authority over the East by resisting its erotic power and at the same time exercising interpretive power over the whole. Through Smith's Orientalist expertise, Rohmer exercises an erotic power over the reader by revealing the unknowable mysteries of the feminized Other, including its apparent silence.

The passage above reminds us that the construction of the Oriental, the denial of subjectivity, takes the form of a sexual domination in which the Orient is constructed as feminine and silent. In this passage, the Orient is not only given gender but also infused with female sexuality and represented as a female object. It is Nayland Smith's mature masculinity, his control over erotic desire, and his appropriation of language and logic that enable him to defeat the clever and cunning Dr. Fu Manchu, who cannot control his own desire to conquer white civilization. Key to the Orientalist's appropriation and control of language is his denial of rationality, sanity, and maturity, all seen as male attributes, to the Oriental. Representing the Orient in terms of female sexuality has been a strategy for establishing the difference between the intellectual, social and historical West and the immature East, caught in the throes of irrationality and unable to exercise self-control. As Smith and Petrie escape yet another trap laid by Fu Manchu, Smith says, "We owe our lives, Petrie, to the natural childishness of the Chinese! A race of ancestor worshippers is capable of anything." [44]

Rescuing Family and Nation at the Movies

If Sax Rohmer gave the Yellow Peril a body and brought him to Chinatown, the movies brought the Yellow Peril from Chinatown into the home. Cecil B. DeMille's *The Cheat* (1915, Paramount) and D. W. Griffith's *Broken Blossoms* (1919, United Artists), two of the earliest feature-length American movies, made explicit what the Fu Manchu stories had only hinted: the Yellow Peril's sexual threat to white civilization. Both *The Cheat* and *Broken Blossoms* constructed and deployed the imagery of sexual relations between Asian men and white women in order to interrogate and ideologically resolve the twin crises of family and nation.

In 1915, David W. Griffith captured the white imagination with his masterwork of racism, *The Birth of A Nation*. The film brought to millions of Americans a historically twisted but emotionally compelling narrative of national redemption through racial revival.[45] *The Birth of A Nation* treated the crisis of a nation still divided by regional loyalties and the politics of race as a crisis of family. The desire to restore a sense of national unity was articulated in terms of national kinship based on racial purity. The divided nation is represented as the white national family, represented in turn by the northern Stonemans and the southern Camerons, who are kin by blood but divided by the politics of race. The white national family is torn asunder by the Civil War, where the cousins are pitted against each other on the battlefield. In a deeply sentimentalized battle scene, two of the cousins are brought together in a dying embrace. The wounded nation can heal only when the attempt to bring blacks into the national family, through emancipation, citizenship, and, worst of all, miscegenation, is brought to an end. Griffith's message was simple and powerful. Black participation in the national family means political corruption and social chaos—in short, the downfall of the white nation. The broken national family can only be redeemed when it recognizes "Negro savagery" and miscegenation as its true enemy. The nation can be reborn in the Klan, where Stonemans and Camerons are reunited in a defense of a "common Aryan birthright." In the flaming Celtic cross, Griffith's Klan deployed a symbol of Christian Anglo-Saxonism in service of a romantic racial nationalism. From the White House, Woodrow Wilson, the first president from the South since Andrew Johnson and a former history professor, enthused that *The Birth of a Nation* was like "writing history with lightning."

The same year that *The Birth of a Nation* celebrated the "redemptive" terror of the old Klan, a new Ku Klux Klan was inaugurated at Stone Mountain, Ga. Although the new Klan found its strongest support in the New South, its popularity spread to all sections of the country. The membership of the new Klan was broadly middle-class; the lawyers, doctors, sheriffs, and bankers who made up the elite of a myriad of small towns provided its institutional core. By 1920, the new Klan could claim the power to mobilize five million defenders of the "Aryan birthright" against not only blacks, but also Catholics, Jews, immigrants, and "deviant" whites.[46]

Wilson's enthusiasm for *The Birth of a Nation* was not merely an expression of appreciation for what he believed to be a vindication of the victimized South, but also a recognition of the power of the movies to mobilize national identity. The movies were the most powerful cultural medium in the first half of the twentieth century. The power of the movies was both social and semiotic. Motion pictures became the main format for the creation of a national audience and the popular articulation of a national narrative. Historian Lary May argues that in the cultural crisis brought about by economic and social changes of the late nineteenth century, the movies provided "both models for an idealized society of consumption and comforting, Victorian reassurances of the perils of indulgence and materialism." [47]

Beginning in the first years of the century, short film strips and one-reelers shown in nickelodeons catered to working-class and immigrant audiences.[48] By the second decade of the century, as movies shifted toward the more complex and novelistic feature-length narrative and as movie theaters were designed to imitate legitimate theaters, the movies began to take on a more reputable image and attract a middle-class audience. When the Lynds began their study of white working-class life in Muncie, Indiana, in 1900, there were no movie theaters in "Middletown"; by 1929, when the study was complete, "Middletown" had seven movie houses. While cinema houses remained rigidly separated by race, the movies began to create a white "national" audience across boundaries of region, class, and ethnicity.[49]

The movies created a new world for their audiences, allowing them to see what previously they had only read, heard, or dreamed about. Visuality could overwrite, undercut, and contradict the verbal narrative; the simplest editing collapsed both time and space. At a moment when the "weightlessness" of middle-class life was being called into question and when the middle-class worried about its lack of "authentic" experience,[50] visuality allowed the movies to intensify everyday life and to manipulate emotions beneath the surface of the written word. Film theorist Raymond Durgnat observes, "For the masses the cinema is dreams and nightmares, or it is nothing. It is an alternative experience freed from the tyranny of the 'old devil consequences'; from the limitation of having only one life to live. One's favored films are one's unlived lives, one's hopes, fear, libido." [51]

From the beginning, films were interested in race and sex and the relationship between the two. A list of D. W. Griffith's one-reelers produced for the Biograph Film Company before 1915 reads like an ethnology text and includes such titles as *The Red Man and the Child, The Hindoo Dagger, the Mexican Sweethearts, A Child of the Ghetto, The Greaser,* and *The Chinaman and the Sunday School Teacher.*[52] Film historian Nick Browne writes that "the imagery of the movie world linked and inter-mingled exoticism and consumerism . . . for cultural possession and in-corporation of the ancient wealth of Asian sexual secrets and material life. The Orient served as the emblem of a deepening reterritorialization of desire."[53]

The Cheat and *Broken Blossoms* brought together the nation's external threat, the Yellow Peril, and the nation's domestic threat, the emergence of the New Woman. To progressive reformers who sought to preserve the family as a sanctuary from the market, the New Woman appeared to be the antithesis of her True Woman mother. She was independent, educated, and liberated; she was a public woman, a consumer, a partici-pant in an autonomous women's public culture, and increasingly a self-conscious sexual being. At the very moment that the over-civilization and weightlessness of middle-class life have weakened the self-confidence of the middle-class male, the New Woman offered a direct challenge to his late-Victorian masculinity.

In her study of maternalist ideology and progressive reform, Eileen Boris argues that in an effort to protect the women and children from the worst effects of capitalism, progressives supported the ideological separation between public and private spheres and consequently rein-forced the treatment of women as dependents.[54] Film historian Gina Marchetti notes that "racial difference, particularly when linked to issues of female sexuality or woman's economic autonomy, has consistently ap-peared in Hollywood's melodramas as an element of disruption to the smooth functioning of the domestic order."[55]

Despite their immediately apparent differences, both *The Cheat* and *Broken Blossoms* used the theme of miscegenation between an Asian man and a white woman to examine domestic crises within a nation already beset by racial and class contradictions. Marchetti observes that "rape or the threat of rape of a Caucasian woman by an Asian man is the narrative pattern of the Yellow Peril as it is portrayed by the Hollywood film."[56] *The Cheat* examined the crisis of consumption and the emergence of the lei-sure class, while *Broken Blossoms* explored the crisis of the working-class family under imperialism. For the audiences of these two early feature-length movies, race rode to the rescue of the national family.

The Cheat: Race, Sex, and Finance Capital

The Cheat, a post-Victorian cautionary tale of seduction and corruption, warns against the hidden dangers of immigration, female sexuality, and the emerging culture of consumption. Its melodramatic plot revolves around an erotic triangle involving Edith Hardy, a young socialite matron (Fannie Ward), her stockbroker husband, Richard Hardy (Jack Dean), and Hisuru Tori, a wealthy Japanese (or after the film's re-release in 1916, a "Burmese") curio merchant (Sessue Hayakawa). Edith Hardy embezzles funds from a charity ball for Belgian War Relief, which she invests on the advice of a friend and then loses when the company goes bankrupt. Desperate, she turns to her friend, Tori, who agrees to lend her the money to make good the loss. Tori, with the expectation of sexual favors, demands that she come to his mansion. In the meantime, Richard Hardy's investments have returned profit and Edith is able to get a check from her husband to pay back Tori. Frustrated in his attempt to extort sex, Tori attempts to rape Edith. He kisses her, rips her blouse, and succeeds in branding her on the shoulder with his seal. Edith shoots Tori, wounding him. Richard comes to Edith's aid only belatedly, after she has already shot Tori and stopped his attack. Later, Richard publicly takes the blame (and credit) for shooting Tori and is put on trial for attempted murder. In a last-ditch effort to save her husband from prison, Edith confesses to shooting Tori and reveals her secret. The courtroom erupts in pandemonium as spectators rise in an attempt to lynch Tori. Thus, in an outburst of violent racial retribution, Edith and Richard are reunited as the white bourgeois family, free to reproduce the new nation.

The Cheat is a melodrama in which psychological development is abandoned in favor of social type. Edith Hardy, a bourgeois matron and "socialite," represents the New Woman as simultaneously consumer (of material goods and of Tori) and consumable (the object of exchange between Richard Hardy and Tori). On one hand, Edith Hardy exercises the independence of the New Woman, going on an outing with Tori without the company of her husband, maintaining an active social life among the local elite, and, of course, shopping. On the other hand, these activities lack a proper Victorian moral center. Edith is not measured by her appropriate role as a reproductive mother or moral anchor for the family, which are the expectations of Victorian True Womanhood; instead, she is defined by consumption. The luxurious clothes that she wears and the company she keeps are fetishized commodities that mark the value that Edith brings to the bourgeois family.

Representing the new capitalist, Richard is not a captain of industry but an investor. He is defined by finance capital, not production. He is trapped in the iron cage of capitalism even more tightly than Edith. Finance capital alienates him from his family and emasculates him. While Edith must seek fulfillment with her "smart set" outside the home, Richard must stay away from family life and even social life to watch over his investments. (When his male friends go to play golf, Richard must stay by the ticker tape.)

In *The Cheat,* Richard (Jack Dean) and Edith Hardy (Fanny Ward) fight over money: a modern bourgeois family caught between accumulation and consumption.
Still courtesy of the Museum of Modern Art Film Archives

The tension in the Hardy household revolves around Richard's absence and preoccupation with his investments and Edith's extravagance. Finance capitalism may be more profitable than production, but it is less stable. Richard Hardy waits nervously for his investments to "come in," unable to assure his family's financial security, while Edith feels compelled to keep up the appearance of secure prosperity through extravagant consumption.

This situation reveals the central tension of gender in the new bourgeois society. At the turn of the century, the new middle-class woman was the entering wedge of consumer culture. By the end of the nineteenth century, it was possible for women who had become middle-class to leave the hearth and loom to create a form of leisured life in which their role shifted to class reproduction. Conspicuous consumption defined the social status of the bourgeois household. Unlike the Victorian True Woman, who had been measured by her role as mother and moral compass, the modern socialite woman was measured by the social capital that she brought to the family. Bourgeois men, on the other hand, worked to ensure that their wives could be maintained in a style to which they had become accustomed and, more important, a style which their neighbors and associates might envy. Women's role as arbiter of taste and fashion was not a mere indulgence, but a critical weapon in the war of social competition. Bourgeois women defined fashion, and fashion defined the bourgeois woman.

The tension between Edith's extravagance and Richard's Puritanism is a reflection of this division of labor. It is manifest not only in their distanced lives but even in their dress. Edith's costumes are lively, luxurious, and sensuous. This extravagance and sensuality are identified with the West's historical source of luxury goods, the Orient. For example, in one scene Edith is shown holding a piece of silk to her skin. On the other hand, Richard is always dressed in dark, sober, stiffly formal business attire. Here dress defines class, gender, and race; the masculine is visually identified with the sober, the rational, and the West, while the feminine is identified with the extravagant, the sensual, and the East.

The Cheat links its narratives of economics and sexuality through the introduction of the Oriental interloper, Tori. In the original version of the film, Tori is identified as Japanese. As a result of protests from the Japanese Association of Southern California, however, Paramount Pictures changed Tori's ethnic identity to Burmese and gave him the name Araku.[57] Notwithstanding the literal intention of the change in subtitles, its effect is to collapse specific Asian national or ethnic identities into a single, collapsed, racialized Oriental identity.

The most complex of the characters, Tori is initially presented as a socially assimilated, well-to-do man about town. He arrives at the Hardy household nattily decked out in a vested sports suit ready for an outing with Edith. Although the audience sees the smiling, handsome Tori as perfectly acceptable, we know in an instant that the domestic economy is about to be disturbed. The flamboyant Tori is presented as the very opposite of the sober Richard. He is dressed in the same bright sporting clothes as Edith, not in the dark business attire of Richard. Tori is immediately identified with the culture of consumption of Edith and her female society. The subtitle tells us that Tori is a "darling of the smart set." In the opening scene, Tori is Edith's Oriental consumable, an attractive lively companion apparently unconnected to Richard's world of capital. Tori's identification with the world of consumption and his sociability with women have the effect of feminizing and sexualizing him, constructing him as the Oriental Other to Richard Hardy's rational Western Man.

The darker side of this Orientalized identity is revealed in the privacy of his own mansion. In this setting, Tori is shot against a dark background, and shadows darken his face. Here, in what may be the archetype of Orientalist lighting technique, DeMille plays light against dark to distinguish white civilization from the Orient. When the boundary separating the Orient from the West is breached, when Tori is shown as neither foreign nor native, his villainous nature as an alien is revealed.[58]

In his darkened study, Tori is shown obsessively "branding" all of his possessions with his seal. A merchant who buys, sells, and owns, Tori is like Richard in that he is not a producer. But Tori represents an insidious Yellow Peril. Unlike Fu Manchu, the agent of a foreign power, Tori operates on a more intimate level, more threatening to the national family. At a moment in which the reproduction of the national family is threatened by bourgeois over-civilization, Tori represents both the seductiveness of Oriental luxury and the danger of over-consumption.

> The West has historically viewed the Orient with desire as the source of luxury, sensuality, and sexuality and thus identified it as erotically female.

At the end of the nineteenth century, commodities associated with the Orient became a central trope of the new feminized consumer culture, through the consumption of Oriental decorative arts and domestic products produced in the "Oriental style." As Mari Yoshihara has recently shown, the Orient was consumed by the middle-class household at the turn of the century.[59] Both *Chinoiserie* and *Japonisme* became popular motifs in women's clothing styles and in household design. The Gorham company designed silver table settings in the "Japanese style"; the silk kimono became a staple in the dressing closet of middle-class women. In 1914, the socialite Mrs. Belmont opened the grand Chinese Teahouse on the grounds of her Newport mansion, Marblehouse, with a tea honoring an international conference of women reformers. On more plebeian ground, Sid Grauman opened his Chinese Theater in Hollywood.

While Fu Manchu may have been the agent of a foreign government, Tori, the merchant, is the agent of Oriental consumption. Tori is identified with *jouissance,* the preoccupation with pleasure. The Orientalized subject is suspected of having the power to seduce its consumer into its ambit of pleasure. The joy and pain of addiction to pleasure is also a central trope of the Orientalist construction of the sensual; thus the opium den is central to descriptions of Chinatowns by virtually every commentator on the Oriental from Charles Nordhoff through Sax Rohmer. In his attempt to rescue Edith from Tori, Richard is protecting her from being Orientalized not only by Tori's sexual assault but by her own addiction to consumption.

Tori does not, of course, seduce Edith, nor does Richard actually rescue her. Tori's "seduction" of Edith is actually an attempted extortion of sexual favors by a man precluded by racial taboo from competing directly for Edith. Tori can realize his desire only through commerce, cash for sex. Tori, the Orientalized male, can only attempt to extort sex from the white woman because he is never to be allowed to be sexually mature. The Orientalized male is assumed to have been hypnotized by the premature pleasures of the senses. His moral development, and therefore his powers of logic, language, and self-control—powers arrogated to Western man—are arrested. The Orientalized male can only vacillate between a superficial boyish charm and sadistic cruelty fueled by frustrated desire. He can only use his IOU as a whip. Tori cannot hope to talk Edith into bed; that would break a taboo stronger than rape. The rape narrative is critical to the maintenance of the racial boundary. Marchetti notes,

> while the [stolen] kiss for women can be looked at as a fulfillment of secret, forbidden desires for the pleasures and freedoms promised by a love affair with a man of another race, it also marks the beginning of Edith's punishment and . . . turns away from any ambivalence about Tori's villainous character.[60]

Tori does not succeed in having his way with Edith, but he does brand her on the shoulder, marking her as his property. The branding scene evokes both the memory of the chattel enslavement of Africans and contemporary fears of white slavery, the coercion of women into prostitution. Since Chinatowns were widely believed to be centers of urban vice such as prostitution and opium smoking, the identification of white

Tori (Sessue Hayakawa) and Edith in *The Cheat:* the cash nexus.
Still courtesy of the Museum of Modern Art Film Archives

slavery with the Oriental was easily made. The marking of Edith as property, as a commodity, can also be read as a warning of the slippery boundary between consumer and consumable. Edith is a consumer *par excellence,* but in the hands of Tori, the expert merchant who knows her desires, she can become the consumed.

Richard Hardy, the New Man of finance capital, fails to protect Edith. He arrives only after she has defended her own honor by shooting and wounding Tori. Edith's shooting of Tori, although it upsets the traditional narrative of patriarchal rescue, is necessary to keep Tori in his racially subordinate status. For Richard to have shot and wounded, or even killed, Tori after Tori had attacked and maimed his wife would only have balanced the moral economy of the movie. After all, Richard has largely abandoned Edith to her own devices and to Tori's advances, and he too shares culpability as a cheat. For Richard to shoot Tori would simply even the masculine exchange. Edith's shooting of Tori, on the other hand, is a decisive racial rejection of Tori's claim to masculinity and bars him from escaping the realm of the feminine.

Richard Hardy's triumph as the patriarch of the new bourgeois family is delayed until he is vindicated in the courtroom. Richard has taken the blame and credit for shooting Tori, and his conviction on assault charges is all but assured until Edith comes to his aid and confesses all. A riot breaks out in the courtroom as a mob rushes forward in an attempt to lynch Tori. At the end of the scene, after Tori has been hustled away, Edith and Richard Hardy are restored as the American family, a restoration made possible only through the re-establishment of the patriarchy. Richard has been restored to his central role as protector of the family and his virility renewed through an authenticating struggle with the racial Other.

Everyone has been a cheat, and the survivors have learned a lesson. Tori is a cheat for having attempted to coerce Edith into having sexual relations with him and for having the pretension of becoming white through acculturation. Edith is a cheat because she has abandoned the moral high ground of True Womanhood and embezzled money, lied to her husband, and cheated Tori of his expected sexual reward. Richard is a cheat because he has abandoned his role as protector of the family in favor of his investments and also because he has taken credit, albeit with honorable intent, for the shooting of Tori. As the new bourgeois family obsessed with consumption, Edith and Richard have cheated their nation, their class, and their race by not having children. The presumed lesson is that Richard and Edith will free themselves from the compulsive consumption that had led them down the Oriental path and return to their home to restore domestic order and to reproduce.

Broken Blossoms: Race, Sex, and Reform

Broken Blossoms followed D. W. Griffith's two spectaculars, the immensely successful but controversial *Birth of A Nation,* in which he articulated his vision of race and national revival, and the hugely expensive failure *Intolerance* (1917), a monumental but disjointed attack on censorship. With *Broken Blossoms,* Griffith turned to another central concern, the family, which was at the center of the progressive reform effort to stabilize the social order.[61] Basing his movie on "The Chink and the Little Girl," a short story by the British writer Thomas Burke, Griffith turned to the "art" movie, the small domestic melodrama, to explore the intersections of class, family, and race.

Broken Blossoms opens in a Hollywood backlot version of a Chinese city. Cheng Huan (Ronald Barthlemes), also called the "Yellow Man," is shown in a Buddhist temple dressed in as a young priest. He is given a mission to take "the message of peace to the warlike Anglo-Saxons," an extension of the antiwar theme in *The Birth of a Nation.* Cheng Huan's first encounter with the West is an attempt to intervene in a fight among a group of sailors; he is beaten for his troubles. Ronald Barthelmes' Yellow Man is slender, delicate in appearance, and timid, the very opposite the imposing, evil of Fu Manchu. Cheng Huan fits perfectly Renan's image of the Oriental male, "like those individuals who possess so little fecundity that, after a gracious childhood, they attain only the most mediocre virility."[62]

The next scene finds Cheng Huan, some years later, standing against a wall in London's Chinatown, now a shopkeeper. Cheng Huan's dejected look and the subtitles tell us that the ideals of his youth lie in shards. Nearby, Battling Burrows (Donald Crisp), a local boxing champion, lives with his stepdaughter, Lucy (Lillian Gish), also called "the Girl." Battling Burrows is the antithesis of Cheng Huan. He is big, crude, strong, and violent, a working-class champion. Burrows' weaknesses, the subtitles tell us, are women and drink. He is also possessed of a "hatred of all persons not born in this great country."

Lucy is bereft of her mother, whose early death has left her unprotected in the face of her stepfather's violent physical abuse. Played by Lillian Gish, Lucy is a waifish fifteen-year-old who appears much younger. Like Cheng Huan, Lucy is delicate, timid, and passive. She is Burrows' slave; he regularly beats her, and implicit in these beatings is sexual abuse.

Lucy has saved scraps of tin foil and the ribbon given to her by her dying mother. Craving beauty even in such degraded circumstances (this symbolizes her inner beauty), Lucy takes the foil and goes to the Yellow

The working-class household in *Broken Blossoms:*
Battling Burrows (Donald Crisp) and The Girl (Lillian Gish).
Still courtesy of the Museum of Modern Art Film Archives

Man's shop to trade it for flowers. Later, after a particularly brutal beating, Lucy again goes to Cheng Huan's shop, where she collapses in the doorway. Cheng Huan takes her into his shop and nurses her back to health, keeping her there overnight and promising to protect her.

Battling Burrows finds out that his daughter is at the Chinaman's store and with three accomplices drags her back to his shack, whereupon he savagely beats her to death. Cheng Huan, notified of her abduction, races to save Lucy but arrives too late. In a rage, Cheng Huan shoots Burrows, and then returns to his rooms with Lucy's body and commits suicide.

The sympathetic treatment of the relationship between Cheng Huan and Lucy allows *Broken Blossoms* to be read as a retreat from *The Birth of a Nation*'s overt and virulent racism. The Yellow Man and his message of Eastern pacifism are contrasted as a positive, albeit insipid, alternative to the self-destructive violence of the West. At the level of the narrative, *Broken Blossoms* portrays the Oriental as a protector of innocence. The film ends in tragedy as a "pure," that is to say unfulfilled, love relationship is destroyed by Burrow's jingoistic hatred and thinly veiled perverse erotic desire.

Notwithstanding the apparent liberalism of the narrative, the melodramatic power of *Broken Blossoms* rests on its play between three powerful taboos: pedophilia, miscegenation, and incest. Linda Gordon notes that public concern about incest and the sexual abuse of children by strangers were linked. At the turn of the century, police and child protection agencies had raised alarms about the incidence of sexual abuse and incest between fathers and daughters, particularly among poor and immigrant families, but by the end of the decade these agencies had shifted their concerns to attacks on younger girls by strangers. She writes,

> The discovery [of stranger attacks] coincided with the diminished visibility of incest. This was not a coincidence but a replacement of one crime by another. Often girls assaulted "on the streets" had been incest victims whose problems were not noticed when they took place within the family.[63]

The sexual abuse of Lucy by her father is implied from the first scene between the two. After Battling Burrows beats Lucy, he forces her to smile for him. This is something Lucy can not accomplish except by pushing her lips into a smile with her fingers. Beaten into complete selflessness, Lucy warns Burrows not that she might die from his abuse, but rather that he might hang for "hitting her once too often."

The incest theme is underscored in the scene of Lucy's murder. In an excruciating scene of domestic violence, Battling Burrows smashes in the door of the closet in which Lucy is cowering, throws her onto the single bed in their household, and beats her with the butt end of a whip. The bed and the obvious phallic symbolism of the butt of the whip aside, the shifting of the camera angle from a close-up shot of abject terror in Lucy face to her view of her father breaking through the closet door is pornographic in its intimate implication of the audience in her violation.

Battling Burrows's role as violent and incestuous father is paralleled by Cheng Huan's role as passive but licentious "dirty old man." In the first decade of the century, the construction of the "dirty old man" played an important role in shifting the focus of child sexual abuse away from incest to sexual attack by strangers. Linda Gordon writes that in Boston,

> The accused [child molesters] were often small businessmen, craftsmen, or employees in shops which provided the physical space for secret activities with children. . . . They were old from the child's point of view. . . . They often appeared as kindly, entertaining children and giving them treats; and it is important to remember the great attraction of small gifts for very poor children.[64]

The threat of rape or molestation is made visible when Cheng Huan professes his adoration of Lucy. The scene of Cheng Huan gazing at and then slowly approaching, the sleeping Lucy is intercut with shots from Battling Burrows' boxing match. When Cheng Huan approaches Lucy, she shrinks from him. He then kisses the hem of her sleeve. Ironically underscoring the sexual implication of this gesture, the title tells us "His love remains pure and holy—even his worst foe says this." This shot is immediately followed by the shot of Battling Burrows winning his boxing match.

The splicing of the slow adoration scene with the brutal boxing match achieves a number of effects. On the level of the narrative, it serves to underscore the difference between the delicate and timid Cheng Huan and the brutal, aggressive Battling Burrows. At the same time, the change of pace from boxing ring to bedroom and back intensifies the parallel sexual tensions that are implicit but, like the incest theme, remain carefully unstated. Cutting from bedroom to boxing ring also enables the audience to imagine the punishment in store for Cheng Huan should he consummate his obvious desire for Lucy.

Cheng Huan's nursing of Lucy is double-edged. He not only brings Lucy back to life but transforms her into a Orientalized woman. This restoration and transformation takes place in his bedroom. Unlike Burrows' sparsely furnished home, where a table and hearth are the focal point, Cheng Huan's rather opulent room is organized around the bed and an elaborate altar to Buddha. Unlike the starkness of the Burrows household, Cheng Huan's quarters are opulent and ornate, redolent of ritual and consumption. Following Manicheaean convention, Burrow's home is starkly lit, while Cheng Huan's apartment is all shadows, soothing and mysterious. Here the film makes reference to another social and pornographic theme of late Victorian society, white slavery (the white woman entrapped into sexual service) and child prostitution (innocence violated).

While the titles declare Cheng Huan's love to be pure and his intentions honorable, visually the audience is led to witness the transformation of the white child into the Orientalized prostitute. Cheng Huan dresses Lucy in a silk robe, the transformative properties of which— "blue and yellow silk caressing white skin"—arouse the sensual in Lucy and the audience. Cheng Huan, who the titles tell us has "dreamt that she is all his own,"[65] spends the night holding her hand. The image of Lucy reclining in the silks of Cheng Huan's bed enables the audience to envision Lucy not only as saved but also as the child prostitute. Lucy takes on the passive but available sensuality of the Orientalized woman described by the French Orientalist Ernest Renan:

The Yellowman's apartment: Cheng Huan (Donald Barthlemes) and Lucy.
Still courtesy of the Museum of Modern Art Film Archives

> The Oriental woman is an occasion and an opportunity for the Orientalist's
> musings; he is entranced by her self-sufficiency, by her emotional careless-
> ness, and also by what, lying next to him, she allows him to think. Less a
> woman than a display of impressive but verbally inexpressive femininity . . .
> a prototype of all the versions of female carnal temptation.[66]

In Cheng Huan's ornate apartment, Lucy's beauty blossoms and she
is transformed into a woman. When she awakes she sees herself amid
the Oriental opulence of the Yellow Man's bedroom. She is then shown
in a close-up, primping as a woman. Transition to womanhood is not a
cause for unalloyed celebration; Lucy has been warned by working-class
women on the street to try to escape the two common fates of prostitution and marriage. Lucy's close examination of her face in the mirror
thus takes on a double meaning. On the one hand, she recognizes herself as a woman, and a beautiful one. On the other hand, given the Victorian belief that the wages of sin and moral turpitude are marked on
the body, Lucy's study of the mirror can be read as a self-examination of
her moral state. For the first and only time, Lucy smiles without the aid

The transformative gaze:
Cheng Huan and Lucy in Cheng Huan's bedroom.
Still courtesy of the Museum of Modern Art Film Archives

of her fingers, suggesting that her simultaneous recovery and fall from innocence please her. As Linda Gordon notes,

> It was part of the mysterious and fetishized nature of sexual experience in the Victorian sexual system that the victim was herself polluted. . . . These fears were associated with childhood "precocity" or "sophistication," synonyms for sexual experience. The sophisticated could never again be naive.[67]

At the same time, the apparent innocence of her question to Cheng Huan, "Why are you so good to me, Chinky?" prompts the audience to doubt the sincerity of her protector's intentions. When Lucy asks Cheng Huan to give her the doll that she has seen in his store window, it is a gesture that reasserts her childhood but can also be seen as the price that she extracts for indulging Cheng Huan's fantasy. The request reminds us of Lucy's vulnerability as a poor child and it ominously foreshadows a future of prostitution. In the final analysis, Lucy is rescued from this imagined "fate worse than death" by death itself.

Containing Chinatown

Before Sax Rohmer made "Chinatown" the headquarters for Oriental evil, Chinatown had already become a well-rehearsed trope for the mysterious and unfathomable Oriental in Charles Hoyt's 1881 *A Trip to Chinatown*, the first Broadway musical smash hit. The play deploys an imaginary trip to Chinatown as a foil in a romantic comedy of manners between two young, white, middle-class couples.

The Cheat and *Broken Blossoms* confirmed visually to white audiences the subtle and intimate dangers of Chinatown as home to the Yellow Peril in their midst. These movies allowed Americans to "see for themselves" what writers could only describe about the Oriental, Chinatown, and the Yellow Peril. Even Asians who might appear assimilated, like Hayakawa's Tori, were, beneath their surfaces, cruel and brutal. Even the wispy and pure-of-heart Cheng Huan could transform a white girl into a prostitute. His intentions were irrelevant; his very presence induced moral decay in everyone with whom he came into intimate contact.

The Cheat and *Broken Blossoms* followed Fu Manchu in consolidating the Oriental as a trope of racial difference. Distinctions between Hisuru Tori, the Japanese (or Araku, the Burmese), and Cheng Huan, the Yellow Man, and the myriad Malays, Dacoits, Thugees, and Tibetan princesses that inhabited Fu Manchu's netherworld were collapsed into the single racial trope of Chinatown. In a wide-angle shot of an opium den deep in Griffith's London Chinatown, a white woman dressed in the masculine mode identified with the New Woman reclines among a motley crew of Orientals who could have come directly from Fu Manchu. Much like the pleasure den described in *The Hand of Fu Manchu*, which also catered to a ethnically mixed Oriental population, "Chinese, Malays, and Indians" and colored men of all sorts mix here easily and scandalously with white women. In this scene, the audience can imagine that Lucy's missing mother is not dead at all, but has merely abandoned the family. She may be this New Woman lost, at the level of the visual at least, to the opium den.

This shot visually confirms the reports Americans had read about Chinatowns as sinks of iniquity since the very establishment of Chinese settlements in the 1870s. Even sympathetic travel narratives from journalists such as Charles Nordhoff in *California for Travellers and Settlers* and Mrs. Frank Leslie's travel accounts in *Leslie's Weekly Magazine* reported in detail on the dark side of the Chinese quarters. In 1880, the virulently anti-Chinese San Francisco Public Health Committee issued a report declaring San Francisco's Chinatown a "public nuisance." In the early years

The absent mother in *Broken Blossoms:* the New Woman among the denizens of
Chinatown.
Still courtesy of the Museum of Modern Art Film Archives

of the twentieth century, journalist Louis Beck in *New York Chinatown,*
the progressive urban social reformers Helen Campbell and Thomas
Knox in *Lights and Shadows of New York,* and Jacob Riis in *How the Other
Half Lives* all described in lurid detail the moral corruption of New York's
Chinatown.

In both the DeMille and Griffith films, Asian immigrant men are not
redeemed either by their social assimilation (*The Cheat*) or by sympathetic and noble behavior (*Broken Blossoms*); their race renders them ir-
redeemable. In both cases, the irreducible difference of race is revealed
through the Asian man's (unrealized) desire for sexual relations with a
white woman. In the critical scene of thwarted desire in each film, the
white heroine "instinctively" draws away, much as the Supreme Court
would later say that the great majority of "our people" will "instinctively
reject assimilation" [with Asians].

Tori's relationship with Edith in *The Cheat* reveals the presumed limits of assimilation. In the bright light of white society, Tori appears as

the totally assimilated, completely acceptable member of the community, which he enters with the eager assistance of middle-class white women. These women are attracted to him, and he is most at ease with them. However, branding his possessions in the shadowy corners of his own house, Tori is unmasked as Fu Manchu. He is driven by a compulsive need to possess and to colonize the white woman. Such consumption and colonization is sterile; it can not reproduce the national family. While Tori is capable of social assimilation, morally he remains unassimilable.

Unlike Tori, whose good looks hide his moral corruption, Cheng Huan, while he appears to be morally acceptable, is physically repulsive. He is the inversion of Fu Manchu and Tori. Cheng Huan, also called the Yellow Man, and who Lucy calls "Chinky," is, at the level of the narrative, a sympathetic protagonist, yet his sickly appearance gives him an almost inhuman quality. Even though he offers himself as Lucy's protector and intervenes when Evil Eye, another denizen of Chinatown, importunes her, Cheng Huan, no matter how moral, cannot hope to assume the heroic mantle of the white man. Unlike Owen Wister's Virginian or Sax Rohmer's Nayland Smith, whose masculinity is defined by emotional control, Cheng Huan is controlled by his desire for Lucy. The Yellow Man's desire, even though it remains repressed, makes the relationship between "The Chink and the Little Girl" (the title of the Thomas Burke short story from which the film was adapted) unacceptable and destined to end in tragedy. Cheng Huan and Lucy cannot be allowed to come to the aid of the nation; their union cannot reproduce the national family. The producer of *The Birth of a Nation,* while captivating his audience with the imagination of interracial love, cannot in the end tolerate miscegenation.

Both *The Cheat* and *Broken Blossoms* portrayed the Asian male immigrant as undermining national strength by seducing the white woman and subverting the already weakened white family. In both films, True Womanhood, in the form of the protective and moral mother and the wifely moral anchor of vital masculinity, is the missing ingredient for the resurrection of the national family. Both films construct a nostalgia for True Womanhood lost to the Oriental. In *The Cheat,* Edith's true womanhood, her moral center and presumed maternal instinct, is lost to the seduction of the consumer culture. Her relationship with Tori is merely an extension of that broader seduction. It is only his attempted rape, and the ensuing open racial struggle, that can bring her back to her senses and reunite Edith with Richard to reconstitute the racially pure national family.

In *The Birth of a Nation,* Griffith also stresses the centrality of the family to the restoration of the nation. The reproduction of the nation can only be accomplished through the restoration of the mother to the family center. It is the mother's death or abandonment that has allowed the family to devolve into violence and exposed the child to the dangers of the street (and marketplace). Linda Gordon observes that "Moving the locus of sexual abuse outside the home let fathers off the hook, but not mothers. 'Incest' or 'carnal abuse' was reclassified as moral neglect, which was by definition a mother's crime." [68] The strong but uncontrolled working-class hero Battling Borrows cannot be the hope for the future of the nation or the race unless the True Woman is returned to provide moral ballast. The warning that a woman on the streets gives to Lucy against marriage and prostitution is a warning to the nation. It warns that a degraded working-class family can not be a source of national rejuvenation.

The Rising Tide of Color

In 1920, Lothrop Stoddard, a founding father of the American eugenics movement, published *The Rising Tide of Color,* a racial jeremiad against immigration. The book was hugely popular and went through fourteen editions in just three years. Stoddard warned of a racial apocalypse: the white world stood at the brink of "the supreme crisis of the ages. . . . The White race and with it a million years of human evolution might soon be irretrievably lost, swamped by the triumphant colored races, who will obliterate the white man by elimination or absorption." [69]

Stoddard believed the principal "colored" threat to white civilization and the white race came from Asia. Stoddard concluded that the question of "Asiatic" immigration was the "Supreme phase of the colored peril. . . . It threatens not merely our supremacy or prosperity, but our very race-existence, the well-springs of being, the sacred heritage of our children." [70]

The Rising Tide of Color used the powerful metaphor of a flood of brown and yellow races threatening to break through what Stoddard called the "inner dikes" (the racial homelands of the Anglo-Saxons) to swamp white civilization. Surrounding the core of white civilization were outer dikes, " the vast areas of the world which were under white political control, but largely inhabited by peoples of color," and the inner dikes, areas including Canada, the United States, and Australia, that were "peopled wholly or largely by whites." These inner dikes, Stoddard insisted, "have become part of the race heritage, which should be defended to the last extremity." [71]

In identifying the threat from the East, Stoddard was in the mainstream of racial geopolitical theory. Stoddard was a protégé of Madison

Grant, a New York patrician lawyer whose 1916 book *The Passing of a Great Race* had popularized the idea that the "Nordic Races," of which the "Anglo-Saxon race" was a branch, were faced with "race suicide." Madison Grant had identified three racial stocks among white Americans: the Nordic, the Alpine, and the Mediterranean. Of these, the Nordic, including its Anglo-Saxon branch, was the physically, morally, and intellectually superior but paradoxically the most endangered race of humankind.

The Passing of a Great Race put in easily understandable if crudely social Darwinist terms the cultural anxieties that beset much of middle-class America in the early decades of the century. The book re-articulated the Anglo-Saxon myth in terms of the anxiety about "race suicide" that had been popular in American culture since the last decades of the nineteenth century. Grant warned that Nordic "blood" was highly "specialized" and therefore more vulnerable to "devaluation" through miscegenation not only with nonwhites but with lesser whites of "Alpine and Mediterranean" stock. In addition, "over-civilization" had weakened the Nordic martial spirit, leaving Anglo-Saxon civilization nearly defenseless. In Grant's pessimistic view, the Nordic bloodline of the United States was being diluted and degraded by the arrival of even those "free white persons"—Italians, Slavs and Jews—whom the Supreme Court in *United States v. Bhagat Singh Thind* (struggling to define whiteness to include Europeans of all hues while excluding Asians no matter what their complexion) described as "dark eyed and swarthy" but also "unquestionably kin, and readily amalgamable by marriage" to those already here.[72]

Although at the turn of the century the idea of a Yellow Peril had been the stock in trade of military strategists and propagandists, Lothrop Stoddard, writing in 1920, did not believe the Yellow Peril to be a threat from foreign arms. In *The Rising Tide of Color*, he summed up his vision of the "colored peril of arms":

> The brown and yellow races possess great military potentialities. These (barring the action of certain ill-understood emotional stimuli) are unlikely to flame out in spontaneous fanaticism, but . . . are very likely to be mobilized for political reasons like revolt against white dominion or for social reasons like overpopulation. The black race offers no real danger except as the tool of Pan-Islamism. As for the red men of the Americas, they are of merely local significance.[73]

For Stoddard, neither military force nor economic competition posed the principal colored threat to white civilization. He believed that white civilization was in imminent danger of being swamped by the rising tide of colored immigration. He saw immigration, assimilation, and miscegenation between yellow and brown and white as the vehicle for the Asiatic swamping of white civilization and, ultimately, for the total absorption of the white race. For Stoddard, the anti-imperialists' turn-of-the-century admonitions had come home to haunt the republic.

The Rising Tide of Color was a eugenicist critique of imperialism as well as a racialist jeremiad against immigration. At the heart of his argument lay the new "science" of eugenics, which held that Nordic blood carried "superior" or "more specialized" genetic material and was vulnerable to "dilution" by the blood of "lesser breeds." Here, Stoddard summed up this "scientific" case against miscegenation. "Of course, the more primitive a type is, the more prepotent it is. This is why crossings with the Negro are uniformly fatal. Whites, Amerindians, or Asiatics—all are alike vanquished by the invincible prepotency of the more primitive, generalized, and lower Negro blood." [74]

Stoddard argued that imperialism, though the inevitable expression of white racial supremacy, had led humanity unwittingly to a "disgenic," potentially disastrous pass. Modern urban and industrial life, he wrote, had been "one sided, abnormal, unhealthy . . . disgenic." In addition to the ill effects of immigration and miscegenation, the modern world was moving toward the "replacement of the more valuable by the less valuable elements of the population. . . . All over the civilized world racial values are diminishing, and the logical end of this disgenic process is racial bankruptcy and the collapse of civilization." [75]

Modernity, imperialism, and technology had shortened the geographical distance between races. The extension of white civilization throughout the world via colonialism had awakened millions in the colored world to the advantages of Western civilization and had aroused their resentment against the imposition of white dominion. At the same time, the expansion of white civilization and Western technology throughout the world had broken down "natural" boundaries and made travel more efficient, making international migration possible for millions. White dominion over Asia was the most significant arena for this change. The immediate danger was, therefore, not miscegenation between white and black, but "that the white stocks may be swamped by Asiatic blood." [76]

Stoddard believed that the defeat of white civilization meant racial death. In the past, the boundaries of civilization had not been coterminous with those of race. The white race could always rely on a reserve army of "white barbarians" (such as Battling Burrows) to forward the militant mission of the race. But by 1920, modernization had spread civilization to all the tribes of the white race and left the race without its redemptive army of "unspoiled, well-endowed barbarians to step forward and 'carry on.'" [77]

For Stoddard, the great threat of Asiatic immigration was exacerbated by a tendency toward race suicide from within the inner dikes. Stoddard, who shared the class elitism of his mentor Madison Grant, saw class struggle in racial terms. Over-civilization, over-consumption, and collapse of purpose had led the middle classes to forget their racial mission. "Two things are necessary for the continued existence of a race," Stoddard warned: "it must remain itself and it must breed its best." Even as the colored tide from the East threatened to breach the inner dikes, the strength of the white race was already threatened by "mongrelization" from within. The mongrelization and "devaluation" of the Nordic bloodline in America had already been brought about both by the migrations of various Alpine and Mediterranean European racial stocks and the "amalgamation with those already here."

For Stoddard, democracy—the dangerously mistaken idea of equality—was another important aspect of the general disgenic tendency in modernity. Echoing *The Birth of a Nation*, Stoddard used the "disastrous" experience of Reconstruction to demonstrate the danger in the fallacy of racial equality. Stoddard, however, did not share Griffith's enthusiasm for a populist racial revival; he saw class struggle in racial terms as well. For Stoddard, the Bolshevik Revolution in 1917 represented both social and racial apocalypse. Should the proletarian revolution, which in another book he calls the revolt of the *untermenschen,* spread, "the [white] race, summarily drained of its good blood, would sink like lead into the depths of degenerate barbarism." However, this degenerate barbarism would not produce the "well endowed" white barbarians that Stoddard believed had come to the aid of the race in the past.

In no less lurid images than those Sax Rohmer used to describe the Orientalized fantasy world of Fu Manchu, whose Asiatic minions maneuvered to "pave a path for the Yellow Peril" into the citadel of white civilization, Stoddard warned that Bolshevism sought to enlist the colored races in its grand assault on civilization.[78] "Meanwhile Lenine [sic], surrounded by his Chinese executioners, sits behind the Kremlin walls, a modern Jenghis Khan plotting the plunder of a world." [79]

For Stoddard, the Red Menace and the Yellow Peril had come together; in his apocalyptic vision, Lenin had become the handmaiden of Fu Manchu.

> In every corner of the globe, in Asia, Africa, Latin America, and the United States, Bolshevik agitators whisper in the ears of discontented colored men their schemes of hatred and revenge. Every nationalist aspiration, every political grievance, every social discrimination, is fuel for Bolshevism's hellish incitement to racial as well as to class war.[80]

For Stoddard, the need to shore up the inner dikes of Northern European white civilization could not have been more desperate. In 1922, the same year that the Supreme Court held that Takao Ozawa could not become white through assimilation, Congress established restrictive quotas on immigration from Southern and Central European nations and ended immigration from all of Asia.

Defining Whiteness: The Limits of the "Common Hurtage"

In 1922 and 1923, two naturalization cases involving Asian immigrants, *Takao Ozawa v. The United States* and *The United States v. Baghat Singh Thind,* brought the struggle to define whiteness and the idea of race itself to the Supreme Court.[81] Ozawa was from Japan and had lived in the United States for twenty-six years. Thind, from India, had already been a naturalized citizen but had it taken away by a federal court.

Takao Ozawa arrived in the United States as a nineteen-year-old from Tanegawa prefecture in Japan in 1894. He worked as a domestic while he attended and graduated from Berkeley High School and then enrolled at the University of California at Berkeley. In 1902, Ozawa filed a declaration of intent to become a naturalized U.S. citizen with the U.S. District Court in Alameda County, Calif. In 1914, Ozawa petitioned to become a naturalized U.S. citizen. After his petitions were turned down by lower federal courts in Northern California and Hawaii where he resided, Ozawa took his case to the United States Supreme Court. When the high court heard his case in 1922, it was two decades after he had first declared his intent to seek citizenship and twenty-eight years after he had first settled in the United States.

In the three decades since Ozawa's arrival in the United States, the country had gone through a period of intense anxiety about "alien" elements in its midst. Immigrants from Europe (who outnumbered Asian immigrants by 100 to 1) swelled America's cities and were viewed by native-born and "old stock" Anglo-Americans with apprehension. In the early decades of the century, concerted efforts were made to assimilate these "foreign elements" into American society through a crash program of "100 Percent Americanization."[82]

Ozawa and his lawyers argued that he was in fact a perfectly assimilated, 100 percent American. The Japanese, they argued, were not like the Chinese, who had been explicitly excluded from immigration to the United States and prohibited from becoming naturalized citizens. Japanese immigrants, the majority of whom were farmers and farm laborers, had begun to immigrate after 1885, just after the Chinese exclusion act had gone into effect and the tide of anti-Chinese violence had reached its apex. Unlike the Chinese government, which had never supervised emigration, the Japanese government, aware of the Chinese experience, took pains to select and prepare Japanese emigrants for life in America. In addition, Japanese emigrants were encouraged to bring their families and to settle in the United States. The Gentlemen's Agreement of 1907, which curtailed Japanese labor immigration, had explicitly exempted women who intended to marry Japanese men already resident in America from its prohibitions on Japanese immigration.

Although the Japanese consulate had not wanted Ozawa to appeal the lower court's denial of his petition, Ozawa had substantial support in the Japanese American community. He drafted his own brief attesting to the extent of his assimilation into American society.

> In name, I am not an American, but at heart I am a true American. . . . (1) I did not report my name, my marriage, or the names of my children to the Japanese consulate in Honolulu, notwithstanding all Japanese subjects are requested to do so. . . . (2) I do not have any connection with any Japanese churches or schools, or any Japanese organizations here or elsewhere. (3) I am sending my children to an American church and American school in place of a Japanese one. (4) Most of the time I use the American (English) language at home, so that my children cannot speak the Japanese language. (5) I educated myself in American schools for nearly eleven years by supporting myself. (6) I have lived continuously within the United States for nearly twenty-eight years. (7) I chose as my wife one educated in American schools . . . instead of one educated in Japan. (8) I have steadily prepared to return the kindness which our Uncle Sam has extended me—so it is my honest hope to do something good to the United States before I bid a farewell to this world.[83]

The US Supreme Court ruled unanimously that no matter how assimilated he was, Ozawa could not become a naturalized American citizen. The issue was race, specifically the meaning of "free white person." Ozawa's attorneys, citing the Dred Scott case among others, had argued that the term "white person" had been constructed by the Court to mean "a person without negro blood."[84] The Court, however, rejected that reasoning and adopted a definition of white person as "a person of what is popularly known as the Caucasian race."[85] This category was a racial category and not a matter of individual color or complexion. Justice Sutherland wrote:

> Manifestly, the test afforded by the mere color of skin of each individual is impracticable as that differs greatly among persons of the same race, even among Anglo-Saxons, ranging by imperceptible gradation from the fair blond to the swarthy brunette, the latter being darker than many of the lighter hued persons of the brown or yellow races. Hence to adopt the color test alone would result in a confused overlapping of races and a gradual merging of one into the other, without any practical line of separation.[86]

In the case of Takao Ozawa, his "100 percent American" habits notwithstanding, the Supreme Court drew a bright line of race between Caucasian and nonwhite. Although Ozawa might well have been more Americanized than the proscribed Chinese, the degree of Ozawa's assimilation was irrelevant to the Court. The principle issue was his claim to whiteness. Differences of complexion could be subsumed within the racial definition of whiteness, which the Court now identified as the "popularly understood Caucasian race"; since the Japanese were not among those included in the "popular" category of Caucasian, Ozawa could not sustain the argument that he was not Negro and therefore white.

In the following year, the Supreme Court took up the case of Bhagat Singh Thind, an immigrant from India. Between 1907 and 1914, some 6,000 Asian Indians had immigrated to the United States from the Indian subcontinent, either directly or via China, the Philippines, or Canada. The majority of these immigrants were Sikhs, mostly farmers who had left the plague-stricken and economically depressed Punjab; others were veterans of the British forces that had suppressed the Boxer Rebellion in China in 1900.[87] The great majority of these immigrants settled in Washington and Oregon, where they were employed in forestry, and in the Central and Imperial valleys of California, where they were farmers and farm workers. A smaller but not insignificant number of Asian Indian immigrants were students, mainly Bengali, many of whom had already become involved in the growing nationalist movement in India. Although the majority of these immigrants practiced the Sikh religion, some were Hindu and others Muslim and Parsee. Regardless of their religious affiliation, the U.S. government classified all immigrants from the Indian subcontinent under the rubric "Hindoo." "Hindoos" were among those who were prohibited from immigration to America under the provisions of the 1917 Immigration Act that had established the Asiatic Barred Zone.

Like Ozawa, Bhagat Thind had come to the United States as a young man. He had attended the University of California and had been granted citizenship by the federal court in Oregon on the grounds that he was able to prove himself Caucasian. His attorney had argued that, as a Hindu of high caste, Thind was descended from Aryan stock and ethnologically speaking was a Caucasian and thus a "free white person," eligible to become a naturalized American. The federal court in Oregon agreed.

Since several scores of Indian immigrants had become naturalized citizens under this reasoning, U.S. government officials saw this "loophole" as threatening, and the federal government appealed the lower court ruling granting Thind naturalization rights. The United States Supreme Court, not wanting "Hindoo" citizens, not withstanding their ethnological status as Caucasians, ruled against Bhagat Thind. The court held that Thind's ethnological argument, while plausible, was irrelevant. It asserted that racial categories were contingent not on ethnology or linguistics but on contemporary popular standards. Writing for the majority, Justice Sutherland asserted that "it may be true that the blonde Scandinavian and the brown Hindu have a common ancestor in the dim reaches of antiquity, but the average man knows perfectly well that there are unmistakable and profound differences between them today." [88]

On the other hand, Sutherland stated that the term Caucasian was a scientific term that had no meaning to the 1790 framers of the first Naturalization Act and thus constituted a poor test of the commonly understood idea of a "free white person." Sutherland held that "free white person" were words of "familiar speech that were used by the original framers of the law . . . intended to include one type of man whom they knew as white." These, Sutherland noted, were immigrants principally from the British Isles and Northern Europe. The Court acknowledged that successive immigration from Southern and Central Europe had brought "the Slavs and dark eyed swarthy people of Alpine and Mediterranean stock" to America but held that these immigrants were "unquestionably kin to those already here and readily amalgamated with them." [89]

With behavior and color (in *Ozawa*) and now science ruled out, the court turned to the ideology of "common sense" as the way in which race would be evaluated. The true test of "whiteness" was in the eyes of the common man. "What we now hold is that the words 'free white person' are words of common speech, to be interpreted in accordance with the understanding of the common man, synonymous with the word 'Caucasian' only as that word is popularly understood." [90]

"Hindoos," regardless of their lineage, were not among those "unquestionably kin" or "readily amalgamated with" that legal fiction the common (white) man. In describing the ethnic assimilation of Americans of European descent and the "instinctive" recognition and rejection of assimilation for American children of Indian immigrants, the court created an impermeable distinction between ethnicity and race.

> The children of English, French, German, Italian, Scandinavian, and other European parentage, quickly merge into the mass of our population and lose the distinctive hallmarks of their European origin. On the other hand, it cannot be doubted that the children born in this country of Hindu parentage would retain indefinitely the clear evidence of their ancestry. . . . What we suggest is merely racial difference, [not superiority or inferiority]

and it is of such character and extent that the great body of our people instinctively recognize it and reject the thought of assimilation.[91]

In the *Ozawa* and *Thind* cases, the Supreme Court articulated the relationship between ethnicity, race, and ideology. In *Ozawa*, the court held that while gradations of color might exist, gradations of race did not. European immigrants from "blond to swarthy brunette" could be amalgamated into a "Caucasian" race; Asian immigrants, however assimilated, could not. Ethnology had its limits, however: despite any common ancestor that he may have shared with modern Caucasians in the "dim reaches of antiquity," Bhagat Thind was declared ineligible for citizenship on the grounds that, although Caucasian, he was not white. The court held that the ultimate arbiter of whiteness is not science but popular ideology. The *Ozawa* and *Thind* rulings established "common understanding" as the popular standard on which "race" was to be defined, impervious to cultural assimilation or science. In cases where the bright line of race might be crossed, as in the case of mixed-race individuals, the "one drop" rule of racial hypo-descent could be invoked. Thus science was brought back into the debate on race but within limits, as the handmaiden of popular ideology. In 1934, in *Morrison et al v. California*, a case involving a conspiracy to violate California's Alien Land Law, which prohibited Asians (as aliens ineligible for citizenship) from purchasing or leasing agricultural land in California, Justice Cardozo, citing both the *Ozawa* and *Thind* decisions, declared that "men are not white if the strain of colored blood in them is a half or a quarter, or, not improbably even less, the governing test always . . . being that of *common understanding*."[92] [emphasis added].

The "common understanding" on which Justice Cardozo relied defined the "inner dikes" of racial purity necessary for the protection of the national family and the reproduction of the race. The cases of Takao Ozawa and Bhagat Thind reflected the judgment of ordinary Americans fully awakened to the Yellow Peril that the "common hurtage" which could bring together Saxon and Celt, Polish, French, Slavs and Italians, African and Armenian, could not admit the Oriental.

5

The Cold War Origins of the Model Minority Myth

Racist Love

n 1974, the writer Frank Chin expressed it this way: "Whites love us because we're not black."[1] The elevation of Asian Americans to the position of model minority had less to do with the actual success of Asian Americans than to the perceived failure—or worse, refusal—of African Americans to assimilate. Asian Americans were "not black" in two significant ways: They were both politically silent and ethnically assimilable.

The Cold War construction of Asian America as a model minority that could become ethnically assimilated, despite what *U.S. News and World Report* euphemistically called its "racial disadvantage," reveals the contradiction between the continuing reproduction of racial difference and the process of ethnic assimilation. The representation of Asian Americans as a *racial* minority whose apparently successful *ethnic* assimilation was a result of stoic patience, political obedience, and self-improvement was a critically important narrative of ethnic liberalism that simultaneously promoted racial equality and sought to contain demands for social transformation. The representation of the Asian American as the paragon of ethnic virtue, who the *U.S. News and World Report* editors thought should be emulated by "Negroes and other minorities," reflected not so much Asian success as the triumph of an emergent discourse of race in which cultural difference replaced biological difference as the new determinant of social outcomes. Although the deployment of Asian Americans as a model minority was made explicit in the mid 1960s, its origins lay in the triumph of liberalism and the racial logic of the Cold War.

The narrative of Asian ethnic assimilation fit the requirements of Cold War containment perfectly. Three specters haunted Cold War America in the 1950s: the red menace of communism, the black menace of race mixing, and the white menace of homosexuality. On the international front, the narrative of ethnic assimilation sent a message to the Third World, especially to Asia where the United States was engaged in increasingly fierce struggles with nationalist and communist insurgencies, that the United States was a liberal democratic state where people of color could enjoy equal rights and upward mobility. On the home front, it sent a message to "Negroes and other minorities" that accommodation would be rewarded while militancy would be contained or crushed.

The successful transformation of the Oriental from the exotic to the acceptable was a narrative of Americanization, a sort of latter-day *Pilgrim's Progress,* through which America's anxieties about communism, race mixing, and transgressive sexuality might be contained and eventually tamed. The narrative of Asian ethnic assimilation helped construct a new national narrative for the atomic age that Walter Lippman had dubbed the American Century.

World War II as Prelude

Ironically, it was Japan's attack on Pearl Harbor and America's entry into the Second World War that began the unraveling of the Yellow Peril myth. The Second World War was a watershed event for Asian Americans. The treatment of Asian American ethnic groups brought into sharp focus the contradiction between their exclusion as racial subjects and the promise of their assimilation as ethnic citizens.

America's entry into the war against Nazi Germany and Imperial Japan made it increasingly difficult to sustain national policies based on theories of white racial supremacy. After Dunkirk, the United States and its allies depended on support from their colonial subjects in India, China (not, strictly speaking, a colony), southeast Asia, and north Africa. The very nationalist movements whose representatives had been summarily dismissed by Woodrow Wilson at Versailles were now actively courted by the United States as allies against the Axis powers. In August 1941, four months before the United States entered the war, Roosevelt and Churchill signed the Atlantic Charter recognizing the right of "peoples" to decide their own form of government. Later that year, in response to the threat by civil rights leader A. Phillip Randolph to lead a massive protest march on Washington, Roosevelt signed an Executive Order outlawing

racial discrimination by companies doing business with the federal government and established a Committee on Fair Employment Practices.

Official pronouncements of racial equality notwithstanding, the
wholesale and brutal incarceration of the Japanese American population
on the west coast underscored, in no uncertain terms, the willingness of
the U.S. government to invoke race as a category of subordination to
achieve its goals.[2] This willingness to use racial categories would result in
physical hardship, economic ruin, family disintegration, and psychological trauma for more than 120,000 Japanese Americans, men and women,
elderly and infant, citizen and immigrant.

After Pearl Harbor, the United States found itself allied with a weak
and divided China. The Yellow Peril, that alliance of Japanese brains
and Chinese bodies that had fired the racial nightmares of turn-of-the-
century strategists of empire from Kaiser Wilhelm to Sax Rohmer, had
remained imaginary. Japan's plans for empire, though couched in Pan-
Asian anticolonial rhetoric, met with resistance in China and elsewhere
in Asia. For the first time, being able to tell one Asian group apart from
another seemed important to white Americans. Two weeks after the Japanese attack on Pearl Harbor brought the United States into the War, *Life*
magazine ran a two-page pictorial entitled "How to Tell Japs from the
Chinese." The reporter for *Life* magazine wrote:

> U.S. citizens have been demonstrating a distressing ignorance on the deli-
> cate question of how to tell a Chinese from a Jap. Innocent victims in cities
> all over the country are many of the 75,000 U.S. Chinese, whose homeland
> is our stanch [sic] ally. . . .
>
> To dispel some of this confusion, *Life* here adduces a rule of thumb
> from the anthropomorphic conformations that distinguish friendly Chi-
> nese from enemy alien Japs.[3]

On the right side of the article, two facial portraits of Orientals are
juxtaposed one above the other. The top picture (of the Minister of Economic Affairs of the Chinese Nationalist government) is captioned "Chinese public servant" while the one below (of Admiral Tojo, the Japanese
Prime Minister) is captioned "Japanese Warrior." Although the pictures
are the same size and the proportions of the facial features virtually identical, the notes tell a vastly different story. The Chinese, *Life* told its readers, has "parchment yellow complexion, more frequent epicanthic fold,
higher bridge, never has rosy cheeks, lighter facial bones, longer narrower
face and scant beard." Tojo, "representative of the Japanese people as
whole . . . betrays aboriginal antecedents, has an earthy yellow complexion, less frequent epicanthic fold, flatter nose, sometimes rosy cheeks,
heavy beard, broader shorter face and massive cheek and jawbone."

In addition, the *Life* article showed two pictures whose captions read, respectively, "Tall Chinese Brothers" and "Short Japanese Admirals." *Life*, taking no chances with its racial taxonomy, supplied the following "field" notes: The Chinese brothers were "tall and slender" with "long legs" while the admirals were "short and squat" with "shorter legs and longer torso." Had *Life* only added blonde hair and blue eyes, it might have created the perfect Aryan Chinaman.

Not wanting to appear unlearned in the matter of racial anthropology, *Life* pointed out that its illustrations were drawn from Northern Chinese. Southern Chinese (at that time, the overwhelming majority of Chinese residents of the United States) the magazine noted, were short, and "when middle aged and fat, they look more like Japs." The *Life* editors went on to tell the reader that

> Southern Chinese have round, broad faces, not as massively boned as the Japanese. Except that their skin is darker, this description fits the Filipinos who are [also] often mistaken for Japs. Chinese sometimes pass for Europeans, but Japs more often approach the Western types.[4]

Lest this confusing racial taxonomy fail Americans in this time of crisis, *Life* reassured its audience that cultural difference could also be identified visually. "An often sounder clue is facial expression, shaped by cultural, not anthropological, factors. Chinese wear the rational calm of tolerant realists. Japs, like General Tojo, show the humorless intensity of ruthless mystics."[5]

Aware that readers might be suspicious that this exercise in racial cataloguing was similar to that being practiced by Nazi social scientists, *Life* assured its audience that American physical anthropologists were "devoted debunkers of race myths." Debunking notwithstanding, *Life* asserted that the ability to measure the difference between the Chinese and Japanese "in millimeters" enabled American scientists to "set apart the special types of each national group." To lend an air of precision, scientific objectivity, and authority to the photos and the accompanying text, *Life*'s editors festooned the pictures with handwritten captions and arrows simulating anthropological field notes.

The same disjuncture between the newly articulated ideals of racial egalitarianism and the practice of racial discrimination can be seen in the Supreme Court's decisions in the Japanese American internment cases. In the case of Gordon Hirabayashi, a student at the University of Washington who had challenged the right of military authorities to establish a curfew applicable only to persons of Japanese ancestry, the court stated that discrimination on the sole basis of race was "odious to a free people." Nevertheless, the court refused to curb the authority of the military in times of national emergency and upheld Hirabayashi's conviction (he had refused to leave the university library at the hour appointed for Japanese Americans to be in their homes). Likewise in the case of Fred Korematsu, a house painter from Oakland who had evaded relocation, the court held that while race was an "inherently invidious" category for discrimination by the state and subject to "strict scrutiny," the court accepted the state's claim of military necessity for the incarceration of Japanese Americans.[6]

Despite its massive mistreatment of Japanese Americans, the still rigidly enforced segregation of African Americans throughout most of American society (not least in the Armed Forces), and the deadly anti-Semitic policy of denying refuge to Europe's Jews, the U.S. government condemned the Nazi's doctrine of racial superiority and identified the defeat of racism as one of the reasons "Why We Fight." While Japanese Americans were singled out on the basis of their "race," other Asian American ethnic groups began to receive favorable treatment from the federal government.

In 1943, Congress voted to repeal the Chinese Exclusion Act, which had for sixty years forbidden Chinese, with few exceptions, to enter the United States. Repeal of exclusion had been a foreign policy goal of successive Chinese governments for more than half a century. Repeal was pushed through the U.S. Congress on the grounds that it would keep the wavering Nationalist Chinese government of Chiang Kai-shek in the war against Japan.[7]

In the next year, two bills were introduced in Congress to establish immigration quotas for India and the Philippines. These two bills were passed in 1946, on the eve of Philippine independence. The repeal of Chinese Exclusion and the effective dismantling of the Asiatic Barred Zone of 1917 had greater symbolic value than immediate demographic effect, since the number of visas issued to Asian countries was still severely restricted. Nevertheless, the ideological statement implied by the dismantling of racially specific barriers signaled an erosion of white supremacy as a national doctrine.[8]

Making the Model Minority Myth

In January 1966, the *New York Times Magazine* published an article with the title "Success Story: Japanese-American Style," and in December *U.S. News and World Report* published an article focusing on Chinese Americans, "Success Story of One Minority in the US."[9] As their titles suggest, both articles told the story of Asians in America as a narrative of triumphant ethnic assimilation.

This new popular representation of Asian Americans as the model of successful "ethnic assimilation" was created in the crisis of racial policy that had surfaced at the highest levels of the federal government the previous year. The policy debate that emerged in 1965 reflected deep ideological division over responses to the demands for racial equality that had developed in the two decades since the end of the Second World War.

The Watts riot in the summer of 1964 and the growing demands of African Americans for economic equity as well as formal political rights, along with the gradual dismantling of Jim Crow segregation in the South, plunged racial policy into crisis. The contours of the crisis can be seen in the conflicting responses of the Johnson Administration to black demands for racial equality. In March 1965, Lyndon Johnson's assistant secretary of Labor, Daniel Patrick Moynihan, published a *Report on the Black Family* which laid much of the blame for black poverty on the "tangle of pathology" of the black family. He admonished African Americans to rehabilitate their dysfunctional families in order to achieve economic and social assimilation. In June, at commencement exercises at all-black Howard University in Washington, D.C., the president articulated a vision of racial equality through sweeping social reconstruction in a massive War on Poverty. Both men genuinely claimed to support racial equality and civil rights, but their two documents could not have been further apart in their analysis and proposed solutions. The conflict between Johnson's response and Moynihan's response forms the ideological context in which the Asian Americans emerged as the model minority.

Johnson's speech emphasized the historical reality of race in America as compelling logic for extending civil rights into the economic sphere. Referring to the disadvantaged position of many blacks in the American economic structure, Johnson declared, "You do not take a person who for years has been hobbled by chains and liberate him, bring him up to the starting line of a race and then say, 'You are free to compete with all the others,' and still justly believe that you have been completely fair." [10] The president went on to lay the principal responsibility for black poverty on white racism, both historical and present, and he outlined an agenda of government-sponsored social change to ameliorate discrimination and poverty.

Moynihan took a radically different political tack. Quoting his former Harvard colleague, sociologist Nathan Glazer, Moynihan complained that "the demand for economic equality is now not the demand for equal opportunities for the equally qualified; it is now the demand for equality of economic results. . . . The demand for equality in education . . . has also become a demand for equality of results, of outcomes." [11]

Moynihan left implicit Glazer's ominous threat that American society, despite a commitment toward the former, would be "ruthless" in suppressing the latter. Moynihan went on to describe a black culture of poverty as a "tangle of pathology" born in slavery but "capable of perpetuating itself without assistance from the white world." [12] In particular, Moynihan identified the prevalence of female-headed households as a barrier to economic success. For Moynihan, the key to both racial integration and economic mobility was not in structural changes or social reorganization that might correct past injustice, but in the rehabilitation of "culturally deprived" black families.

The *U.S. News* article was quite explicit about the political context of its report when it asserted, "At a time when it is being proposed that hundreds of billions be spent on uplifting Negroes and other minorities, the nation's 300,000 Chinese Americans are moving ahead on their own with no help from anyone else." Foreshadowing an obsession that was to shape Richard Nixon's campaign rhetoric a year later, the writer of the *U.S. News* article described America's Chinatowns as "havens for law and order" and made no fewer than six references to low rates of delinquency among Chinese American youth. [13]

Making the Silent Minority

The construction of the model minority was based on the political silence of Asian America. An often cited example of Asian American self-reliance was the underutilization of welfare programs in 1970. Despite the fact that 15 percent of Chinese families in New York city had incomes below the federal poverty level, only 3.4 percent had enrolled to receive public assistance. This statistic has often been used as an example of a cultural trait of self-reliance and family cohesion. An alternative explanation, grounded in recent Asian American history, would stress apprehension and mistrust of the state's intentions toward them.

Wartime incarceration had left deep wounds in the Japanese American communities. The removal to fairgrounds and racetracks, the relocation to remote, barbed-wired camps, the uncertainty of loyalty oaths, the separation of family members, all traumatized the Japanese American community. The Japanese American Citizens League's policy of accommodation with the War Relocation Authority and its role in suppressing dissent within the camps had left bitter divisions among many Japanese Americans. Japanese Americans, for the most part, were anxious to rebuild their lives and livelihoods and reluctant to relive their experience. In particular, the American-born Nisei generation remained remarkably silent about its camp experience until the emergence of the Asian American movement in the 1970s and the Redress Movement of the 1980s. Social psychologists have likened the response of Japanese Americans who had been unjustly incarcerated to that of victims of rape or other physical violation. They demonstrated anger, resentment, self-doubt, and guilt, all symptoms of post-traumatic stress syndrome.[14]

While postwar Japan became America's junior partner, the People's Republic of China became its principal enemy. After the Korean War broke out in 1950, and especially after China entered the war in 1951, the United States made every effort to isolate communist China, economically and diplomatically, and embarked on a military policy of confrontation aimed at "containing" the expansion of Chinese influence throughout Asia and the Third World.

The fear of Red China extended to the Chinese American community. In 1949, Chinese communities in the United States were divided in their attitudes toward the communist revolution. Although the number of communists in Chinese American communities was tiny, many who were not communist or even leftist nonetheless found some satisfaction in the fact that a genuinely nationalist, reputedly honest, and apparently more democratic government had finally united China after a century of political chaos, weakness, and humiliation. On the other hand, Chiang Kai-shek's Kuomintang Party had long enjoyed the support of the traditional elites in the larger Chinatowns.[15]

When the Korean War broke out in 1950, Congress passed the Emergency Detention Act, which vested the U.S. Attorney General with the authority to establish concentration camps for any who might be deemed a domestic threat in a national emergency. The mere authorization of such sweeping powers of detention served as a stark warning to Chinese Americans that what had been done to Japanese Americans a decade earlier could also be done to them without effort.

The pro–Chiang Kai-shek Chinatown elite, working with the FBI, launched a systematic attempt to suppress any expression of support for the new communist regime in China. The Trading with the Enemy Act, which prohibited any currency transfers to the Peoples Republic of China, including remittances to family, was used as a tool to attempt to deport suspected communist sympathizers. Although only a few leftists and labor leaders were actually deported, the threat of deportation had a deeply chilling effect, since many hundreds of Chinese had come to the United States as "paper sons" during the long decades of exclusion and were in the United States under false pretenses.

In 1952 Congress passed the McCarran-Walter Immigration and Nationality Act, which dismantled racial prohibitions on immigration and established an Asian-Pacific Triangle with an immigration quota cap of two thousand visas. Even though McCarran-Walter still strictly limited Asian immigration, the red scare that was its impetus was contagious.

In 1955, Everett F. Drumwright, the U.S. consul in Hong Kong, issued a report warning that Communist China was making use of "massive" fraud and deception to infiltrate agents into the United States under cover as immigrants. Drumwright's hysterical and largely unsubstantiated report provided the rationale for massive FBI and INS raids into Chinatowns around the country to search out pro-China subversives. Chinatowns were flooded with public notices and street flyers warning of potential spies and subversives, while "innocent residents" were encouraged to report suspected subversives to the FBI.

In 1957 Congress authorized the Chinese Confession Program. Chinese Americans who had come as paper sons were encouraged to confess their illegal entry. In return for consideration for an appropriate (but not guaranteed) adjustment of their status, the applicant had also to make a full disclosure on every relative and friend. The information gathered in the Chinese Confession Program was used to try to deport those who were identified by the FBI's informants as supporters of China or as domestic troublemakers. Membership in leftist support organizations, in labor unions, in "pro-China" organizations melted away in the face of the sustained harassment and attack from the conservative elite within Chinatowns, and the FBI and INS from without.[16]

Containing The Red Menace: The Fordist Compromise

At the close of the Second World War, American labor was infused with a renewed militancy. During the war years union membership had grown from nine million in 1940 to about fifteen million in 1945. This represented almost thirty six percent of the non-agricultural work force, the highest proportion of unionized labor in the country's history. During the war years, organized labor had agreed to a no strike policy and to curb wage demands as a patriotic obligation to the war effort. However, at the war's end pent-up wage demands and the problems of reabsorption of millions of men leaving the service led to a resurgence of demands for wages and a reassertion of control over work conditions. Labor strife soon boiled over at General Motors and in the oil industry. In 1945 forty-five hundred work stoppages, mainly wildcat strikes and sitdowns, involved five million workers. Some of these work stoppages took the form of hate strikes aimed at driving women and black workers from the factory positions they had earned during the war.[17]

In 1946, the steelworkers went on strike, then the miners. Strike fever spread when a general strike was called in Stamford, Connecticut. In 1947 militant labor called general strikes to shut down business in Houston, Rochester, Pittsburgh and Oakland.

In May 1946, President Truman seized the railroads to prevent a strike.

Altogether Truman would seize and operate nine industries under powers granted the executive branch by the War Labor Disputes Act. Management launched a massive attack on radical, particularly Communist Party, leadership within the labor movement. Their most effective tool was the Taft-Hartley Act, passed in 1948, which outlawed the closed shop, secondary boycotts, and jurisdictional strikes in violation of decisions of the National Labor Relations Board; jointly administered welfare funds; and made unions subject to suit in federal courts for violation of contracts. The Taft-Hartley law stripped collective bargaining rights from unions having communists among their leadership and resulted in successive purges of the labor movement. Employers and employees could petition for decertification elections, and federal employees were forbidden to strike. State right-to-work laws were legalized, and the president was given power to enforce eighty-day cooling off periods during which labor would be compelled to return to work.

The long period of economic growth that sustained America's rise to hegemonic power depended on a sustained accord between labor and management. This pattern of cooperation has been called the Fordist Compromise, since it seemed to usher in that stage of capitalism which Henry Ford had envisioned, in which working-class demand for durable consumer goods would drive economic growth. The Fordist Compromise permanently institutionalized many of the features of "scientific management" that had been introduced during the war. Under the new production-oriented union leadership, labor contracts developed a pattern of close collaboration between labor leadership and management on issues of supervision, productivity, and work rules.[18] In return, management and the state worked together to create a working class that had the social characteristics of a middle class. Real income rose by 30 percent between 1945 and 1960. The Fordist Compromise also called for a relatively high degree of state intervention, from the mediation of labor relations through the National Labor Relations Board, to the regulation of working conditions through agencies such as the Occupational Safety and Health Administration, to the organization of a "welfare state" of permanent entitlements for the new "middle" class, such as social security, subsidized housing, educational financing, unemployment insurance, and increased public higher education. The state also took on an expanded role in intervening in the economy through an ever-wider range of fiscal control policies and by exercising its economic power as the purchaser of last resort.

The sustained economic growth on which the Fordist Compromise depended was fueled by several sources, but initially it was $40 billion in wartime personal savings and a pent-up demand for durable consumer products that drove production. This required the reinvigoration of the patriarchal nuclear family. Wartime production had increased the number of women in the labor force from just under fourteen million in 1940 to just over nineteen million in 1945.[19] Both management and federal agencies worked to encourage and sometimes force women back into the home while work assignments in many plants were resegregated along racial lines.[20] As men returned from war and started families, the birth rate in the United States grew for the first time in several decades, leading to the sustained growth of a domestic market for housing, education, and durable consumer goods. The nuclear family was the necessary social unit of consumption for durable goods—the automobiles (fifty-eight million sold in the 1950s), refrigerators, toasters, and televisions whose production drove the economy.

The realization of the Fordist Compromise could only be imagined in a world in which the United States had reconstructed a sphere of influence based on free trade and open markets. In the late 1930s and '40s, American policy planners in the State Department and the Council on Foreign Relations had initially imagined a "Grand Area" of American influence, to include the Western Hemisphere and the Asia-Pacific area. By the of the war, the United States was in position to supplant Britain, France, and the Netherlands in many, if not all, of their colonial territories.[21] The American postwar project of global transformation supplanted European colonial administrations in Asia with nationalist elites whose economic interests and political allegiances were aligned with American interests. By the end of the 1940s, one-third of all manufactured goods in the world were made in America, and U.S. officials emphasized a high level of exports as a critical factor in avoiding a postwar depression.[22] American policymakers therefore took it as an article of faith that the reconstruction of a stable, multilateral, capitalist economic system would rely on the unobstructed movement of capital and labor.

America's strategy for global reconstruction required the reconstruction of both western Europe and Japan as major industrialized trading partners. In Europe, the Marshall Plan funneled millions of dollars into the rebuilding of western Europe. Financing the reconstruction of Europe could not be funded solely through European-American trade, however; imports from Europe only amounted to one third of one percent of the U.S. gross national product. The United States therefore looked to Asia and the Pacific to close the "dollar gap."

The development of a Pacific Rim economic strategy therefore became a central requirement for American policy planners directly at the war's end. Although MacArthur had begun to dismantle prewar cartels such as Mitsui and Mitsubishi as a means of democratizing the Japanese economy along with its political system, by 1947 the reverse decision was made to reconstruct Japan's prewar economic machine as a foil to a possible revolutionary China. Japanese manufacturing was to become what the Council on Foreign Relations called "the workshop of the American lake." Japan was to play a critical role as a junior partner in the Pacific Rim strategy. After the "loss" of China, Japan, with American encouragement, focused its economic attention on southeast Asia. In its report on Asian economic development in 1952, the Institute for Pacific Relations spelled out the role that Japan was to play between the United States and the Southeast Asian market.

> There can be little question that . . . the best area for Japanese economic expansion is in Southeast Asia, with its demands for capital and consumer goods, its raw materials and rice surplus. . . . It would seem that Japan should be encouraged to develop trading outlets there in the interest of the overall structure of Pacific security. Japan has herself shown keen interest in these trade possibilities, especially in Thailand, Malaysia, Indonesia, and India.[23]

The Pacific Rim was not only a crucial market for American goods but also a highly profitable region for export of capital. In addition to the redeployment of Japanese capital, direct U.S. investment in the Pacific Rim was a major source of profits for American corporations. While overseas investments grew at about 10 percent per annum—twice the growth rate of domestic investment—American investment in the Pacific Rim outside Japan brought a 25.5 percent return on investment, and investment in the Japanese economy brought in 11.3 percent. Between 1951 and 1976, the book value of American investments in the Pacific Rim grew from $16 billion to $80.3 billion.[24]

Containing The Black Menace: Ethnic Assimilation

In 1944, the same year in which the Supreme Court heard the Japanese internment cases, Gunnar Myrdal published *An American Dilemma: The Negro Problem and Modern Democracy,* a massive collaborative study of American race relations. Drawing on the work of a generation of American liberal social scientists, notably sociologist Robert E. Park and his students, *An American Dilemma* signaled the intellectual discrediting of biological theories of racial superiority and the triumph of the concept of ethnicity as the dominant paradigm for explaining and transforming race relations. Myrdal's report to the Carnegie Foundation focused on the disparity between the egalitarian ethos articulated in the nation's founding documents and the practice of racial discrimination in American society. Myrdal was clear about the implications of the "American dilemma" for America's role as the principal organizer of the postwar world order: "If America in actual practice could show the world a progressive trend by which the Negro finally became integrated into modern democracy, all mankind would have reason to believe that peace, progress, and order are feasible." [25]

Myrdal's hope was a statement of liberal faith. The triumph of liberalism, including ethnic liberalism, was made possible by the victory of the United States and its allies over the Axis powers and necessary to the rise of a *Pax Americana* in the postwar era.

The Cold War provided a national security dimension to the "race problem." Although Soviet communism was perceived as the greatest threat to the established order, after the Soviet Union exploded its own atomic bomb in 1949 the struggle against the Soviet Union was limited to a war of containment. [26] Since the establishment of relatively stable opposing blocs in Europe in the mid-1950s, the struggle between the U.S. and the Soviet Union was played out principally in Asia, Africa, and Latin America. In 1954, the term "Third World" was coined as India, the People's Republic of China, and Indonesia (with the tacit support of the Soviet Union) sponsored a conference of non-aligned nations at Bandung, Indonesia. The demands of the Third World nations, largely peoples of color, for independence, self-determination, and economic development became the ideological arena in the contest between the Soviet Union and the United States.

It is not surprising, then, to find federal intervention on behalf of civil rights expressed in the language and logic of the Cold War. As early as 1948, in *Shelley v. Kraemer,* a case involving restrictive covenants in real estate, the federal government's brief supporting the dismantling of racial restrictions on housing "relied" on the State Department's view that "the United States has been embarrassed in the conduct of foreign relations by acts of [racial] discrimination in this country." [27] In the most significant postwar desegregation case, *Brown v. Board of Education,* both the Justice Department and the NAACP briefs emphasized the important foreign policy implications of the case. The Justice Department's *amicus* brief stated the foreign policy case explicitly:

> The existence of discrimination against minority groups in the U.S. has an adverse effect upon our relations with other countries. . . . Racial discrimination furnishes grist for the Communist propaganda mills and it raises doubts even among friendly nations as to the intensity of our devotion to the democratic faith. [28]

A decade later, in the aftermath of the Watts riots, both Johnson's Howard University speech and the preface to Moynihan's *Report* referred to this ideological struggle and framed the problem of civil rights and social justice in the United States within the global context of the Cold War. Both initially emphasized the need to provide the world with a model of the "true American revolution" as an alternative to communism. The president opened his speech by declaring,

> Our earth is the home of revolution. . . . Our enemies may occasionally seize the day of change. But it is the banner of our movement which they take. And our own future is linked to this process of change in many lands in the world. But nothing in any country touches us more profoundly, nothing is freighted with meaning for our own destiny, than the revolution of the Negro American.[29]

Moynihan opened his report with the observation that "the [Black] movement has profound international implications, . . . [and that] it was not a matter of chance that the Negro movement caught fire in America at just that moment when the nations of Africa were gaining their freedom."[30] He went on to invoke the threat of perceived separatist Black Muslim doctrines or the "attractiveness of Chinese communism" to American blacks.

Anxious to replace the invidious category of race, for which there was little scientific justification and significant political cost, liberal theorists subsumed race relations to ethnicity. Ethnicity theory was grounded in the belief that while certain historically anachronistic patterns of racial segregation persisted, modern American society was open to the full participation of all who were willing to participate. Liberal social scientists who promoted the ethnicity paradigm argued that the desired assimilation of blacks into modern American society could be achieved in two steps. The barriers of Jim Crow segregation had to be dismantled (over the objections of "pre-modern" segregationists like the Klan, the White Citizens Councils, and an entrenched Southern power structure), and non-whites had to accommodate themselves to the "universal" demands of modernity.

The blueprint for ethnic assimilation was Robert Park's theory of a four-stage ethnic or race relations cycle. Park identified four stages in a natural and irreversible process of ethnic assimilation: initial contact between the outsider and the host society, economic and political competition, economic and cultural accommodation of the ethnic to the host society, and finally, assimilation into the host society. These patterns of cultural assimilation and integration were assumed to be universally applicable to all "newcomers" into the modern city and applicable to racial as well as ethnic relations. This was a narrative of modernization drawn from studies of the historical experiences of European immigrant groups in American cities. The ethnic component of cultural identity was identified with the Old World. Seen as pre-modern and dysfunctional, ethnic differences of language, custom, and religion were transcended as the immigrant became modern and American.

Since the stages of assimilation were based on a narrative of universal modernization and not on a theory of subordination, the burden was on the latecomer to modernization to accommodate the host society. It did not occur to assimilation theorists that racially subordinated people might be reluctant to abandon cultures of survival that had been developed over centuries of oppression. The black sociologist E. Franklin Frazier, a student of Park and one of the most important contributors to *The American Dilemma*, wrote:

> Since the institutions, the social stratification, and the culture of the Negro community are essentially the same as those of the larger community, it is not strange that the Negro minority belongs among the assimilationist rather than the pluralist, secessionist, or militant minorities. It is seldom that one finds Negroes who think of themselves as possessing a different culture from whites and that their culture should be preserved.[31]

Assimilationists supported the civil rights movement in the dismantling of Southern Jim Crow segregation and encouraged voting rights and electoral political participation. Assimilation theory, however, suggested that the duty of the state was limited to the dismantling of formal, legislated barriers to participation. Since the greater part of assimilation rested on the accommodation of the minority to the host society, state regulation of private activity in the interest of equal condition was seen to have little positive and possibly greater negative effect. The sociologist Milton Gordon, who in the early 1960s elaborated and refined Park's race relations cycle into a seven-stage theory of ethnic assimilation, warned explicitly:

> The government *must not* use racial criteria positively in order to impose desegregation upon public facilities in an institutional area where such segregation is not a function of racial discrimination directly, but results from discrimination operating in another institutional area or from some other causes.[32] [Emphasis added.]

In the 1950s and early 1960s, liberalism, with its universalist claims on science and progress, became the hegemonic ideology of the American imperium. The political requirements of the Cold War and the logic of liberal universalism required an adherence to a doctrine of racial equality. Liberal social scientists articulated a theory of modernization that could be deployed as an ideological alternative to communism in resolving the problem of the Third World. Its domestic version, ethnic assimilation, would provide a similar nonradical solution to the "Negro problem."

Ethnicity theory met the requirements of liberalism by articulating a doctrine of individual competition in a "colorblind" society or, in Milton Gordon's view, a society in which the state played a neutral role. Ethnicity theory articulated a vision of the colorblind society but evaded a critique of the historical category of race altogether. Ethnicity theory offered a promise of equality that could be achieved, not through political organization and community empowerment, but only through individual effort, cultural assimilation, and political accommodation. For liberals who sought both to develop the Negro and to contain black demands for the systematic and structural dismantling of racial discrimination, the representation of Asian-American communities as self-contained, safe, and politically acquiescent became a powerful example of the success of the American creed in resolving the problems of race.

In 1955, less than a year after the Supreme Court had shocked the system of Southern segregation by declaring separate but equal education inherently unequal and unconstitutional, the torture, lynching, and mutilation of Emmett Till, a black fourteen-year-old who was accused of flirting with a white woman, shocked the world. The exoneration of Till's killers by a jury of their white peers signaled a strategy of "massive resistance" to racial equality in the South. The murder of Emmett Till served as the counternarrative of racial intolerance and violence that threatened to undermine the liberal narrative of Myrdal's American creed so painstakingly assembled and elaborately articulated.

Containing The White Menace:
The Nuclear Family as Civil Defense

In 1948, Alfred Kinsey shocked America by reporting that a third of American men had engaged in some homosexual activity during the course of their lives and that a majority had experienced homoerotic desire. The news should not have come as a surprise. The 1940s had witnessed a marked expansion of sexual freedom and experimentation with new definitions of gender relations. During the war years, millions of young men went into the armed forces and millions of young women went into the factories. These young people established new patterns of dating and had a more relaxed attitude toward premarital sex than did their parents. During the same period, gay and lesbian public cultures emerged in cities around the country.[33]

Kinsey's study, *The Sexual Behavior of the Human Male,* a dry sociological survey of 12,000 respondents, became an immediate best seller. It also drew the ire of conservative churchmen and politicians. For reporting these activities of Americans, Kinsey was accused of aiding and abetting the communist cause and was investigated by the House Committee on Un-American Activities.

In the Cold War search for traitors and subversives, homophobia and anticommunism went hand in hand. Following on the heels of Senator Joe McCarthy's search for communist agents, the Senate launched investigations to root out homosexuals in the federal government. Nonreproductive sexuality, homosexuality in particular, was seen as a threat to the national security. Anticommunist crusaders warned that homosexuality weakened the nation's "moral fiber," making it susceptible to both sexual and political seduction. Just as communism was considered a perversion of the natural economic order, homosexuality was considered a perversion of the natural biological order. When the sudden turn from American triumph in the Second World War to the high anxiety of the Cold War could only be explained by treason, homosexuals were seen to have secret lives much likes spies or foreign agents. Shortly after his inauguration as president in 1953, Dwight Eisenhower issued an executive order barring gay men and lesbians from Federal employment.[34]

The link between anticommunism and homophobia was not merely psychological or metaphorical; in the atomic age, reproducing the nuclear family was understood to be the key to national survival. In the 1950s and early 1960s, seeking to take advantage of America's advantage in nuclear weapons, strategic planners stressed survivability in nuclear war. This strategic doctrine relied on a program of civil defense, the mass mobilization and education of the civilian population regarding their duties during nuclear war. At the heart of civil defense was the belief that the nuclear family was the primary social unit through which the American way of life could be preserved or resurrected.[35] Talcott Parsons, perhaps the most influential American sociologist between 1940 and the 1960s, argued that the middle-class family, with its "natural" division of labor between the sexes, was the most efficient and implicitly the highest form of social organization. In the absence of a state apparatus that might be obliterated or cut off from its people by nuclear war, the nuclear family was a natural social unit that would reproduce America.

Sayonara: War Bride as Pocahontas

Sayonara, a 1956 film directed by Joshua Logan, is a drama about the trials of interracial romance in the Cold War era. The movie, based on James Michener's novel of the same title (published in 1953), is a narrative in which "modern" interracial love triumphs over anachronistic racial bigotry. *Sayonara* establishes the anticommunist necessity of ethnic liberalism and presents the war bride as a model of ethnic assimilation. This triumph of ethnic liberalism opens up the way for the rebirth of a nation, America as protector of the postwar global order.

The War Brides Act of 1945 had made it possible for American military personnel to bring their spouses and dependent children to the United States as nonquota immigrants. In the five years between 1947 (when the War Brides Act was amended to include Chinese and Japanese wives of American citizens) and 1952 (when its provisions ended), some 6,000 Chinese women came to the United States. Between 1945 and 1975, some 45,000 Japanese wives of American servicemen immigrated to the United States.[36] Only a few Japanese women came to the U.S. under the War Brides Act itself. It was only after the McCarran-Walters Immigration and Nationality Act of 1952, which allowed the naturalization of Japanese and Korean immigrants and provided nonquota visas for spouses and children of American citizens, that many Japanese spouses of American service personnel began to arrive.[37] Japanese "war brides" were among thousands of women from Asia who took advantage of the dismantling of immigration laws that had restricted their entry into the United States since the Page Act of 1870. Thousands of Filipino wives accompanied American servicemen to the United States or joined husbands who had immigrated earlier. In the 1950s and '60s women made up the great majority of immigrants from Asia.[38]

The relationship of gender and sexuality to the process of ethnic assimilation and racial segregation has always been a troubled one. In *An American Dilemma*, Myrdal identified the preservation of a taboo on marriage and sexual relations between black men and white women as the single highest priority of white Southerners. A decade later, Emmett Till paid with his life after being accused of breaking that taboo. The Americanization of the Asian war bride—Orientalism domesticated—was the Cold War narrative of ethnic assimilation and domesticity that could restore credibility to the "American creed" that reconstructed the American family as modern, universal, and multi-ethnic, if not exactly multiracial. In this tale of Americanization, the Oriental woman was transformed from dangerously transgressive into a symbol of domesticity and a stalwart of a restored postwar patriarchy. Meanwhile Asian men remained outside the American family, marginalized, invisible, and racially Other.

Shot against the serene background of a lush Japanese garden, with gracefully arched footbridges and a watercourse, *Sayonara*'s title sequence establishes the tension between the modern West and the premodern East. The classically Orientalist image of Japan—aestheticized, unchanging, pastoral, and ahistorical—is immediately displaced by the opening scene, which sets up the historical context for *Sayonara*'s narrative of Cold War modernization. The opening shot shows a fighter jet landing on an airstrip in Korea (the caption tells us the year is 1951), signaling the arrival of the active, masculine, and modern American Century. The scene is careful to underscore the fact that the Korean War is not the Second World War and that the relationship between Asia and America has changed. The Sabrejet lands in front of two ground crewmen working on an older, propeller-driven plane, an obsolete reminder of the Second World War and an earlier era. When Major "Ace" Gruver (Marlon Brando) opens his hatch, his war weariness is immediately apparent. He admits to moral fatigue. Gruver comments to his ground crewman, Airman Kelly (Red Buttons), that this time "there was a guy with a face in that [enemy] plane." Gruver's admission articulates his ambivalence about the war in Korea, which, though it is a war against communism, is merely a "police action," a war of containment and not a total war.

Although the Korean War occasions the *Sayonara* story, apart from the introductory scenes virtually no further mention is made of the war itself. *Sayonara* is a garrison drama, as such its themes are domestic. The struggle against Soviet communism is not only on the battlefront in Korea but also, perhaps principally, within the American empire. Racial attitudes are critical to the way in which the conduct of Americans in Japan and elsewhere in the Free World are judged.

Gruver is told by his commanding officer that he must dissuade Kelly from marrying Katsumi (Miyoshi Umeki), the Japanese woman with whom he is in love. While it winks at casual sexual relations between American service personnel and Japanese women, the military establishment strongly discourages marriage between Americans and Japanese and forbids servicemen from bringing their wives to the United States. When Kelly enthusiastically shows Gruver a photo of Katsumi, Gruver— a West Pointer, the son of a general, and a Southerner—responds with blunt racism. "I don't understand how a normal American can marry a Japanese. . . . Go ahead and marry this slant-eyed runt if you like." Gruver shows Kelly a picture of his fiancée, Eileen Webster (Patricia Owens), the daughter of another general, and catalogues the qualities that make her a good potential wife for a "normal" American. Eileen is "an American girl [with] fine character, with good background, good education, good family, [and] good blood." If not precisely an Aryan superwoman, Eileen is the white middle-class ideal of its social elite. The racial and class differences between Katsumi and Eileen are marked immediately on the body. When they exchange pictures of their respective objects of desire,

Gruver remains silent on Katsumi while Kelly comments enthusiastically on Eileen's figure in a swimsuit.

In response to Gruver's racist slur, Kelly's sharp retort, "Don't ever talk to me like that again," signals his independence and principled fearlessness in the face of a superior. It establishes Kelly's role as representative of the working class in this film. Class differences, coded as military rank, are underscored by the revelation that Kelly, a forthright but devoted and hardworking soldier, has been promoted and demoted four times for insubordination. Kelly shows Gruver the military's pamphlets warning about "the dangers" of intermarriage. Kelly defies the military bureaucracy by writing his congressman to get permission to marry. His class analysis is straightforward and populist: "There's the generals for the officers and congressmen for the peasants." This secures Kelly's position as spokesman for the workingman and helps to mobilize populist legitimacy for his desire to marry Katsumi.

In what seems an absurd irony, after forcing Gruver to apologize for his racist slur toward his intended, Kelly asks him to serve as best man at his wedding. This is where the film's liberal individualism exerts itself as a containment of a more radical structural critique. While Airman Kelly is measured both by his principled stand against the undemocratic state (represented by the military authorities) and by his personal fealty to his superior officer, Gruver is measured by his personal loyalty to his men over and above his obedience to the rules. Kelly and Gruver share a possessive individualism that is offended by the state's intervention in the (private) decision to take a wife. At the same time, this reliance on individualism safely contains the radical potential of Kelly's protests, both against racism and against the privilege of class or rank.

Japan is presented as a sexual wonderland, beginning with Kelly's first description of an all-male Kabuki theater and an all-female Matsubayara dance troupe (based, presumably, on Tokyo's famous Takarazuka Theater). The exoticism of Japan is ironically underscored by the surprise arrival of Gruver's fiancée, Eileen, the daughter of his new commanding general. Eileen Webster represents the conventional white middle-class ideal of sexual attractiveness. Yet it soon becomes apparent that Eileen is dissatisfied with the prospect of a conventional family life shaped by the demands of a shared military career "like our parents have." However Eileen's rebelliousness is contained by her intense romanticism; she can identify her own pleasure and fulfillment only through a husband. She explains to a somewhat befuddled Gruver, "No woman wants to live any way except body and soul with the man she loves."

Gruver's first introduction into Japanese high culture is a trip to the Kabuki Theater arranged by Eileen. Kabuki is a classical and highly ritualized theater in which male actors play both male and female roles ("Just like they do at Princeton," chirps Eileen's mother). While Gruver appears discomfited by the idea, Eileen seems clearly titillated and enthusiastic about the exotic and potentially transgressive nature of the performance; she reads aloud from a brochure that the Kabuki actors combine "the grace of a woman and the power of a man" in one body. Gruver becomes clearly uncomfortable with the homoerotic potential in the Kabuki performance and, in what appears to be a homophobic panic, insists on a disruptive public display of heterosexual affection. Eileen, on the other hand, uses the performance to prod Gruver's sexual anxiety. When Nakamura turns the character of the lady into a lion in a powerful dance, Eileen twits Gruver, "Is he man enough for you now, Lloyd?" [39]

The first view of the Kabuki actor Nakamura (Ricardo Montalban) is an elaborate costuming scene that interjects an extraordinarily disruptive moment into what, until this point, has been a densely heterosexual discourse focusing on the exchange values of Japanese and American women. In the course of putting on his heavy white face and body paint, and his female costume, Nakamura's race and sex are simultaneously transformed and deconstructed. As a male actor playing a female role, Nakamura's sex is temporarily obscured. Nevertheless, when Nakamura is displayed in a direct frontal shot wearing a codpiece, there remains little doubt as to his physical sexual identity as a male.

Preparing for the stage, Nakamura applies a heavy white greasepaint that obscures his visual identification as Asian, although the ritual underscores his cultural identity as Japanese. The whiteness of the Kabuki makeup also marks Nakamura as potentially racially transgressive. This is a double masquerade, since Nakamura is played by Ricardo Montalban in yellowface. The casting of Montalban in this role achieves a number of purposes. It uses the Cuban-born actor's image as a romantic sophisticate (based on another ethnic stereotype) to create an ethnically exotic yet racially acceptable potential rival to Gruver. The audience is thus reassured that if Nakamura *née* Montalban does have an affair with Eileen Webster, no racial taboo will have been broken, since beneath the white paint and the yellow paint there is a white man.

The film next turns to its second spectacle of Japanese sexuality, the dance of the Matsubayara showgirls. The dancers first appear dressed in prim kimonos marching from their dormitory to their theater like school girls. The single exception to this display of demure femininity is their chief dancer, Hana Ogi, who is dressed in pants, turtleneck sweater, and feathered hat. Hana Ogi, a transvestite woman, is the mirror image of Nakamura. Gruver is told that "the tall ones play men's parts."

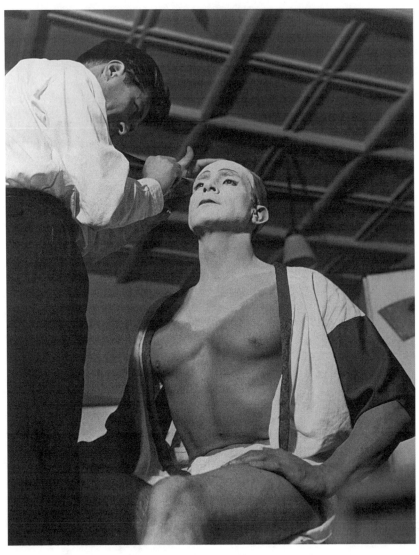

White face on yellow face:
Ricardo Montalban as Nakamura in *Sayonara*.
Still courtesy of the Museum of Modern Art Film Archives

Postwar spectacles:
The Matsubayara Dancing Girls with Hana Ogi (Miko Tara) center stage in *Sayonara*
Still courtesy of the Museum of Modern Art Film Archives

The Matsubayara performance displays an virtual buffet of imagined Japanese sexuality. Against a line of dancers in lamé tights, Hana Ogi first appears in a sheer kimono as a Geisha; then, in short succession, in top hat and tails, a western-style ball gown, a formal kimono, the costume of a Shinto priest, in Samurai costume, and finally as a princess. The sexual fantasy that she represents and appears to offer crosses gender, racial, and cultural boundaries. Although she refuses to meet him, over the course of the next few months, Hana Ogi parades in front of Gruver on her way to and from the dormitory. This parade reproduces the male drag fantasy of her dance performance as she wears a variety of sexually signifying men's hats: a brown fedora, a golfing cap, a straw hat, and a gaucho hat.

Contrasted to the rigidly heterosexual gender and family codes of the United States, represented by General and Mrs. Webster, Japan is polymorphous, transgressive, and exotic. Both Nakamura and Hana Ogi represent a sexuality that is transgendered and unpredictably dangerous.

"The tall ones play the men's parts": Hana Ogi in male drag meets Gruver (Marlon Brando).
Still courtesy of the Museum of Modern Art Film Archives

The homosocial tension between Gruver and Nakamura in a potential rivalry over Eileen (whose fascination with Nakamura is made evident) is overwhelmed by the homoerotic tension between the two characters. Gruver and Nakamura mirror each other visually and narratively. The scene that introduces Nakamura pays close attention to makeup and robing as an elaborate transgendering ritual. In this scene, Nakamura sits erect and appears energized by the erotic power expressed in his acting. This astounding fetishization of the "Japanese" male body stands in stark contrast to a parallel introduction of Gruver. In that scene—Gruver's post-flight medical examination—Gruver sits on examination table, also naked from the waist up. But his body, in contrast to the erect Nakamura, is slouched, flaccid with physical and moral fatigue. In a later scene, Gruver confides to a Marine Corps officer (James Garner) that an acting experience in high school had "changed [his] world" but that he had repressed his youthful desire to be an actor (like Nakamura) in favor of West Point and the military career chosen for him by this father.

The scene in which Hana Ogi and Gruver are finally introduced is an exercise in Orientalist shtick. The meeting is arranged to take place in Kelly's small Japanese-style house. There is the traditional bumping of Western heads on low ceilings; much is made of the ritualized etiquette of sake drinking (in contrast to the two-fisted whisky drinker that Gruver is presumed to be—signified by the bottle of whiskey he brings as a gift). Hana Ogi is presented in formal kimono; predictably the introductions take place over the mutual pouring of sake. Despite her former aloofness, Hana Ogi immediately and unconditionally assumes the subordinate Orientalized position. She asks Gruver's forgiveness for hating Americans because she has held them responsible for the deaths of her family. To this reminder of America's still recent encounter with Japan, it must have been unsettling for audiences to hear Gruver reply simply, "there were a whole lot of Americans killed too and it's best we forget." [40]

In the West, the gaze is traditionally appropriated to masculine power. Therefore, when Hana Ogi says, "I have been watching you, too, and you have not looked like a savage," and adds, "Katsumi-san [whom Gruver has kissed, somewhat reluctantly, at her wedding] has told me how gently you kiss," it is a startling moment for Gruver. The admission by the Native Woman of looking and inquiring captures the eroticism of the exotic. On one hand, the admission seems to betray innocence; Hana Ogi appears not to know better than to reveal her interest in Gruver. On the other hand, it reveals her appropriation of the gaze; she can exercise the power of surveillance. She can categorize him as "not a savage." Hana Ogi goes on to spin a fantasy of innocence, danger, and devotion that would make Madame Butterfly blush: "I have never been in love, though I have dreamed and thought about it. . . . There is danger of discovery for both of us, danger of weakness when it is over. . . . I will never fall in love again, but I will love you, Lloyd-san, if that is your desire." This combination of submissive innocence and assertive sexuality is the epitome of Orientalist fantasy.

The gauzy romanticism of the affair between Gruver and Hana Ogi is sharply contrasted to the Kellys' marriage and subsequent double suicide. Kelly and Katsumi settle into a small house off base in what appears to be a working-class neighborhood. Kelly makes an attempt to learn Japanese and takes great pride in knowing about Japan and things Japanese. Katsumi is portrayed as an ideally devoted Japanese wife—submissive, docile, and obedient. It is not out of any gesture of independence or individuality on Katsumi's part, but precisely out of her obsequiousness, that the only occasion for Kelly's anger with his "model" wife arises. Kelly is angered by Katsumi's suggestion that she wants to have an operation to remove the epicanthic folds from her eyelids, a literal self-effacement to make herself acceptably "white."

Kelly takes great umbrage at this self-denying and naive idea and commands that she remain as she is. Kelly's objection and command reveal the disparate power relations between the white American husband and the Japanese wife. First, it underscores Kelly's complete domination over the supine Katsumi, who is willing to undergo mutilation to please him and then meekly accepts his decision to veto the idea. Second, although it signals Kelly's resistance to racist assumptions about beauty, Kelly's refusal of permission can also be read as a sign of his desire for Katsumi to remain exotically "Japanese." Third, Kelly accepts Katsumi for who she is, or at least how he, and not others, has created her. Katsumi's aborted plan to have her eyelids "fixed" and Kelly's difficulty in learning to speak Japanese are meant to suggest that the utopian dream of "going native" or "passing" is not a viable alternative.

The Kellys, and all the other interracial couples under military command, are made to endure increasing harassment ordered by a bigoted Southern colonel who is the executive officer under General Webster. Symbolic of this pressure and representative of the ostracism that may face interracial couples on their return to the States, the colonel places their homes off-limits to other American personnel.

Faced with sudden orders to return to the States, and unable to bring Katsumi with him, Kelly commits suicide with Katsumi. Their suicide is literally foreshadowed in *bunraku,* a shadow puppet performance that ends with a romantic double suicide. Short of having the couples attend *Madame Butterfly,* the audience could be given no clearer notice of the inevitable. Suicide is Kelly's final utopian, Butterfly-like gesture. Kelly, who has been portrayed as rigidly principled, cannot now think of any pragmatic response that will preserve his sense of honor and justice. Kelly must make some final gesture, however futile and romantic, of resistance. Of course, he takes a stereotypically Japanese course of action.

It is only in the wake of the Kellys' suicide that the anticommunist logic of ethnic liberalism explicitly reveals itself. After Gruver's initial racist comment in Korea, he is gradually transformed from a Southern racial bigot to a national racial liberal. Racism is clearly identified as a Southern pathology; the racist villains of the film are General Webster's executive officer, a colonel, and Eileen's self-serving and status-conscious mother. Both are Southerners who represent an anachronistic, if still persistent, racial bigotry. In an early scene, where the marine officer played by James Garner and his Japanese date are turned away from the officers' club by the colonel at Mrs. Webster's insistence, it is made clear that her bigotry is damaging to the political alliance between the United States and Japan.

The colonel then orchestrates the harassment of interracial families and the sudden transfer of Kelly to the States, making the Kellys' suicide inevitable. The Kellys' suicide touches off anti-American demonstrations and a near riot (assumed to be communist-inspired). Witnessing this, Gruver is given to understand the global importance of ethnic liberalism. Racial bigotry of the old Southern variety is thus revealed to provide "grist for the communist propaganda mills." It is the Kellys' suicide and the subsequent recognition of the political significance of their own relationship that finally brings Gruver and Hana Ogi together permanently. Despite her embarrassingly obsequious professions of selfless and undying love and devotion, Hana Ogi is more Pocahontas than Madame Butterfly.

The Pocahontas legend, repeated and embellished over three centuries, has assumed the status of a myth of national origins.[41] Pocahontas could be viewed as the sexual, maternal, self-sacrificing, fertile native woman who symbolizes the fruit of conquest. She can serve as a triumphal metaphor for the assimilation of the "ethnic" woman into the benevolent paternalism of American society.[42] In these narratives, the native woman, the princess of a defeated or soon-to-be defeated nation, falls in love with the white conquering hero and realizes the moral superiority and liberation of American society. The native woman becomes a true woman through her love of the white man. Having become a true woman via this transformative love, she becomes a candidate for the motherhood of the new nation.

As in the legend of Pocahontas and John Smith, Hana Ogi "saves" Gruver. Hana Ogi saves Gruver from himself, from his own exhaustion, self-doubt, and "Southern" racism, and from his crisis of masculinity, through his heterosexual affair with her. Since Hana Ogi's dance has assured us of her desirability as a heterosexual object of desire, her apparent transvestitism allows Gruver to simultaneously express and contain his repressed desire for Nakamura. The triumph of Gruver's "natural" heterosexuality is realized in the domestication of Hana Ogi's previously transgendered sexuality. When Hana Ogi declares finally that Gruver's love has made her, as she says, a "real woman," it signals the triumph over his own suppressed homoerotic desire for Nakamura. In declaring that Gruver has made her a real woman, Hana Ogi has made him a real man.

If Eileen is the conventional definition of the ideal American woman, Hana Ogi is her opposite. Eileen demands a romantic break from

In a love scene in *Sayonara,* Hana Ogi is dressed in a traditional kimono.
Still courtesy of the Museum of Modern Art Film Archives

middle-class family life and an escape into the exotic (although her flir-
tatious relationship with Nakamura is deflected). On the other hand,
Hana Ogi (for whom the theater has been family and the source of order
since the death of her father and brother) breaks from the exotic to
reconstruct a familial life with Gruver. Ultimately Hana Ogi, like Pocahontas, will give up status and prestige in her native land to live in the
imperial metropole, where she will represent the domesticated exotic.
Assimilated, with her transgressive sexuality in check, she is now a real
woman. In the last scene of the film, when Hana Ogi and Gruver decide
that love will conquer all, they resolve the question of their (future)
multiracial children by making them America's future. Like Pocahontas
portrayed as a lady of the Elizabethan court, Hana Ogi, with Gruver as
husband, is now portrayed as the mother of a new nation.[43]

"I Enjoy Being A Girl": *Flower Drum Song*

In 1960, four years after *Sayonara* was released, the film *Flower Drum Song*
showed Asians in America as, if not yet a model minority, at least perfectly suitable candidates for ethnic assimilation. The musical comedy—

about romantic misalliances among a group of young Chinese Americans and the conflicts that arise when their hopes for romance confront the traditional expectations of their immigrant parents—promoted a popular vision of the universal possibilities of ethnic assimilation.

The Rodgers and Hammerstein musical was loosely based on the novel of the same title by the Chinese American author C. Y. Lee. Lee's novel was a more dark-humored exploration of the difficulties of assimilation and generational conflict among American-born Chinese and their immigrant parents. When *Flower Drum Song* opened on Broadway as a light-hearted musical, the reviewer for *Time* magazine said that the theme of romantic triumph over cultural conflict had already become hackneyed after *South Pacific* and *The King and I,* both Rodgers and Hammerstein productions. Besides, the *Times* reviewer noted, San Francisco's Chinatown was less genuinely exotic than the "real" Asians of *The King and I.*[44] *Commonweal,* a liberal journal that had long actively promoted ethnic assimilation and racial harmony, praised the musical's emphasis on virtue and its civility.[45] The reviewer for the *New Yorker* was less kind when she wrote,

> The authors' attitude toward exotic peoples in general seems to have changed hardly at all since they wrote "South Pacific" and "The King and I." If friendly, the natives have a simple, primitive, childlike sweetness. If girls, they do not know how to kiss, but once they have been taught they are wild about it. They also beg to inquire, please, just what it is that is said with flowers. In their conversation, as you may have gleaned, there is more than a smidgen of pidgin. . . . It seems to have worried neither Mr. Rodgers nor Mr. Hammerstein very much that the behavior of war-torn Pacific islanders and nineteenth-century Siamese might be slightly different from that of Chinese residents of present-day California, where "Flower Drum Song" is fictionally sung.[46]

Flower Drum Song's Chinatown is a yellowface version of *State Fair*'s small-town America. Set down on San Francisco Bay, Chinese America is representative of ethnic Americans generally. Ironically, in a film in which ethnicity displaces race and cultural transformation is a measure of assimilation, it is race—and the tradition of not being able to tell one Asian from another—that lends the film its supposed authenticity.

Although the all-Asian casting of *Flower Drum Song* represented a breakthrough for Asian American performers (with the exception of Juanita Hall, a veteran African-American singer cast as Auntie Liang); none of the actors, except Benson Fong, who played the patriarch of the Wang clan, was actually Chinese American. The cast included Miyoshi Umeki (from Japan) as Mei Li, a recent arrival from China; James Shigeta (Japanese from Hawaii) as Wang Ta, the serious and sincere eldest son of the Wang clan; Patrick Adiarte (Filipino American) as Wang San, the hyperassimilated teenage son of the Wang family; Jack Soo (Korean American) as Sammy Fong, a somewhat sleazy, somewhat hip nightclub owner; and Nancy Kwan (Scots-Irish and Chinese from Hong Kong) as Linda Low, the femme fatale nightclub dancer. The complete reliance on the racial appearance of the actors in establishing the show's ethnic credentials is underscored by the use of stage sets. In the opening number, when Mei Li sings "One Hundred Million Miracles" in a "Chinatown" park, the Asian passers-by who gather are, without exception, dressed as middle-class white Americans of the period; men in suits and ties, women wearing sensible Republican cloth coats. The crowd in Chinatown includes an apparently Chinese policeman who gives them directions to the Fong household.

The film's premise is set by the arrival in San Francisco of Mei Li and her father (Kam Tong) as undocumented immigrants. They have come to the United States so that Mei Li can be married to Sammy Fong, a somewhat spoiled nightclub owner whose mother has arranged their betrothal. Sammy, however, is not ready to get married and has a girlfriend besides, the exotic dancer Linda Low. He tries to pawn off Mei Li on the wealthy Wang family. Master Wang, or Wang Chi-yang, who is looking for an appropriately traditional wife for his eldest son Wang Ta, approves of the obedient and respectful Mei Li. However since Sammy has resisted a commitment to marriage, Linda Low, with an eye to the main chance, has been going out with Wang Ta. Resolving the plot complications is a matter of appropriately matching up the marriage pairs.

With the hope of introducing Mei Li and Wang Ta, Master Wang invites the girl to a party to celebrate Wang Ta's college graduation and Auntie Liang's American citizenship. Much to everyone's surprise, Wang Ta announces his engagement to Linda Low. Sammy Fong sabotages the engagement by inviting the Wang family to the nightclub, where they discover that Linda is an exotic dancer. Scandalized, Wang Chi-yang forces Wang Ta to break their engagement. Meantime, Mei Li has fallen in love with Wang Ta at first sight, but believing that he loves his devoted friend Helen (Reiko Sato), Mei Li forces Sammy to honor his contract of marriage to her.

Wang Ta now realizes that he really does love Mei Li, despite the fact that she is his father's choice for him. Finally, all is resolved when Mei Li announces that she must release Sammy from his obligation to marry her because she has deceived him by coming to America as an illegal "wetback." This allows Wang Ta to marry her voluntarily and with full knowledge of her immigration status. In a double wedding ceremony, Wang Ta then marries Mei Li and Sammy Fong marries Linda Low. All's well that ends well.

These alliances set up a universal generational confrontation in ethnic families between the modern American-born second generation and the traditional immigrant generation. In *Flower Drum Song* the musical comedy, the theme of an ethnic generation gap is substituted for the interrogation of racial exclusion that organizes the novel. *Flower Drum Song* creates a paper tiger conflict between an anachronistic (if quaint), stultifying (if wise), oppressive (if loving), traditional world view held by the immigrant generation of Chinese parents versus the shallow (yet glamorous), modern (yet materialist), romantic (yet rootless) world view of American-born Chinese kids. This is played out in a song and dance routine, "What Are We Going to Do About the Other Generation."

Flower Drum Song's generation-gap depiction of ethnic assimilation is weak tea, however. It provides neither space for Wang Ta to negotiate between the sterile traditionalism of his father and the vacuous rootlessness of his younger brother, nor the racial history which might enable him to critique Chinese America. At the graduation/citizenship party in which the Wang family celebrates its entry into American society, the family organizes a square dance to a song titled "Chop Suey." Not only is the square dance, like the quilting bee or barn raising, a nostalgic icon of American culture, it is popularly identified with a specifically white American rural community. Chop suey, the hash invented in San Francisco and served in Chinese restaurants throughout the country, is emblematic of the inventedness of ethnic identity. Performed together, song and dance simultaneously celebrate the absorptive capacity of the American melting pot and underscore its rootlessness. America is a vast chop suey joint in which anyone can consume an ethnic identity. Chop suey ethnicity erases from memory the history of the Chinese in America as a racialized minority, a history that makes Mei Li and her father illegal immigrants and constructs Chinatown as an Oriental fantasy world in the first place. Chinese Americanness is reduced to little more than paper lanterns and chopstick hairsticks.[47]

In *Flower Drum Song*'s world of assimilation, it is the women who know the way out. Linda Low, Mei Li, and Auntie Liang, despite their obvious differences, are all liberal pragmatists. They hold the keys to successful ethnic assimilation. Like Hana Ogi in *Sayonara*, Linda Low represents the desired exotic. It is no accident that Nancy Kwan, who had just made her movie debut as a Hong Kong bar hostess in the *World of Suzie Wong* (1960, also directed by Joshua Logan), was brought in to replace the exuberant but considerably less sultry Pat Suzuki, who had played the

"Chop Suey" square dance: the naturalization/graduation party
at the Wangs' in *Flower Drum Song*.

part on Broadway. Despite the fact that Miyoshi Umeki had won an
Academy Award for her earlier role as Katsumi in *Sayonara,* it was Nancy
Kwan and her image as Suzie Wong that was featured prominently in all
of the billboards and promotionals for *Flower Drum Song*.

Like Hana Ogi, Linda Low is the personification of sexual fantasy;
indeed the fact that both are dancers allows the use of the dance to display the exotic. The dance scene at the nightclub is similar to that of the
Matsubayara review in *Sayonara;* it presents a pastiche of international
sexual commodification. The song and dance that defines Linda Low,
however, is not transgendered in the way that Hana Ogi's dance was.
"I Enjoy Being a Girl" is uncompromisingly—and, to its presumed audience, reassuringly—heterosexual. Linda Low's sexuality is contained
and domesticated by its transformation into consumption. The song fe-
tishizes the female body, which the Barbie doll (a new hit on the toy
market that year) was making into a new vehicle of consumption. Like
Barbie, which had started out as an "adult novelty" in Germany but had
been cleaned up for her debut in the United States, Linda Low is sexy
but not dangerous. Like those of the American Barbie, Linda Low's
desires are transparent, understandable, and (for the middle-class male

wage earner) readily satisfied. Being a "girl" means being a consumer of furs, perfume, a sporty car, and a nice house.

To be sure, Linda Low represents a modern girl. She is independent and sexually assertive, but what she wants is a husband. For Linda Low, it is less "a man to share her life with" than a man with whom to share a lifestyle. In the dream sequence "Sunday" [picture here], Linda and Sammy lounge in nightclothes, surrounded by the luxuries of middle-class life, including children playing cowboys and Indians. In *Sayonara*, Hana Ogi must be domesticated before she is allowed entry into the American family, and her sexual domestication is itself a sign of American triumph. In *Flower Drum Song*, Linda Low is already safely domesticated; in her we see what Hana Ogi can become.

On the surface, Miyoshi Umeki's Mei Li is a reprise of her role as Katsumi in *Sayonara:* a "traditional" Asian immigrant woman, self-effacing and self-denying. Like Katsumi, who thinks that an eyelid operation will fool her oppressors, Mei Li is always positive, willing, and innocent in the face of adversity. Her theme song is, after all, "One Hundred Million Miracles."

While Mei Li is portrayed throughout the film as traditional and

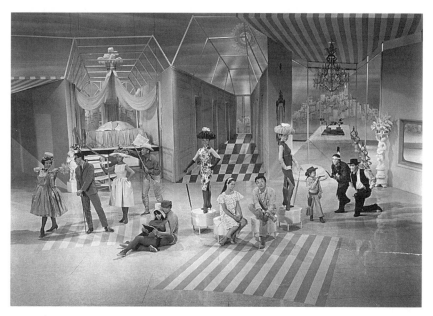

Sunday morning in the American dream:
Linda Low (Nancy Kwan) and Sammy Fong (Jack Soo) daydream of assimilation into 1950's suburbia in *Flower Drum Song*.

respectful of her elders, the wealthy, and men in general, her story suggests more agency than is conveyed on the surface. It is she who has brought her aging and somewhat ineffectual father to the United States, stowing away in a ship. She demands that Sammy Fong uphold his agreement to marry her, and she decides to break off the impending wedding ceremony.

While Mei Li and Linda Low are played as opposites, they ultimately share many of the same characteristics. Both Mei Li and Linda Low demonstrate the same instrumental need for husbands. In 1960, finding a husband is the expected route into the world of middle-class consumption and assimilation. A husband is required for a life in the United States.

For Mei Li, like Linda, it is the consumption of American popular culture that makes her American. Linda's status as an All-American girl is measured by her clothes, perfume, jewelry, and cars, items that transform the Asian body into an American body. Mei Li is transformed into an American by television. The solution that Mei Li comes up with to free herself (to marry Wang Ta) and Sammy (to marry Linda) comes from a TV show. Mei Li, it is revealed, has been an inveterate consumer of television since her arrival in the United States. Through television, she has absorbed the plain language (the ironic reference to wetbacks) and pragmatic values and solutions of American liberalism.

Auntie Liang is the liberal pragmatist and paragon of ethnic assimilation who mediates between older and younger generations. Unlike Wang Chi-yang, who hides his money under his bed, she is not afraid of modernity. She shares Wang Chi-yang's conservative goals (the marriage of Wang Ta and Mei Li), but she recognizes the need for new modes of behavior to achieve them. She admonishes the elder Wang to let the children decide for themselves whom they will marry, just as she scolds him for not trusting in banks. Marriage for love, and savings accounts, are part of the modern world with which one must come to terms.

The liberal pragmatism represented in these women is critical to *Flower Drum Song*'s narrative of ethnic assimilation. Unlike the men who struggle over the meaning of tradition, the women use it or ignore it as it suits their purpose. Mei Li invokes traditional forms of deference and television, as the situation dictates. Tradition is good only as it is useful; it is only the individual freed of the burden of history who can successfully negotiate modernity. Nevertheless, *Flower Drum Song*'s liberal pragmatism is only instrumental; the ends of its ethnic assimilation saga are conservative. The musical's Oriental women have become American without making a sound in American society.

Sayonara in 1956 and *Flower Drum Song* in 1960 were Hollywood's new liberal narratives of national origin. Liberalism was the ideological core of the decentralized political structure of American imperialism. Less a national ideology than a world view, liberalism is the ideology of modernity, deeply identified and aligned with science and, like Marxism, universalist.[48] As a science of modernity, liberalism could be deployed domestically as a progressive but moderate response to the demand for racial equality and internationally as an alternative to the anticolonialist critique and socialist promise of Lenin and Marx.

Sayonara and *Flower Drum Song* both celebrate American liberalism. In these films, ethnic assimilation is the vehicle through which the social identities of race, class, sex, and nationality can be displaced by the individual embrace of the modern. The "naturalized" (heterosexual and Americanized) nuclear families simultaneously fetishize ethnicity as cultural artifact and render race invisible as a social relationship of power. The nuclear family, the end result of both these films, is expected to produce a new American: a liberal individualist who transcends social origin. Before they can become the mothers of the new American nation, Hana Ogi and Linda Low must be domesticated, naturalized, transformed from exotics into American girls suitable for marriage and motherhood.

Sayonara and *Flower Drum Song* follow in the Pocahontas tradition as narratives in which the woman of color becomes mother of the nation through a process of ethnic assimilation; the history of race relations is effaced in favor of romance and individual transformation. The Oriental woman is assimilated through the domestication of her exotic (racialized) sexuality. In *Sayonara* as in the Pocahontas legend, marriage between the woman of color and white man embodies the highest stage of assimilation. Hana Ogi is the native daughter of a conquered tribe whose erotic difference is domesticated by her devotion to her white man. In *Flower Drum Song*, the Oriental woman is assimilated through the consumption of American culture and marriage. Linda Low's all-American sexuality is revealed to be only an expression of her safe (satiable) desire for durable consumer goods. In both cases, the domestication of exotic sexuality re-creates the Oriental woman as a naturalized woman, ready to assume the mantle of mother of a new American empire.

6

The Model Minority as Gook

n *Year of the Dragon,* Michael Cimino's 1982 film about organized crime in New York's Chinatown, an elderly Chinese woman and her teenage granddaughter have an audience with Joey Tai, a prominent businessman and ruthless mobster. The grandmother asks Tai for money to send the young woman to Columbia University. Tai gives her the tuition money and, in good Chinese avuncular fashion, admonishes the young woman to work hard and listen to her grandmother. We next see this teenage honor student, now dressed in a tight silver lamé miniskirt, shooting up a restaurant with an Uzi. After a wild, running gunfight, the white hero of the story, Stanley White, a decorated Vietnam veteran who is now captain of the Chinatown precinct, shoots the girl down in the streets of Chinatown.

The contradictory figure of this young woman, simultaneously an honor-roll student and a "gangsta," replays the popular Vietnam War trope of the female Viet Cong fighter emerging from a crowd of friendly villagers to kill or try to kill the American savior. She is symbolic of the deeply contradictory and contested representation of the Asian American as permanent resident alien: both model minority, productive and acquiescent, and yellow peril, the Viet Cong, invisible and destructive.

The Crisis: The Long Year of 1974

The year 1974 encompassed Watergate, the OPEC oil crisis, and the fall of Saigon. On August 9, 1974, millions of American television viewers watched as their president, the disgraced Richard Milhous Nixon, stepped into a waiting helicopter and escaped into exile in California. Nine months later, millions of American viewers saw Graham Martin, the last American proconsul in Vietnam, clamber aboard another waiting helicopter, abandoning hundreds of "loyal" Vietnamese in the embassy compound below. Defeat in Vietnam signified the early end of the American Century.

By 1974, inflation fueled by Vietnam war spending, the Eurodollar crisis, the OPEC oil crisis, and the end of the Bretton Woods international monetary system all signaled the erosion of the structure of accumulation that had been shaped by the Fordist Compromise. The downturn in the American economy, which coincided with a long downturn in the world economy, was experienced as "stagflation," an unprecedented combination of flat growth and double-digit inflation. By the end of the 1970s, the attempt to dampen inflation had also resulted in a double-digit unemployment rate; in the election campaign of 1979, Ronald Reagan could campaign on the issue of a "misery index" for the U.S. economy.

The crises of the mid-1970s set the stage for the global restructuring of capital and the process of "de-industrialization" in the United States, which dominated the economic news in the 1980s and 1990s.[1] In the massive reorganization of the social structure of accumulation that began in the early 1970s, Fordism was replaced by what geographer David Harvey has called flexible accumulation.[2] Dominated by multinational corporations and the almost instantaneous transfer of funds across the globe, flexible accumulation has been marked by a shift of economic growth to new commanding sectors of the economy—financial and professional services, which are marked by a high rate of return and a short turnaround time on investment.

The reorganization of the social structure of accumulation has entailed the relocation of manufacturing from high-wage to low-wage environments, both across national boundaries and from region to region within a country. Heavy industry and the manufacturing of durable consumer goods, traditionally the strongholds of high-wage organized labor, have been either abandoned to imports or shifted overseas or to the areas where organized labor is weakest. In the manufacturing sector, the use of outsourced materials has become an increasingly large part of the production process. By 1990, imported components were used in more than half of domestic manufacturing.[3] Akira Morita, the former chairman of the Sony Corporation, called this dramatic expansion of outsourcing the "Hollowing of America."[4]

Since the mid-1970s, the process of de-industrialization in America and the failure of attendant Keynesian approaches to solve the dilemma of capitalist economic crisis has been marked by a struggle over the dismantling of the democratic welfare state and the restoration of bourgeois class hegemony.[5] Since the 1970s, management has fiercely pressured organized labor to give back many of the gains in wages, retirement, and health care benefits that had been made under Fordism and to accept the reassertion of management control over production schedules, mandatory overtime, and work rules. Despite the continued gap between union and nonunion wages, membership in unions dropped in the 1980s from 23.8 percent to 16.3 percent among nonagricultural workers.[6] The only sector of the economy where labor did make gains in membership was in the expanding low-wage, service sector of the labor force among hotel and food service, clerical, health care, and public employees.

By 1980, the state had retreated from intervention on behalf of the Fordist Compromise to support capital's attack on labor. The state's retreat from the Fordist Compromise has included the sharp reduction, if not abandonment, of its regulatory responsibilities in the work place, and its mediation between labor and management. In the 1980s, the state became openly hostile toward organized labor and the unorganized poor. In the wake of its abandonment of the most privileged stratum of the working class (organized manufacturing labor) the state is in the process in the 1990s of ending subsidies to the poor, racial minorities, children, and the elderly—those who had not originally been included in the Fordist Compromise but who had demanded a place at the table in the wake of the civil rights movement and the War on Poverty in the 1960s.

David Harvey observes that the collapse of the Fordist structure of accumulation, with its large-scale production and long-term planning, and the emergence of flexible accumulation, with its emphasis on the rapid transfers of capital, technology, and short run production, is experienced culturally as a crisis of time and space: a collapse of boundaries—particularly national boundaries—and standards, and the rise of relativism and multiculturalism.[7] Both restorationist narratives, which represent Asian Americans as the model minority, and dystopic narratives, which depict Asian Americans as the domestic Viet Cong, articulate the collapse of the Fordist structure of accumulation as a boundary crisis, a breakdown both of national borders and of internal boundaries.

The Model Minority and the Neoconservative Racial Project

In the neoconservative narrative of post-Fordist national restoration, Asian America embodies the nation's hope for a return to hegemony in the global marketplace through discipline, obedience, and return to family values. The restorationist narrative constructs a nostalgic imagery of American society and culture that the model minority is mobilized to revivify. Asian American habits of behavior are seen as the secret weapons of national restoration; on the other hand, it is precisely from their otherness that this behavior is supposed to originate. The Asian American model minority is thus a simulacrum of both an imaginary Asian tradition from which it is wishfully constructed and an American culture for which it serves as a nostalgic mirror. The model minority can operate as the paragon of conservative virtues that all Americans should emulate only if Asian Americans remain *like* "us" but utterly are *not* "us."

Howard Winant observes that the conservative strategy has been to dress up class as race and to return to a Social Darwinian war of all against all. As the Edsalls and others have shown, conservatives since the Nixon administration have used race as a wedge issue to split the alliance between working-class whites and racial minorities that had ensured congressional Democratic majorities in the post-war era.[8] Neoconservatives could not deploy an overt appeal to a theory of racial supremacy, however. Liberalism's great achievement has been to relieve race, at least in so far as it could be defined in biological terms, of its explanatory power over behavior, substituting culture or ethnicity. Displacing race with ethnicity, however, invited a social amnesia with respect to race as a historical experience and a social reality for millions. Once race is set aside as a false category, an appeal to a color-blind ideal can invoke the principle of racial equality without addressing the claims of historically racialized minorities. In the process of honing a covert appeal to white racial privilege, conservatives turned the liberal discourse of racial equality on its head. The color-blind society of Myrdal's American creed is not understood as a promise but assumed to be the actually existing condition of American society. The race problem is assumed to have been resolved with the dismantling of state-sponsored racial discrimination in the 1960s.

Although the intent of liberal ethnicity theorists had been to substitute culture for race as a means of opening up social mobility through ethnic assimilation, the rhetoric of culture could also reify cultural difference as immutable and resistant to historical change. In the current crisis, the family, both as a socioeconomic unit and as a trope of nationhood, has become the principal site of ideological struggle. Conservatives have encoded the appeal to race in terms of the family, allowing race to be at the same time ubiquitous and publicly invisible. Debates around labor force issues, wage structure, reproductive rights, racial equity, and national identity have all become encoded in the Right's effort to reconstruct "traditional family values" as an ideological response to the crisis of post-Fordism.

Even Moynihan's early characterization of the matriarchal black family as "a tangle of pathology" able to reproduce itself "without help from white racism" suggested that the "culture of poverty" could be understood without reference to poverty itself. Increasingly the discussion of poverty focused on the multigenerational and self-reproducing. The metaphor of black pathology displaced analysis of social crisis, the effects of massive unemployment, poverty, and the collapse of family life. Since it was the dysfunctionality of the black family, and not genetics, that determined black behavior (not, of course poverty or discrimination), race could be encoded as cultural difference into public debates over social policy.

In the 1980s, African Americans were constantly identified with social chaos and violence: witness Ronald Reagan's invocation of the infamous unnamed "welfare queen," George Bush's use of black rapist Willie Horton in ads during his first presidential campaign, tales of "wilding" black teenagers, even the sexual harassment charges against Clarence Thomas, President Bush's black conservative nominee to the Supreme Court. Although race was made to disappear as a category of analysis, dressed up as cultural difference it became ubiquitous as a coded trope in the discussion of social policy; it is nowhere and yet everywhere. Although the appeal to culture appears to be non-biological, hence non-racist, in fact it has become a mode of perpetuating race as a category of immutable cultural difference.

The model minority representation of Asian Americans that had originated in the Cold War and gained visibility in the mid-1960s has been expanded and transformed to fit the current crisis. Asian cultural difference is held to be a source of social capital. A mythic Asian American family, the imagined product of an ahistorical and reified Asian "traditional" culture, is a central image, expanded to fit a wider target. Increasingly, the imagined Asian American family has been upheld as a model not only to blacks and Latinos but to working-class and middle-class whites as well. In the updated model minority story fitted to the ideological demands of the post-Fordist crisis, not only social conservatism but also productivity is emphasized. Recent articles in the national press on Asian Americans emphasize their persistence in overcoming language barriers, their superior disciplinary and motivational roles as parents, and their "intact" families' success at savings.[9]

Twenty years after Asian Americans were first heralded as a potential model for the upward mobility of nonwhites in American society, David Bell theorized Asian American success in an 1985 essay in the *New Republic,* "The Triumph of Asian Americans." Bell summarized Asian American virtues as "self-sufficiency" and proclaimed this the secret to Asian

American success. At the center of such self-sufficiency he placed the traditional Asian American family, an "intact" family, significant in three ways: It provides a secure environment for children; it pushes those children to work harder; and it fosters savings.[10]

The *New Republic* did not hesitate to make an invidious comparison between Asian and African Americans. Bell's article characterizing Asian Americans as a self-sufficient racial minority that made no demands for institutional change followed an article in the same issue titled "Brown's Blacks." This article excoriated black students at Brown University for protesting a recent spate of assaults on minority students on campus and demanding greater representation among the faculty and in the curriculum. While the student protesters at Brown had been a broad coalition of Asian, Latino, and black students and had gained substantial support among white students at the liberal campus, the *New Republic* article ignored the multiracial aspect of the protest and chose to characterize the movement as solely a black protest, the black students as malcontents, and the troubles on campus as yet another negative result of misguided affirmative action. When read back to back, the comparison between the "good," self-disciplined and submissive Asian Americans and the ungrateful and complaining blacks could not have been made more clear.

In 1988, a news report that ten of the twelve winners of the prestigious Westinghouse Prizes for achievement in science among high school students were Asian American prompted Stephen Graubard, a history professor at Brown University and the editor of *Daedalus,* the prestigious journal of the American Academy of Arts and Sciences, to publish an essay in the *New York Times* titled "Why Do Asian Pupils Win Those Prizes?" In a series of paradigmatic questions, Graubard laid out the implications of the traditional Asian American family model for all other Americans.

> Is the "stability" [of a dual parent family and a single family home] almost a prerequisite for school accomplishment? . . .
>
> If so, what is to be done for those hundreds of thousands of other New York children, many of illegitimate birth, who live with one parent, often in public housing, knowing little outside their dilapidated housing and decaying neighborhoods?

Graubard does not answer his own questions, but the family to which his questions lead us is unmistakable. It is the traditional Asian American family, presumed to be intact and self sufficient, and certain to be disciplinary and motivational.

> Do [non-Asian students] have teachers prepared to tell them that personal appearance matters, that a price is paid for spiked hair and blue lipstick? . . .

Who, for the impoverished black or Puerto Rican student, advises something other than the conventional educational path?

In Graubard's view it is not only African American and Latino families who will do well to learn from Asian Americans. In a peculiar formulation of racial and ethnic difference, Graubard asks, "What would it take for Puerto Rican, black and *white children of certain ethnic origins* to become serious competitors for such honors, and what would such an academic 'revolution' mean?" [Emphasis added.]

In Graubard's view, it is not only racial and ethnic minorities (including those mysterious "white children of certain ethnic origins") who should learn from the disciplined and motivated traditional Asian American family; America's middle class can also improve its performance by taking a lesson from Asian America. After all, the glittering prizes now captured by Asian American students had once been the patrimony of middle-class white students. Graubard asks what has happened to those students: "What about the others [of the middle class]? . . . Are the children of such families reaching out and securing the great prizes? . . . The children of the middle class, who are much more privileged but appear both indolent and incompetent . . ."[11]

For both Bell and Graubard, Asian American "success" is a product of an unspecified and decontextualized traditional Asian culture. Tradition is reduced to the values of obedience, discipline, and motivation enacted by the family, those traditions most valued in the late capitalist economy. In contrast, at the heart of the economic and academic difficulties of black, Hispanic, working-class, and even middle-class America is the cultural pathology of family structures that tolerate spiked hair and blue lipstick.

What distinguishes the model minority myth as a hegemonic mode of racial representation is not primarily its distance from reality but rather its power to dominate or displace other social facts. Ideological hegemony operates through its power to absorb, co-opt, or displace oppositional views, to tie a diverse and sometimes contradictory set of images and representations into an explanatory whole. It is the location of specific images and representations within the hegemonic paradigm that endows those images with ideological power.

The hegemonic power of culture as the new defining category of difference can be seen in an August 1987 cover story of *Time* Magazine, "The New Whiz Kids." This article attempts to provide a more balanced and informed picture of the educational achievements of young Asian Americans. It showcases their scholastic triumphs but also discusses both the institutional barriers that still stand in the way of Asian American students and the cost in stress that many pay for such success.

The article quotes extensively from a variety of experts on education, including scholars who study Asian American communities. Nevertheless, both the structure of the inquiry and the outcome of the article's conclusions are built around the reified concept of the "traditional" Asian family. The *Time* writers cite Professor William Liu of the University of Illinois at Chicago who asserts that Japanese, Korean, Chinese, and Vietnamese students perform better because "the Confucian ethic drives people to work, excel and repay the debt they owe their parents." The article contrasts this information to the observation of Professor Ruben G. Rumbaut, a sociologist at San Diego State University, that "Laotians and Cambodians, who do somewhat less well, have a gentler Buddhist approach to life." [12]

Assigning the differences in achievement and social mobility of various Asian American ethnic groups to assumed differences between a disciplined Confucian tradition (supposedly shared by Japanese, Koreans, Chinese, and Vietnamese) and a "gentler" Buddhist tradition (shared by Laotians and Cambodians) is, at best, astoundingly simplistic. Whatever impact a millennium of Buddhism may have had on China, Japan, or Vietnam is gently ignored. The high proportion of ethnic Chinese among the Cambodian and Laotian immigrant communities is also ignored. The high proportion of second-, third-, and fourth-generation American-born and middle-class Japanese Americans is ignored. Perhaps the most important ignored factor is the higher educational and occupational skill levels, and greater capital, that Chinese, Korean, and first-wave Vietnamese brought with them to the United States. Indeed, the entire history of Asia, a region in which social and cultural change has been nothing less than revolutionary in the twentieth century, is ignored in this rush to reify traditional culture as the key to Asian American success.

In their rush to judgment on the cultural superiority of Asian Americans, these commentators almost completely ignore recent Asian American history. Indeed, although these articles draw heavily on the images of recent Asian immigrants, all but the most self-evident facts about the revolutionary changes in the demography of Asian America since 1965 are elided by the hegemonic status of culture as the determining variable of social mobility. Bell, Graubard, and *Time* Magazine fail to ask even the most basic questions about the American economy and the place of Asians, blacks, Latinos, or "whites of certain ethnic origins" within it.

Recent Asian American history offers a different interpretative paradigm for understanding patterns of Asian American economic success and hardship. Since 1970, the Asian/Pacific Islander population (to use the Census Bureau's designation) has been the fastest growing nonwhite minority in America. Between 1970 and 1994, the Asian American population grew from 1.4 million to 8.8 million people.[13] The huge growth through immigration of the Asian American population has not been evenly distributed across ethnic groups, class, or sex. While there has been considerable economic success among Asian Americans, they also experience undeniable poverty. Both phenomena can be explained more accurately by the realities of Asian immigration patterns than by the secrets of traditional Asian family values.[14]

The explosion of the Asian/Pacific Islander population was due primarily to massive immigration from Asia after the passage of Immigration Reform Act of 1965. In addition to dismantling the national quota system that had been designed to exclude Asian immigration, the Immigration Reform Act of 1965 contained two provisions that encouraged immigration from Asia. The new policy favored the entry of scientific, technical, and professional personnel, and it gave preference to family members of immigrants already resident in the United States.

The most significant factor in accounting for Asian American economic prosperity—and that undermines the notion of Asian American cultural superiority—is the fact that a large proportion of this new Asian immigration was already middle-class on arrival in the United States. The 1965 immigration act favoring technical and scientific personnel and those who met specific occupational needs (particularly medical personnel) not only encouraged immigration from Asia, where economic development policies had created a pool of well-educated technical personnel eager to emigrate, but it also made likely the successful economic integration of Asian immigrants in the 1970s. Between 1965 and the mid-1970s, the majority of immigrants from Asia were middle-class professionals.[15]

In addition to their immediate integration into the professional, technical, and managerial sectors of the work force, the large proportion of middle-class immigrants among Asian Americans resulted in a second generation of children who were academically advantaged. Thus the "brain drain" from Asia in the 1970s resulted in an Asian American population that was already highly educated. According to the Census Bureau's 1994 statistics, slightly more Asian Americans than non-Hispanic whites over the age of twenty-five had completed four years of high school, and almost twice as many had completed college.[16]

In some respects Asian immigration has matched the demand for capital and labor at both ends of the post-Fordist economy. Since the late 1970s, the demand for semiskilled, unskilled, and entrepreneurial labor in the new low-wage manufacturing and service sectors of the post-Fordist economy has been met in large part by Asian and Latin American immigrants. Although the absolute number of professionals among

Asian immigrants has remained high, since the mid 1970s they no longer make up the majority of immigrants from Asia. Working-class immigrants and refugees now make up the majority of Asian immigrants. In particular, women now outnumber men among immigrants from Asian countries. Some come independently as workers; others come as spouses to American citizens and as permanent resident aliens. Many have had work experience in Asia—in the needle trades, electronic assembly work, institutional custodial or housekeeping work, or food service. Some come with semiprofessional skills, particularly in the health industry, as nurses and technicians.[17] In sum, Asian Americans, particularly immigrant Asian workers, have a highly visible position in both ends of the post-Fordist economy, in what urban sociologist Saskia Sassen has called "global cities"—the command centers for serving the financial needs of the new transnational economy.

The suggestion of parity between Asian Americans and non-Hispanic white Americans is, therefore, deceptive. The figure cited most often to illustrate the Asian American success story is the median income of Asian American families ($42,250 in the 1980s and -90s), slightly higher than the median income for white families. When controlled for geography and the number of wage earners per family, however, the income of Asian Americans falls short of that for non-Hispanic white Americans.[18]

Despite the fact that a large number of Asian Americans are successful, a disproportionate number of Asian Americans are poor. In 1990, while 8 percent of non-Hispanic white families had incomes below the Federal poverty guidelines, 11 percent of Asian/Pacific Islander families had incomes below the poverty guidelines. In 1994, despite their higher educational attainment and similar family income, the poverty rate for Asian/Pacific Islander families was almost double that of non-Hispanic white families. Among families with high school educated householders, the poverty rate was almost twice that of non-Hispanic white families; among college-educated householders, the poverty rate of Asian/Pacific Islander families was almost three times that of non-Hispanic white families. The poverty rate for Asian/Pacific Islander married couples was more than twice that of white married couples.[19]

The Asian American as Gook

The model minority concept as theorized by Bell, Graubard, and *Time* Magazine singles out for praise those values most closely identified with the Protestant work ethic. Obedience, self-control, individualism, and loyalty to the needs of the nuclear family, as opposed to either anarchic libertarianism (spiked hair and blue lipstick) or social consciousness (black radicalisms), are mobilized in an imagined Asian American tradition that is deployed in the attempt to restore American hegemony in the global marketplace.

The model minority has two faces. The myth presents Asian Americans as silent and disciplined; this is their secret to success. At the same time, this silence and discipline is used in constructing the Asian American as a new yellow peril. In contemporary dystopian narratives of post-Fordist urban America, the Asian American is both identified with the enemy that defeated the United States in Vietnam and figured as the agent of the current collapse of the American empire. The Vietnam War story, told as the tragedy of America's lost innocence, works as a master narrative of national collapse while defining the post-Fordist crisis as a product of invasion and betrayal.

The constant refrain in Vietnam War narratives is that the Americans are unable to see and know, and thereby to conquer, the Viet Cong—reason enough for My Lai, free fire zones, tiger cages, and, ultimately, defeat. The supposed invisibility of the Viet Cong led to the racialization of the Vietnam War. "Gook" became the most common racial epithet used by Americans to describe Vietnamese, enemy and ally alike. Indeed, the supposed invisibility of the communist enemy led American soldiers, who measured the war in body counts, to invoke the "mere gook rule," whereby any dead Vietnamese could be counted as a dead enemy.

The term "gook" has a long history in the American vocabulary of race and in the American imperial career in Asia and the Pacific. A bastardization of the Korean *hankuk* (Korean), or *mikuk* (American), it was used by Americans in the Korean War to refer to North and South Koreans and Chinese alike. The term also has links to "goo-goo," used by American soldiers used to describe Filipino insurgents at the turn of the century.

Such broad ethnic inclusiveness makes this racial epithet emblematic in describing Asian Americans as the ubiquitous and invisible enemy. Asian Americans, figured as gooks, the flip side of the model minority, become the scapegoats onto which anxiety over economic decline and the psychic trauma of the Vietnam War can be transferred. They appear silently, like the Viet Cong, as an alien threat in these narratives of multicultural dystopia and besieged nationhood, at once ubiquitous and invisible, ersatz and inauthentic.

The myth that America lost the war in southeast Asia because it had been betrayed by the liberal elite mobilizes a populist working-class rejection of liberal economic and social policy and lays the foundation for an attempt to restore American hegemony by revitalizing an undivided American people. The theme of betrayal as the cause of America's fall from grace attributes the defeat of the United States in southeast Asia to the sapping of American strength as a result of radical divisiveness and liberal tolerance. This breakdown of American unity is reflected in the breakdown of the traditional American nuclear family. The embattled nuclear family becomes a trope for national unity beset by the divisiveness of feminism, multiculturalism, and class conflict. In this dystopian vision of post-Vietnam America, the Asian American model minority becomes the enemy within, economically productive but culturally inauthentic, and thus unsuitable as model for national restoration.

Race Wars in the Global City: *Blade Runner*

Four towering blast furnaces belch flame and smoke into the night air over densely built Los Angeles in the year 2019. Shot from above the city, the opening scene of Ridley Scott's dystopian vision of the post-Fordist City of Angels recalls J.M.W. Turner's painting of satanic mills lighting up the night over the English midlands at beginning of the industrial revolution. No longer the low-slung, endlessly expanding metropolis crisscrossed with sprawling freeways, Scott's LA is a dense, dark, constricted cityscape, the imploding dark star of the American empire. *Blade Runner*'s vision of the global city as a social Darwinist nightmare is a catastrophic representation of the crisis of the post-Fordist present.

In the global cities—New York, London, Los Angeles, Hong Kong—are concentrated huge numbers of financial service agents and a corps of professional and semiprofessional support personnel ranging from stockbrokers, lawyers, and bankers to media consultants, medical personnel, and celebrity chefs. Supporting this professional and managerial elite are the new hewers of wood and drawers of water: millions of low-wage, mostly unorganized, mostly nonwhite, mostly immigrant army of waiters, chambermaids, housekeepers, orderlies, and day-care workers.

Sassen observes that in the 1980s foreign capital flowed into the new manufacturing sectors in Los Angeles and New York, making the United States a net importer of capital.[20] Of particular importance in the transition to flexible accumulation has been the rapid relocation of production, accompanied by the rise of competitive capitalist centers in east Asia—not only reconstructed Japan, but also Hong Kong, Singapore, Taiwan, and South Korea. The internationalization of capital means that immigrant workers in Los Angeles and New York are not exploited by U.S. capital alone. Industrial LA is just as much an imperial venture as plants in the Philippines. Los Angeles is thus both a First World and a Third World city.

While industrial production in the older, more highly organized, more capital-intensive sectors of the manufacturing economy (heavy industry, automotive and durable goods) has been transferred overseas or to non-union regions of the United States, a new manufacturing sector has enjoyed phenomenal growth in the global cities. Since the early 1970s, manufacturing industries have increasingly relied on rapid changes in fashion to keep up demand in periods of real income decline. This has resulted in the introduction of on-demand production in many areas of manufacturing. New technologies in communications, design, and production allow the rapid transfer of capital and reorientation of machinery to produce new products.

This also means that the highest profit margins occur during the early phases of production, rather than in the giant mass production associated with the Fordist economy. David Harvey observes that in the new manufacturing sectors that do not rely on high technology, capitalists have reintroduced pre-Fordist decentralized systems of production, such as family-directed home sweatshops and semi-coerced labor at underground subcontracting plants employing illegal immigrants. The shift to on-demand and decentralized manufacturing processes has created huge new markets for temporary, part-time, and migrant labor. The system of decentralized production is also highly ethnicized, with ethnic networks of capital formation, business associations, supply networks, and labor recruitment. Paul Ong and Edna Bonacich report that as many as 85 percent of garment industry subcontractors in Los Angeles are Korean, Chinese, or Vietnamese immigrants, and the great majority of their workers are Latino.[21] In other cities, such as San Francisco and New York, Asian immigrants make up a large percentage of garment workers.

David Harvey has observed that *Blade Runner* maps the post-Fordist economic geography of the global city, with its dense imagery of the totalizing multinational corporation and its decentralized mode of production that relies on a myriad of small ethnic subcontractors and armies of Third-World manufacturing and service workers. At the apex of *Blade Runner*'s LA is the totalitarian Tyrell Corporation, a giant postnational biotechnology conglomerate. Tyrell produces life itself, albeit synthetic life. Its project is to replace all authentic life with simulacra (true copies for which no originals exist). At the top of this synthetic chain of beings are replicants, genetically engineered androids. The corporation's control over human life is symbolized in its headquarters building, a fortress of massive proportions that visually recalls an Aztec temple of human sacrifice. State and civil society are collapsed and subsumed to the totalitarian power of the Tyrell Corporation. Just as LAPD helicopters do today, police hovercraft skim over the future city, keeping vigilance from a distance over the teeming masses on the ground. Reflecting the huge growth in the 1980s and 1990s of what David Gordon calls the guardian sector of the economy and the increasing privatization of security, police, and prisons, the state is reduced to its role as guardian of order and brought under the aegis of the corporation.

Reflecting contemporary Los Angeles, *Blade Runner*'s decentralized mode of production is elaborately racialized. At the service and manufacturing end, the work force is principally Oriental, represented by Chew (Phillip Hong) the specialized producer of replicant eyes ("I only do eyes"). The economy that supplies parts to the giant Tyrell Corporation is made up of small workshops peopled in the main by ethnic, mainly Asian, labor. A Cambodian woman, a specialist in exotic animals, is the lab technician who examines simulated reptile scales. On the street, beneath garish neon lights and a giant video screen on whose soundtrack a female announcer hawks the opportunity to remake life "off world," the multiracial denizens of Los Angeles buy synthetic fish at a sushi stand from a Japanese vendor. Only the weak, the diseased, the perverse, and the cops are left in the city; the powerful, wealthy, and healthy have all abandoned America with Richard Nixon for off world, the galactic suburbs. Once the epicenter of the golden California dream, the City of Angels is now a congested hybrid of downtown Tokyo and New York. The giant video screen advertises the only good life. The disembodied voice intones, "A new life awaits you in the off-world colonies. The chance to begin again in a golden land of opportunity and adventure. New climate, recreational facilities . . . absolutely free." Off world is not only a chance to rebuild and reinvigorate the body with new climate and adventure; it also offers nostalgic possibilities of racial and class restoration. The advertisement goes on to encourage would-be pioneers to bring a slave, in the body of a replicant, with them. "Use your new friend as a personal body servant or a tireless field hand—the custom-tailored genetically engineered humanoid replicant designed especially for your needs."

The United States might no longer be the unchallenged master of the post-Fordist global political economy, but the colonization of off world is still couched in nationalist terms. "So come on America, let's put our team up there." The director's cut of the film, released in 1992, added the following line, underscoring America's dependence on Asian and Latino capital and labor: "This announcement is brought to you by the Shimato-Dominguez Corporation—helping America into the New World."

Blade Runner signifies a post-Vietnam multiculturalism as racial degeneration. A 1980s pop song boasted that it never rains in southern California, but in Ridley Scott's Los Angeles, it always rains. In 2019 the city lives in a impenetrable smog, its environmental degradation an emblem of the social degeneracy brought about by the domination of global capital and labor migration. Apart from the Asian worker drones, the police, and the street urchins, the only humans left in LA are freaks of nature or freaks of culture. Scott's vision of the multiculturalism of the global city is a visualization of what Lothrop Stoddard sixty years earlier had called "disgenic mongrelization."

In this film adaptation of Philip K. Dick's novel *Do Androids Dream of Electric Sheep?*, Decker (Harrison Ford) is a blade runner, a twenty-first-century bounty hunter, expert in identifying and killing replicants who have slipped back to Earth from off-world space colonies where they perform labor as coolies, mercenaries, and body servants. Brought out of retirement for a special assignment, Decker sets out to hunt down and exterminate a group of six replicants who have returned to Earth to find a way to extend their foreshortened lifespan.

At one level, as a story told from the ambivalent point of view of the blade runner, replicants can be seen as escaped slaves from the off-world mining and plantation colonies. At another level, set against the context of the American Century's end, replicants can also be seen as representing the betrayed victims of America's imperial adventures coming home to roost: the Vietnamese abandoned at the American embassy, the Hmong warriors of the CIA's secret war in Laos, traumatized black and white GIs, victims of Agent Orange, hundreds if not thousands of POWs and MIAs, the assassinated Diem brothers. "Retirement," the euphemism for the assassination of replicants, is reminiscent of "termination with extreme prejudice," the U.S. government's euphemism for assassination. Like Vietnam War survivors who can bear witness to My Lai, free fire zones, Project Phoenix, and the Hanoi Hilton, the replicants serve as witnesses to America's betrayal of its liberal promise. Roy Batty (Rutger Hauer), the leader of the replicants, confesses to having carried out unnamed but morally distasteful tasks for his human masters. "I've done . . . questionable things. [But] nothing the god of biomechanics wouldn't let you into heaven for." In his dying soliloquy, Batty tells Decker, "I've seen things you people wouldn't believe. Attack ships on fire off the shoulder of Orion. I watched C-beams glitter in the dark near the Tannhauser gate. All those moments will be lost in time, like tears in rain. Time to die."

Like the Asian American model minority, replicants are the perfect workers, virtually indistinguishable from humans (to all but their owners and the blade runners) yet completely inauthentic. Replicants can be expected to perform humanly, yet need not be treated humanely. Since they are products of genetic engineering, replicants are, materially, human. Genetically customized to their assigned tasks, replicant humans are more efficient than actual humans in their physical capacities. Like the model minority, replicants can represent perfectibility and perfect malleability; since they are simulacra, they are completely inauthentic.

In a movie in which considerable attention is paid to the creation of polyglot ethnicities (the police captain, played by Edward Olmos, is a mulatto of unspecified origins who speaks a creole that sounds like Malay-Indonesian; street urchins speak ersatz German), the ubiquitous Asian paraphernalia and a conspicuous absence of black bodies underscores the role of the Asian as the alien, an Orientalizing presence. The extremely pale hue of the two principal replicants, Batty and Pris (Darryl Hannah), underscores the social constructedness of race and its markers, the effect of whiteface minstrelsy.

As in Bierce's "The Haunted Valley," the use of the eyes as the sole physical marker of difference accentuates the constructed nature of the difference between replicant humans and natural humans. The two are indistinguishable except for a faint glow in the eyes of the replicant. This glow can be discerned only with the use of high technology in an examination. The examination scene brings to mind the interrogation of thousands of Chinese immigrants detained at Angel Island. Eye symbolism is visible everywhere in *Blade Runner,* from the opening scene to replicant owls to the light bulbs on the broken-down Bradbury building. The symbol of authenticity, eyes are a fetishized commodity. In Chew's shop, called Eye World, Chew and one of his replicants, Leon, handle the eyes. Batty, the leader of the renegade replicants, plays with glass-encased eyes in his apartment. In his search for Tyrell, his creator, Batty tries to get answers from Chew, the eye maker. In an ironic statement, Batty says to Chew, "If only you could see what I have seen with your eyes." Batty has been a witness through the eyes that Chew has manufactured for him. If eyes are the principal markers of authenticity, they are also a vulnerable target. Tyrell has huge glasses, both to make his eyes appear bigger and to protect them. Leon tries to kill Decker by poking out his eyes. Batty finally kills Tyrell, pressing his thumbs into his creator's eyes.

The Tyrell Corporation has given the replicants life but has purposely truncated that life. The physical difference that is engineered into the replicant and that motivates the replicants' search for their history is a genetic code that gives them only four years of life. In the view of their creator, Tyrell, their truncated lifespans are compensated for by the intensity of the lives they are given. When Batty finally confronts him as son to father, Tyrell tells him, "The light that burns twice as bright burns half as long . . . and you have burned so very, very brightly, Roy." The replicant's key to solving their problem of survival is to construct a history for themselves as individuals, to identify their inception dates, and as a group to find the design of their system—a desperate search for assimilation.

The critical difference between natural humans and replicants parallels the difference between "real Americans" and the Oriental American. Both the android "new friend" and the model minority are people without history; both are simulacra whom a programmed historical memory simultaneously renders functional and inauthentic. Both replicant and model minority are critical to production but, lacking history, are necessarily sterile in the reproduction of a national narrative. The paradox of economic productivity and cultural sterility is underscored in *Blade Runner* through the highlighted role of the Asian worker in producing replicants. This reproduction of labor power can be understood as the literal reproduction of labor, in which the original model minority produces an improved, more productive work force, one that cannot threaten the national identity by reproducing itself.

New York as Saigon: *Year of the Dragon*

If *Blade Runner* is a parable of the backwash of the Vietnam War, Michael Cimino's *Year of the Dragon,* released in 1985, is its literal reenactment. New York's Chinatown is the last domino of the Vietnam War. While sharing *Blade Runner*'s penchant for Orientalizing spectacle and pastiche, *Year of the Dragon* (screenplay by Michael Cimino and Oliver Stone) situates the new Asian immigration squarely within the Vietnam War narrative. In Manhattan in 1985, as in southeast Asia a decade earlier, the spectacle of the Orient masks revolution and invasion.

The film opens with the spectacle of a lion dance and a lunar new year's parade complete with synthesized, Orientalized jazz soundtrack. Ornately costumed, masked dancers and firecrackers contribute to detailed and absorbing visual and aural spectacle. In a nearby restaurant, Jackie Wong, a longtime Chinatown crime boss, is assassinated. As the lion dance turns into a gang fight and shoot-out, the dancing and the fighting, the dancers and the fighters become indistinguishable. Later, during Jackie Wong's funeral, two teenage Chinese gang members shake down an Italian American shopkeeper across Canal Street. The shopkeeper, invoking what heretofore had been a Mafia-protected Little Italy, dismissively curses them: "Cross Canal Street, you little chink scumbag, you're going to end up with a wire around your neck." The "little chink scumbags" curse him in a patois of Chinese-English and then shoot him. The shooting signals the armed crossing of old ethnic boundaries and the invasion of new Chinese immigrants into old ethnic American turf.

As one police official warns, "Chinese are coming across Canal Street and taking over the drug trade, banks, and real estate."

The introduction of the film's antihero protagonist, Stanley White, a Vietnam veteran, makes explicit the film's argument that the struggle to contain the Chinese in New York is a chapter of the Vietnam War. White is the new sheriff in town; given the command of the Chinatown precinct, he takes it upon himself to clean up Chinatown. For him, Asian Americans, and new immigrants in particular, are the enemy. White's superiors warn him to proceed cautiously, lest he upset the comfortable relationship between the police and old Chinatown bosses. They warn him that organized crime is an integral part of ancient Chinese culture. "The Mafia concept is not even Italian, it's Chinese," says his superior. For White, his police superiors are like the liberals who dictated Vietnam War policy. They want Chinese expansion to be contained but not defeated. They warn him, "You want to attack Chinatown with the Eighty-second Airborne. This isn't Vietnam."

But for White, New York's Chinatown *is* Vietnam; Asian America *is* the ground on which the Vietnam War can be fought again and again, and this time won for white America. Echoing the accusation that liberal elites abandoned America in southeast Asia, White asks, "Will they let us win this time?" White mobilizes the central myth around which the master narrative of the Vietnam War is organized: the ubiquitousness and invisibility of the Asian enemy. White fiddles with his Marine lapel pin, looks through the window at an American flag, and baldly conflating Asian Americans with his former Vietnamese enemies, declares, "The difference was, there I never saw the goddamned enemy, here they are right in front of your eyes—they don't have a jungle to hide in."

Although *Year of the Dragon* trades on the themes of the Vietnam War, it makes use of many of the same narrative conventions that Sax Rohmer deployed in his Fu Manchu series. The contemporary yellow peril, the invasion of new Chinese immigrants and their gangs, are embodied in the figure of Joey Tai (John Lone). His physical appearance and mannerisms recall Fu Manchu's; he is tall, slender, elegant, and androgynous, hinting at sadomasochistic sexual ambivalence.

Much like Sax Rohmer, Cimino deploys spectacle and makes use of a pastiche imagery of different Asian cultures to create a universal Oriental otherness. Like Fu Manchu, Joey Tai is presented as an urbane and sophisticated criminal mastermind. Both avoid personal violence, preferring to send out their multiethnic minions to do their bidding. (Though Tai's thugs are principally Asian, his chief lieutenant is a Mandarin-speaking African American.) Both Fu Manchu and Joey Tai command Oriental

"At least here we can see them": Stanley White (Mickey Rourke) faces off with Joey Tai (John Lone) in *Year of the Dragon*.
Still courtesy of the Museum of Modern Art Film Archives

gangs in the West and secret armies in southeast Asia. In a scene of extraordinary Orientalist excess, Joey Tai is shown surrounded by a teeming horde of armed guerrillas, entering the camp of an aging Kuomintang Chinese warlord who is his heroin supplier in the Thai hinterlands.

Just as Nayland Smith, the former agent of empire in Burma, "knows" the otherwise unknowable Orient, Stanley White, the Vietnam veteran, "knows" Asians and therefore Chinatown. White recruits an ambitious, if vacuous, female Asian American television reporter, Tracy Tzu (Ariane), by telling her the inside story of Chinatown. In juxtaposing White's intimate knowledge of the Chinese community with Tracy Tzu's ignorance of it, Cimino establishes White's Orientalist authority over the Asian American story.

Cimino uses the gaze of Tracy Tzu's television camera to colonize Chinatown. In a scene reminiscent of Nayland Smith exposing the dark corridors of opium dens in Fu Manchu's Limehouse, Tzu's television camera penetrates the veil of Chinatown, moving from banks above ground to subterranean gambling dens, from gaudy gilt and red restaurants to the dark and dank cellars where workers toil below ground. The audience is led to believe that it can see both the public exterior and secret interior of Asian American life.

Much as Sax Rohmer uses a bigoted and ignorant policeman as a buffoonish foil for Nayland Smith's Orientalist erudition, Cimino deploys Stanley White's own overt racism as a foil for the film's Orientalist position. The criticism and rejection of White's most overtly racist comments and views by his own colleagues and supporters paradoxically serve to reinforce the essential correctness of his viewpoint. His racism is presented as excessive and potentially damaging to his righteous crusade against the Chinese. In the end, Stanley White, for all his racism, is validated by the two "good" Chinese, Tracy Tzu, who submits to his rape, and his rookie subordinate, Herbert, who submits to his racism.

At the heart of the confrontation between Stanley White and Joey Tai is the class struggle in the post-Fordist political economy. Both Joey Tai and Stanley White are in rebellion against their immigrant elders. Both are brash and ruthless: Tai, the new immigrant, and White, the new white ethnic. Both challenge the old, corrupt, venal, and compliant older immigrant generation. Both Tai and White strive to break out of their respective ethnic ghettos into the American dream. Outwardly Joey Tai is a successful young businessman, a pillar of the Chinese community, a model of the emergent new immigrant success story. Lone's Joey Tai, like Hayakawa's Hisuru Tori in *The Cheat*, is contemporary, modish, and sophisticated. Joey Tai is impeccably dressed and elegant, while Stanley White sports a designer haircut and, most important, has changed his name from Wyscinski to White. It is Joey Tai who seems to be most at ease with the privilege that his power and wealth have given him. White, on the other hand, is mired in bitter class resentments against both the upper classes and the recent immigrants who aspire to upper-class privilege. Joey Tai represents the new ethnic entrepreneurial capital. His resources are global: his extended family and his financial network. Stanley White represents the abandoned rust-belt economy. His resources are local: his nuclear family and his racist instincts. The class struggle between Joey Tai and Stanley White is overdetermined by race, Stanley Wyscinski's trump card in the class struggle. The son of Polish immigrants, Wyscinski can become white, a transformation that Joey Tai can never make.

Ultimately the class struggle between Stanley White and Joey Tai is fought out in the arena of sexuality. As Gina Marchetti observes, it is presented as an explicitly homosocial struggle over the control of women and an implicitly homoerotic sadomasochistic relationship between the two men.[22] Class has long been a common signifier of difference within the homoerotic, simultaneously expressing and containing class struggle within the realm of the sexual. In *Year of the Dragon,* this veiled, homo-erotically charged class struggle gives us a restorationist narrative of patriarchy and racial subordination in populist drag.

Stanley White is torn between two women: his wife Connie, a white ethnic working-class feminist, and Tracy Tzu, the yuppie Oriental television reporter. To White, the Vietnam vet, Connie is the embodiment of an unwelcomed post-Vietnam feminism. When Stanley returns home late, after his first meeting with Tracy, Connie emerges from the kitchen, not with a hot dinner, but with a monkey wrench in her greasy hands. She announces angrily that the washing machine is broken, that she has to go to work, and that Stanley can fix it.

When Stanley follows Connie up to the bedroom, his Marine fatigue jacket is left hanging on the newel post of the staircase and carries the emasculating weight of the defeat in Vietnam.[23] Connie is emblematic of the new feminism; she is financially independent, a nurse, and moreover, she is in control of her sexuality. Connie demands sex timed for reproduction, but Stanley has continually arrived too late or has been otherwise unable to perform. Connie's anger is palpable. When Stanley misreads Connie's anger and, oblivious to the real issue, says that he will

"You're living in the past": Connie White (Caroline Cava) confronts Stanley White in the bedroom.
Still courtesy of the Museum of Modern Art Film Archives

buy her a new washing machine, she, echoing the sentiments of his police superiors, snaps, "You're living in the past."

The figure of Tracy Tzu is created in stark contrast to that of Connie
White. Tracy Tzu is a junior member of the media elite, another emergent class stratum of the post-Fordist political economy, and one that
Stanley White, as a precinct captain, must learn to deal with. Tracy Tzu
is played with remarkable woodenness by Ariane, a model with little acting experience. Although controversial at the time, this casting precisely
fits the requirements of the Orientalized female as newscaster. Epito-
mized by Connie Chung, though now simulated in virtually every major
television market in the nation, the Orientalized female, constructed
without subjectivity, is perfectly suited to be a news reader. She is attractive and reliable, not only because she can be spoken to and through,
but also because she can be trusted not to speak for herself.

Tracy Tzu comes from an upper-class family, not unlike the ones that
abandoned White and his friends in Vietnam. Unlike White, who went
to Vietnam, Tracy Tzu has gone to the university. She flaunts both her
upper-class privilege and her sexuality before White. Stanley White says
that he hated her "kind" when he was in Vietnam. Stanley's sexual conquest of Tracy Tzu is an act of both racial and class revenge and, by extension, may be seen as a homosexual rape of Joey Tai. Tracy Tzu appears
as androgynous as Joey Tai. Her pale skin, aquiline nose, and slim hips,
her short-cropped, slicked-back hair, and elegant clothes make her a virtual double for Tai.

The androgyny of Tracy Tzu is accentuated by her stark black costumes, which contrast with the casual house clothes or nurses' whites of
the earthier and potentially reproductive Connie. Tracy Tzu's apartment
is appointed in minimalist white and black; Connie White's house is in
what appears to be a working-class white ethnic neighborhood. (When
Stanley White returns home after dinner with Tracy Tzu, the block is lit
by the light of the neighborhood Catholic church.) The upper-class sterility of Tracy Tzu's apartment is directly contrasted to the fecundity of
the ethnic home with its pictures of Jesus, a cross, medallions of saints,
and pictures of family on the bedroom wall.

It is only after avenging America's defeat in southeast Asia on Tracy
Tzu's body that Stanley White can return home to Connie and attempt
to fulfill his role as husband and protector, although this gesture comes
too late. Joey Tai has sent assassins who kill Connie. Later Tai sends a
gang of Asian thugs to rape Tracy Tzu, thereby asserting Tai's claim over
the Asian woman. In this post-Vietnam scenario, Stanley White, the Vietnam vet, fails both as husband and protector, while the new immigrant,

Chinatown spectacle: Stanley White with Tracy Tzu (Arianne) in a Chinese restaurant. Still courtesy of the Museum of Modern Art Film Archives

Joey Tai, his family visible in the background in photographs and at ceremonies, is able to adopt a public persona as a generous and respected father and community leader.

Year of the Dragon rejects the claim that Asian Americans are a model minority. Instead, it figures them as gooks. Far from providing the model for the patriarchal restoration, which Stanley White yearns for, the new Asian immigrant godfather, Joey Tai, destroys the "real American" family and replaces it with a simulacrum. The figure of the honor student turned "gangbanger" reveals the model minority to be the Viet Cong.

The three "good" Asian American characters underscore the film's rejection of Asian immigrant claims to America. Tracy Tzu's ambivalent position as both object of desire and seductive destroyer of the family is only redeemed by her collaboration with White and her ultimate devotion to him. The second "good" Chinese is Herbert Kuang, a recently immigrated police cadet, who is dragooned into Stanley White's service. Like most sidekicks, Kuang is a buffoonish character whose worth is measured only in his Gunga Din–like devotion to his racial superior. But even Kuang grows weary of White's racial abuse. He launches into a short soliloquy on Asian Americans, asserting that Chinese are no longer coolies or houseboys and that he will not die for White. Of course, after White cajoles him into spying on Joey Tai, he is discovered and does die for White. Kuang's gesture of resistance, momentarily compelling, becomes completely irrelevant as an intervention against White's racism, and his death paradoxically ratifies White's racist judgments.

The third "good Chinese" is an elderly worker in an underground bean sprout factory who discovers the bodies of several gang members and reports his discovery to the police. He later appears at Connie White's funeral and is acknowledged in passing by Stanley White. This character, who remains silent except for his dutiful report to the police, represents the good, older generation of Chinese immigrants who knew their place.

In the early 1980s, the mounting trade deficit with Japan, driven in no small part by the preference of American consumers for Japanese automobiles, prompted some American business and labor leaders, especially in the auto industry, to accuse Japan of waging an undeclared trade war. In 1984, Lee Iaccoca, a former president of the Ford Motor Company and self-styled populist maverick, elaborated on this theme of invisible war and elite betrayal in his immensely popular autobiography:

> Right now we're in the midst of another major war with Japan. This time it's not a shooting war and I guess we can be thankful for that. The current conflict is a trade war. But because our government refuses to see this war for what it really is, we're well on the road to defeat.[24]

Year of the Dragon is an attempt to "bring the war home," this time to win it. While Stanley White's overt racism is dutifully condemned by all of his associates—his superiors, Connie, Tracy, Herbert—they are all figured as liberals, well-meaning but hopelessly naive. In the task of exposing the model minority as a new incarnation of the Viet Cong, race is the only lens that allows White, and the audience, to flush the invisible enemy out of the jungle into the city where "here, at least, you could see them."

In 1985, in Iacocca's Detroit, two furloughed autoworkers, Ronald Ebens and Michael Nitze, encountered Vincent Chin, a Chinese American automotive engineer, in a strip club. Ebens and Nitze taunted Chin as a "Jap," the enemy of the American auto industry. Chin took exception, and a fight ensued. After retreating to a nearby McDonald's, Eben and Nitze armed themselves with baseball bats and went in search of Chin. They found him a block away and beat him to death on the spot. After their conviction for manslaughter, trial judge Irving Kaufman released both men with a fine, stating that they were good citizens and represented no threat to the community.

1

After LA

Los Angeles, 1992

Between April 29 and May 2, 1992, the South Central, Korea-town, and Pico Union neighborhoods of Los Angeles became free-fire zones. Confronted with a massive outburst of rage over the acquittal of the four white Los Angeles police officers whose beating of black motorist Rodney King had been spectacularly broadcast to the nation, the LAPD sealed off the "colored" zones of the city from White LA and let them burn. The LAPD's strategy of containment was effective in protecting white LA; it brought massive destruction and death to LA's "Third World."

The mass violence in Los Angeles has been called a slave rebellion, a bread riot, and an urban uprising.[1] The causes for the urban uprising are multiple and complex; in Los Angeles in 1992, there was plenty to be angry about. The outrage over the not-guilty verdict handed down by the all-white jury to the white police officers who had savagely beaten Rodney King reflected the deep racial and class chasm that split the city. The highly militarized LAPD had a long history of treating nonwhite communities as enemy hamlets requiring pacification and containment. Simi Valley, where the trial took place, is one of those white middle-class suburbs that had been developed in the 1970s and -80s while Watts, Central LA, and Compton were being abandoned; an extraordinary 2,000 LAPD officers and their families lived in Simi Valley. Deep recession and structural changes in the political economy of Los Angeles had left the poor black and Latino communities in the inner city more impoverished and more disempowered than ever before.

The outbreak of mass violence in Los Angeles could, however, also be called a pogrom. Although stores owned by many blacks, whites, Latinos, and other Asian Americans were also wrecked, Korean immigrant merchants sustained fully one half of the $850 million of property loss in the three days of looting and arson. An estimated 2,300 Korean-owned businesses were destroyed.

The events of Los Angeles between April 29 and May 2, 1992, America's first multiracial riots, cannot be fully understood without taking into account the crisis of post-Fordism in the economic sphere and the emergence of a racial discourse that constructed Asian Americans as agents of Orientalized capital.[2] In this construction of the Oriental, it is not only the Asian American who is Orientalized; multinational capital itself is _cyberpunk_ imbued with Oriental cultural difference. In Los Angeles' globalized capitalism, Asian Americans appear ominously everywhere on the urban landscape, from the glittering skyscraper downtown to the corner liquor store in the ghetto.

Orientalizing Capital: *Rising Sun*

In the 1980s, spurred by the rapid growth of Pacific Rim economies and heavy immigration flows from Asia and Latin America, Los Angeles was transformed into a global city. Los Angeles County became the largest manufacturing metropolitan area in the United States and a financial hub of the Pacific Rim economy. By the late 1980s, Asian and Asian American capital had become a visible presence at every level of Los Angeles life. Most visible were the Japanese banks and trading houses that dotted the LA cityscape. Japanese corporations reinvested much of their huge trade surplus in the American economy. The revaluation of the yen drove down the U.S. trade deficit with Japan from about $52 billion in 1987 to $38 billion in 1990. However, more valuable yen made Japanese investment in U.S. real estate and corporations a bargain. In 1989, Japanese corporations made several big purchases, which made headlines and the evening news: Mitsubishi bought Rockefeller Center, Sony bought Columbia Pictures, Matsushita bought MCA. Other, lesser icons of old-stock American culture, like the Pebble Beach Golf Club and Brooks Brothers were also sold to Japanese investors.

By the end of the decade, the shift from trade imbalance to investment touched off a new round of cultural panic, despite the fact that Japanese investments in the United States were only half those of Great Britain and on a par with those of the Netherlands. *Time* Magazine ran a cover with a faceless personification of corporate Japan in Samurai armor. Suddenly the Japanese businessman was not only a Samurai competitor; he might also be your boss. Japanese management techniques became the rage in the popular business literature and, for a short time, *The Book of Five Rings,* a seventeenth-century book on swordplay, became the "little Red Book" of American business managers.[3]

At the end of the decade, a spate of books characterized Japanese economic growth as a distortion of capitalist development. Unlike earlier studies of the 1970s, which had put Japan forward as a model of economic dynamism founded on democratic-institution building, free markets, and conservative politics, the new studies argued that Japanese capitalism was a predatory reflection of a much darker aspect of an essentialized Japanese character. The epitome of this new trend was Karel van Wolfren's *The Japanese Enigma.*[4] Van Wolfren, a Dutch journalist based in Tokyo, saw Japan as a closed society where individual initiative was completely stifled in service of a rigidly hierarchical and monolithic system, "as inescapable as the political system of the Soviet Union." At the heart of the "Japan Problem" was not capitalism, but the culture that legitimated this totalitarian system. The central failing of Japanese culture was that it was not Western. Van Wolfren contended that Japanese culture was not sufficiently committed to transcendent truths and thus left the Japanese people "less free than they should be." Japanese culture, in his view, is at odds with the "one single demand that has reverberated throughout Western intellectual development ever since the Greeks: 'Thou shalt not cherish contradictions.'" The failure of Japanese society to have grasped the central tenet of the European enlightenment had therefore rendered them constitutionally incapable of rationality, logic, and individuality, qualities which defined Western man.

In a 1989 essay, "The Clash of Civilizations," published in *Foreign Affairs,* the flagship journal of the elite Council on Foreign Relations, Samuel Huntington proposed a new paradigm for understanding international relations in the post–Cold War era. Huntington, a distinguished defense intellectual and director of Harvard University's Center for International Studies, proposed a theory of post–Cold War international relations in which the principal threat to global order is a clash of essentialized cultures—Western civilization confronted by an unholy alliance of militant Islamic and Confucian capitalism. In this scenario, immigration and multiculturalism pose a critical threat to national unity which, Huntington insists, is based on the essential European character of liberal democracy. Within this paradigm, the Asian American can be figured not as the model minority but as a potential agent of disorder, the yellow peril.

Echoing Lothrop Stoddard's *The Rising Tide of Color,* Huntington argues that "civilization" is the paradigmatic social unit of the twenty-first century.[5] Huntington's major claim is that "the most important conflicts of the future will occur along the cultural fault lines separating these civilizations from one another."[6] Like Stoddard, Huntington identifies seven or eight civilizations in his mapping of the contemporary world: Western (of which Huntington sees two variants, western European and North American), Confucian, Japanese, Islamic, Hindu, Slavic-Orthodox, Latin American, and "possibly" African civilization. However, as in Stoddard's scenario, the principal threat to Western civilization is from the East. Echoing Stoddard's warning about the rising tide of brown and yellow peoples, Huntington argues that the West is threatened by the possible, even likely, alliance between militant Islam and the economic powerhouses of Confucian East Asian civilization.

Although Huntington does not mention race, much less genetics, his civilization is no less a category of reduction. Huntington constructs civilization as the defining category of basic, insurmountable difference, impervious to historical change. Huntington defines civilization as "the highest cultural grouping of people and the broadest level of cultural identity people have, short of that which distinguishes humans from other species."[7] "[Civilizational] differences," he asserts "are the product of centuries" (yet are somehow now resistant to change). Cultural differences are "far more fundamental than differences among political ideologies and political regimes."[8] In Huntington's view, an individual might or might not choose to be a socialist, a Catholic, a worker, but the individual cannot transcend his or her "essential" Armenianness, Italianness, or Japaneseness. "In the conflicts between civilizations, the question is 'What are you?' That is a given that cannot be changed."[9]

In Huntington's view, the United States is threatened with becoming a "torn society" by a rising tide of multiculturalism. Just as Stoddard saw Asiatic immigration as a threat to the inner dikes of white civilization, Huntington sees immigration from the non-Western world (both Asia and Latin America) as threatening to undermine western civilization. Responding to critics, Huntington asserts that the national unity of the United States has historically rested on "the twin bedrocks of European culture and political democracy," and he sounds the alarm against the "weakening of the European character of American society and culture through non-European immigration and multiculturalism."[10] Following Nathan Glazer, Huntington looks nostalgically toward European immigrant assimilation as the master narrative of the nation.

Huntington argues that America is threatened by the demand of non-European Americans for racial equity and social recognition, which he characterizes as "special rights (affirmative action and similar measures) for blacks and other groups." Such claims, he asserts, undermine "the principles that have been the basis of American political unity." Simultaneously, "multiculturalism" insists on "rewriting American political, social, and literary history from the viewpoint of non-European groups," thereby encouraging "a clash of civilizations within the United States."[11]

At the heart of Huntington's conflation of civilization and race is the fear that Western civilization (the North American variant) is threatened by a demographic revolution. The Hispanic and nonwhite populations that Huntington fears will soon be a majority in the United States threaten to "de-Westernize" America.[12] His North American variant of Western civilization apparently includes Canada and the United States, but not Mexico or the Caribbean. Hispanics are part of a Latin American civilization that is not, in his view, part of Western civilization. Neither are African Americans, whose ancestors arrived as early as 1620. Huntington seems to believe that African Americans understand American civilization less well for having experienced it as "non-Westerners" for almost 400 years.

In Huntington's view, Hispanics and nonwhites have nothing to add to liberal democracy, which is an immutable product of a Western civilization, to which they do not or cannot belong. Huntington sees the call for systematic dismantling of economic and political barriers to racial equality and cultural recognition as a rejection of the western European essence of liberal democracy. Having effectively equated Western civilization with Lothrop Stoddard's white civilization, Huntington asks rhetorically,

> Will the de-Westernization of the United States, if it occurs, also mean its de-Americanization? If it does and Americans cease to adhere to their liberal democratic and European-rooted political ideology, the United States as we have known it will cease to exist and will follow the other ideologically defined superpower [the Soviet Union] on the ash heap of history.[13]

In this world view, essentialized cultural difference—the very cultural difference that marked Asian Americans as role models for Bell and Graubard—defines Asian Americans as inauthentic and the potential agents of a dreaded de-Westernization of American society. Huntington's essay theorizes the narrative of American vulnerability and the erosion of a national unity by the demands of fake Americans on the traditional social order. In the heated debate over immigration, Huntington thus aligns himself with cultural conservatives (such as William F. Buckley and Allen Brimelow) who have argued against economic conservatives (such as Bill Bennett and Jack Kemp) that regardless of the economic advantages that accrue from immigration, non-European immigrants represent a threat to the nation's cultural core.[14] In *Alien Nation: Common Sense About America's Immigration Disaster,* Allen Brimelow, a senior editor at the *National Review* and himself an immigrant from Britain, echoes Huntington's linking of non-European immigration and multiculturalism. He attacks the historian Ronald Takaki, an outspoken proponent of a multiracial interpretation of American history. Brimelow quotes from the preface to Takaki's text, *A Different Mirror: A History of Multicultural America,* which emphasizes the everyday importance of understanding America as a multiracial society. In Brimelow's paranoid account, Takaki is transformed into a latter-day Fu Manchu, bent on nothing less than the destruction of white civilization. Brimelow writes, "To the extent that there is any content to Takaki's complaint, it is that he is Asian in a predominately white society. And there is no cure for that except radically increasing the numbers of minorities and breaking down white America's sense of identity." [15]

Michael Crichton's novel *Rising Sun,* published in 1991 and released as a movie in 1993,[16] identified Japan as the particular threat from the East, whose specter haunted the landscape of late capitalist America. Although it appears to be about unraveling the murder of young (blonde) American woman found dead in the boardroom of a Japanese corporation's brand-new LA headquarters, *Rising Sun* is less a detective thriller than a jeremiad against an economic and cultural threat from Japan. Crichton attempts to validate his depiction of U.S.-Japan relations by appropriating the work of academic and journalistic Japan watchers, chief among them Karel van Wolfren. At the end of the novel, Crichton appends a three-page bibliography on Japan and its relations with the United States. At the heart of *Rising Sun* is Karel van Wolfren's dark vision of a predatory and destructive capitalism distorted by a crypto-fascist social system.

In *Rising Sun,* Crichton mobilizes the same narratives of nationhood, cultural identity, and business that are at work in the dominant academic discourse about Japan. Echoing Iacocca's claim that Japan has launched a silent war on the United States, Crichton claims that the Japanese have invented "a new kind of trade—adversarial trade, trade like war, trade intended to wipe out the competition." [17]

Throughout the novel we are presented with a narrative of Japanese economic warfare and its unscrupulous strategies and tactics. The homicide is linked to the proposed sale of an American computer equipment company, Microcon, to a subsidiary of the Nakamoto Corporation and "Japan Inc.," which would give the Japanese a monopoly over the production of computer chips and control over computer manufacturing

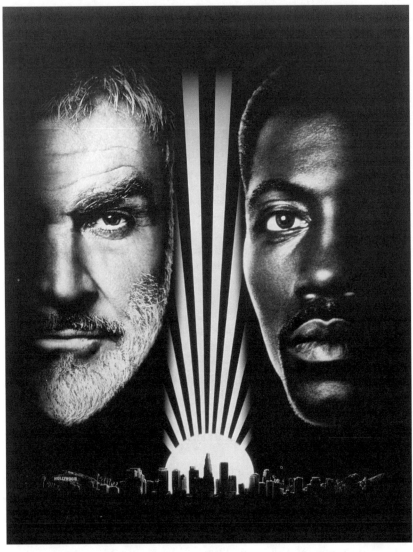

The yellow peril and national unity: *Rising Sun* poster showing Sean Connery and Wesley Snipes.
Still courtesy of the Museum of Modern Art Film Archives

in America. The sale is being blocked in Congress by Senator Morton, one of the few Americans who sees the Japanese challenge. It is revealed that the Senator has had an illicit affair with the murder victim, has been tricked into believing that he is guilty of her death, and is being blackmailed by the Japanese into dropping his opposition to the Microcon sale.

Rising Sun follows very closely the tropes of the Fu Manchu narrative. The hero is an archetype of Orientalist expertise. The novels narrate both a mystery plot and a parallel political message. The plot of the first Sax Rohmer novel concerns the serial murders of the handful of Orientalist experts who are about to warn the West of the Yellow Peril. There is one significant difference, however. In the Fu Manchu stories, as well as in *The Year of the Dragon*, a single Oriental man bent on world domination embodies Asiatic evil. In *Rising Sun*, it is Japanese culture, with its interchangeable minions, that is the villain. The closest Crichton comes to a Fu Manchu character is Ishigura, a low-level corporate bureaucrat and nervous bungler who gets mixed up with the murder and its cover-up. Ishigura's motivations have nothing to do with a desire for world domination, but rather stem solely from a desire to prove himself to his superiors. Behind the buffoonish figure of Ishigura is the Nakamoto Company, Crichton's real yellow peril and an obscure and shadowy confluence of forces often working to contradictory ends. This image follows Karel van Wolfren's description of Japan as a rudderless society bereft of individual initiative or moral compass. In this view, Japan's orientation toward unscrupulous practices in the international trade arena is less an unfolding of a master plan than the natural outcome of Japanese culture.

Rising Sun is infused with the tension and anxiety over the decline of the American hegemony and the dismantling of the Fordist social order. Los Angeles, once the destination of the American dream and now a magnet for labor, a strategic point on the circuit of Pacific Rim capital, is the prime site for such a radical dislocation. Crichton reminds us, with an opening quotation from Phillip Sanders, that "We are entering a world where the old rules no longer apply." [18] Los Angeles is a harrowing, smog-filled site of radical confusion, a society in flux beyond our capacity to understand or change. Crichton writes, "Think back to the fifties, when American workers could own a house, raise a family and send the kids to college, all on a single paycheck. . . . [now p]eople struggle to hold on to what they have. They can't get ahead." [19]

The story's narrator, Peter Smith, a detective newly assigned to the LAPD's Special Services unit, which handles politically sensitive cases, recalls, "I had gone out looking for a house, hoping to get a backyard for Michelle [his daughter]. But housing prices were just impossible in L.A. . . . I was never going to be able to afford one." [20]

Middle-class anxiety over the collapse of the single-income household and the impossibility of finding affordable housing for the middle class contrasts with to the opening of the newest edifice of Japanese capital in downtown LA. This is the Nakamoto Building, all glass, chrome, steel, and marble, with two-way mirrors surrounding the inner office spaces and elevators that speak Japanese. For the Los Angelenos who enter it, the Nakamoto Building, all gleaming surface, is a profound reflection of postmodern anxiety and dislocation.

Rising Sun attempts to remap categories of culture and nation in a world "where the old rules no longer apply." The key narrative at work in *Rising Sun* is the foregrounding of cultural difference as the ultimate determinant of the rules of the game in the late capitalist world order. According to the logic of the novel, the radical dislocation felt in Los Angeles is the result of the radical alienness of Japanese culture and America's grave misunderstanding of the nature of Japanese competition. In order to explicate otherwise unknowable Japanese difference, Crichton resorts to the tropes of Fu Manchu and Nayland Smith. Just as Sax Rohmer's narrator, Dr. Petrie, is guided through the sinister underworld of Fu Manchu by the Orientalist expert Nayland Smith, Crichton's narrator, Peter Smith, is mentored and guided through the mystery by John Connor, a retired Special Services officer and an expert on Japanese culture. Like Nayland Smith, who served the Empire in Burma, Connor knows the Orient from having lived in Japan for some time and becoming fluent in the language and culture of the Japanese. It is intimated that Connor's retirement is at least partly due to the fact that he has gone native and can no longer be trusted. "There were times when I thought Connor had become Japanese himself. He had that reserve, that secretive manner." [21] A measure of how far Connor has gone native is his apartment, described as furnished in "the Japanese style: *tatami* mats, *shoji* screens, and paper-and wood-paneled walls. A calligraphy scroll, a black lacquer table, a vase with a single splash of white orchid." [22] Nonetheless, the measure of Connor's trustworthiness is the distance that he can continue to maintain between himself and the Japanese culture that he clearly admires.

It is only by establishing a formal Japanese relation of mentor and pupil that Connor can communicate to Smith his expert insight into Japanese culture, customs, and behavior, reserving judgment in his objective description of a culture-driven Japanese economy that is "fundamentally different" from that of America. Thus Connor occupies the privileged position of the Japanologist, the informed expert whose objective understanding of Japanese society and culture allows him to authoritatively deploy a particular kind of narrative of Japan.

As a foil to the charge that his essentializing of Japanese society and culture is racist, Crichton, following Rohmer, provides his Orientalist expert with a racist straw man. Connor's Zen-like equanimity is set in stark contrast to the figure of Tom Graham (Harvey Keitel), the police officer officially in charge of the murder investigation. Graham is a vulgar racist whose open hostility and contempt of the Japanese render him ineffective. His language is rife with slurs and epithets toward the Japanese, and his investigation of the case is thrown off course by his single-minded desire to persecute a Japanese offender. Graham is dismissed by Connor for his misunderstanding of the Japanese: "Graham has no real knowledge, no first-hand experience. He just has a collection of prejudices and media fantasies. . . . He doesn't know anything about the Japanese—and it never occurs to him to find out." [23]

Although Graham's figure of the raving Japan basher is set up as a foil for Connor's authority, Connor's "objective" understanding of the Japanese leads him to some of the same conclusions Graham has arrived at through "common-sense" racism. In a conversation with Connor, Smith expresses his confusion as to the motivations behind all the machinations of their Japanese adversaries. Connor, the more sophisticated liberal, who genuinely knows the Japanese and admires their aesthetics, confirms Graham's opinion that Japan has launched another undeclared war. Smith: "Graham thinks its a war." Connor: "Well, that's true. We are definitely at war with Japan." [24]

It becomes clear that at the core of Connor's expertise on Japanese culture is his clarity about Japan's adversarial relation with America and his alignment with the project of reestablishing U.S. hegemony. Connor warns that the fundamental and insurmountable difference between Japanese culture and American culture lies in the Japanese belief that "trade [is] intended to wipe out the competition." Connor tells us that this is not common to capitalist behavior but is peculiar to the Japanese. For Crichton, like Huntington, culture is essential, impervious to change, and determinative of behavior. Even as the discourse of biological race is discredited through the figure of Graham, a reified culture is substituted for genetics; race is reformulated as essentialized cultural difference that keeps Americans and Japanese immutably different. As Connor explains to Smith, "Americans don't understand . . . because the Japanese system is fundamentally different." [25]

There are several scenes in the novel in which Connor instructs his student on this immutably different Japanese culture. Having been informed about a Japanese style of business negotiation involving extensive use of bribes and favors, Smith asks why this is so. Connor's answer: "Why do they eat sushi? It's the way they conduct business." As to why Americans fail to deal adequately with the Japanese style of business: "Why do they eat hamburgers? It's the way they are." [26]

These immutable differences are only one component of Crichton's representation of the new social order. The decline of the United States as world leader has been accompanied by a decay of the domestic social order. Despite the fact that *Rising Sun* purports to expose the Japanese political and economic threat to the United States, the entire history of global capitalism is suppressed in favor of narratives of culture and sex.

In *Rising Sun,* the collapse of the family is central to the collapse of the nation. The decline of the moral order at home is a central reason for the inability of the United States to assert itself in the world. While American men like Senator Morton put themselves and the nation at risk with their sexual peccadilloes, Crichton's Japanese men are obsessed with white women, especially blondes. Much attention is paid to the ways in which Japanese money is used to pay for American sex. Bars that cater to Japanese businessmen and a dormitory of white women reserved for Japanese executives become exhibits in an indictment of Japanese sexuality—and reproduce the opium dens and dives of Fu Manchu's Chinatown. The murder investigation reveals that Cheryl Austin, a once-wholesome girl from the Midwest, has been lured into prostitution and introduced to the pleasures of rough sex by Ishigura. However, Crichton reserves his greatest scorn for Smith's ex-wife, represented as an amoral, careerist attorney who has abandoned her young daughter to Smith's care as a beleaguered but loving single father. She has gone to work in the district attorney's office, which has prostituted itself to the interests of Japanese capital. Although she has long ago abandoned family in favor of career, she goes so far as to threaten to have Smith's custody of his daughter revoked if he does not back off his investigation of Nakamoto.

The substitution of culture for race is made all the more apparent in the film version of *Rising Sun.* In response to criticism that the novel's polemics trade in racist stereotypes, the producers decided to cast Wesley Snipes as Peter Smith, the narrator and disciple of John Connor, played by Sean Connery. Crichton goes to great pains to point out that Japanese are themselves deeply racist, but nothing is made of this with regard to Smith. There is no clue in the novel to suggest that Smith is black, but the decision to cast a black actor in the narrator's role deflected the charge of racism from the film.

Indeed, the partnership of Snipes and Connery, despite the obvious stereotype that marries black brawn and hip style with white brains and control, allows for new racial alignments in the global city. The principal poster ad for the movie shows Connery and Snipes on either side of a stylized World War II Imperial Japanese battle flag that looms over an LA skyline [illustration here]. In one scene, the American heroes are chased by a car full of Japanese gangsters through the bleak low-rise urban landscape far from the polished marble, chrome, and glass facades of the Nakamoto tower. Just as it appears that they will be captured by the Japanese, Smith, who until this moment has been marginalized as Connor's sidekick, calls upon a group of black inner-city youths to intervene to save them. Although the scene is played for low humor, the notion of a black and white alliance against an alien threat is resonant. In this bombed-out landscape—devastated by multinational capital, identified in *Rising Sun* with Japanese culture—the crisis of race between white and black can be resolved in a new alliance that restores national unity against the alien. It was precisely in these neighborhoods of the global city that thousands of Asian-owned stores were looted and set ablaze in 1992.

Orientalizing Capital II: The Mere Gook Rule

In the 1980s, Los Angeles county became the nation's largest manufacturing center. This was due in large measure to the influx of migrant workers and capitalists from Asia and Latin America into the LA basin. Although less visible than the Japanese skyscrapers, the presence of hundreds of thousands of Asian immigrant entrepreneurs was felt at every level of the Los Angeles economy.

Some Asian immigrants have come with enough capital, or are able to borrow enough here, to enter the secondary retail sector abandoned by national chain stores and earlier ethnic retailers. For example, in Los Angeles, Korean liquor store owners often bought their stores from African American entrepreneurs, who had bought the stores from Jewish owners who had been burned out in the Watts riots of 1964. These entrepreneurs—Korean retailers, Indian motel keepers, Thai restaurateurs, Vietnamese garment subcontractors, and others—make up for a low level of capital investment with a high rate of exploited labor, often commandeering the underpaid or unpaid labor of family members.

Asian entrepreneurs have also helped create a new manufacturing sector that responds to the demands of flexible accumulation for small batch production, custom designs, and quick turnover. This demand and the small-scale capital available to many of these immigrant entrepreneurs has resulted in a manufacturing landscape filled with thousands of small subcontractors. In Los Angeles, the garment industry has played a central role in this development. Despite the fact that apparel manufacturing declined by 20 percent nationally in the 1980s as production was transferred overseas, garment manufacturing in Los Angeles grew by a remarkable 60 percent during that period. Not only has a labor force of Latinos and Asian immigrant workers been mobilized to compete with foreign suppliers; Korean, Chinese, and Vietnamese immigrants make up an overwhelming proportion of the subcontractors in the industry. In sum, Asian Americans, particularly immigrant Asian workers, have a highly visible position on both sides of the post-Fordist urban economy.

In the 1992 riots, there were specific local reasons why Asian American businesses were targeted. Antagonisms between African Americans and Korean merchants in Los Angeles were widely publicized. There was anger in the African American community over the killing of Latasha Harlins, a black teenager, by Soon Ja-Du, a Korean female shop owner, over a disputed bottle of orange juice. Although Soon Ja-Du was convicted of manslaughter, the white judge refused to sentence Soon Ja-du to any time in prison, asserting that she represented no threat to the community. This leniency confirmed a persistent belief in the black community that Asian-owned businesses got favored treatment from the government and the banks. There was the broader charge that Korean merchants exploited and did not give back to the communities in which they did business. Most immediately, many blacks and Latinos felt they were rudely treated and singled out for surveillance when they patronized Korean-owned stores.[27]

Korean-American shopkeepers were, however, merely the gook of the moment. The mere gook rule (from the Vietnam War, wherein any dead Vietnamese could be counted as a dead enemy) was in play, and Koreans were the closest and most vulnerable Asian Americans in sight. Koreans were not the only Asians targeted; 300 Chinese-owned stores were destroyed, as were several dozen shops owned by Filipinos and South Asians. In nearby Long Beach, Vietnamese shops were targeted and looted. Despite television and radio characterization of the event as a black riot, the looting was a multicultural affair. To be sure, in areas such as South Central where African Americans made up a majority of the residents, they constituted a majority of the looters. But in such areas as Pico-Union, where Latinos made up a majority of residents, they did the looting, and in still other neighborhoods non-Hispanic whites joined in.

The massive attack on Asian Americans by their fellow Los Angelenos in 1992 was stunning and unsurpassed in its scale but not unpredictable or unprecedented in the focus of its fury. Since the beginning of the 1980s, racially motivated hate crimes against Asian Americans had been growing in every part of the country. In New York city, hate crimes against Asian Americans rose by an astounding 680 percent between 1985 and 1990. Between 1989 and 1990 alone, hate crime against Asian Americans more than doubled, and subway crime against Asian Americans rose by 206 percent.[28] Although differences in definition, recordkeeping, and monitoring make it difficult to systematically observe the nationwide rise of hate crimes against Asian Americans, several well publicized, racially motivated murders during the 1980s and 1990s are an indicator of an alarming rise in hate crimes and violence against Asian Americans. Asians of every ethnicity have been its victims; Americans of every other race are among the assailants. Most notorious have been the murders of Vincent Chin in Detroit; Navorze Mody, an Indian American, in New Jersey; and Vandy Phorng, a Cambodian American, in Massachusetts in 1987; Jim Loo, a Chinese American, in North Carolina, and five Cambodian and Laotian American children in a Stockton, Calif., schoolyard, in 1989; Hung Trong, a Vietnamese American, in Houston in 1990; and Thien Minh Ly, a Vietnamese American, in Los Angeles in 1996. Not always classified as racially motivated, and therefore less well publicized, are the killings of scores of Asian American shopkeepers and cabdrivers. In Los Angeles in the two years before the riots, twenty-five Korean American shopkeepers were killed by non-Korean assailants.[29]

In several of these cases and in many others, it did not matter that the victim was Chinese, or Korean, or Vietnamese; the mere gook rule overrode ethnicity. Vincent Chin, a Chinese American, was taken to be Japanese and killed by two white, furloughed autoworkers in Detroit. Jim Loo, also a Chinese American, was killed by two white men who thought he was Vietnamese. In 1990, Tuan Ana Cao, a Vietnamese American, was beaten and severely injured by a group of black men who thought he was Korean. In January of 1996, Thien Minh Ly, a Vietnamese American, was killed by two White drifters who called him a Jap. In these cases it didn't matter what ethnicity or nationality the victims really were; the only significant issue was that they were the gook.

While *Rising Sun*'s glittering Japanese skyscrapers symbolized the yellow peril to corporate America in the 1980s, Korean shopkeepers embody Oriental capital in the decaying neighborhoods of the inner city. Two films that were released just before and after the LA riots exemplify this new construction of the Oriental. *Falling Down* (1992, Warner Bros., directed by Alan Schumacher) and *Menace II Society* (1993, New Line Cinema, directed by Allen and Albert Hughes) supply their audiences with brutal, dystopian visions of Los Angeles. Both films mobilize frustration and anger against the political economy of late capitalist Los Angeles into narratives of beset manhood and rage against the Oriental alien.

Both films present a vision of Los Angeles that is made up of Asian-immigrant capitalists, black and Latino gangbangers, skinheads, rude motorists, and impersonal fast-food joints. *Falling Down* and *Menace II Society* map—by foot, bus, and automobile—the city as a multiracial nightmare in which civil society, both public society and the family, has collapsed.

At the surface, these two films seem worlds apart; *Falling Down* is about beset whiteness, while *Menace II Society* is about beset blackness. What draws the two films together is their treatment of the gook. Both films open with an act of retributive violence against the alien. In both films, the alien is the Korean merchant. In *Falling Down*, a laid-off white defense worker (Michael Douglas), known by the vanity license plates on his car ("D-FENS"), enters a corner convenience store in a desolate corner of Los Angeles looking for change with which to phone home. The Korean shopkeeper points to a "No change will be given without a purchase" sign and then charges what D-fens takes to be an exorbitant amount for a soda. In a rage, D-fens takes a baseball bat and destroys the interior of the store. *Menace II Society* opens with the murder of two Korean shopkeepers. Two young black men, Caine (Tyrin Turner) and O-Dog (Laurenz Tate), enter a neighborhood store to buy malt liquor. The "boyz" are kept under close surveillance by the shopkeeper. They return his suspicion with hostility and begin to leave without paying for the beer. As they approach the door, the shopkeeper mutters that he feels sorry for their mothers. O-Dog turns, walks back to the shopkeeper, and shoots him point blank in the head. Mugging at the surveillance video camera, O-Dog goes into the back of the store where he shoots and kills the shopkeeper's cowering wife and grabs the videotape from the camera.

Falling Down takes up the nostalgic banner of the angry white male, identifying the frustrations of urban life with "multiculturalism" and articulating white populist rage as a restorationist revolt against the erosion of urban civility. Following the convention of Clint Eastwood's "man with no name," the antihero of the film, a white Everyman, is known only as D-fens. He is one of the heroes of the Cold War, now abandoned by the society he has helped to defend, a victim of the triumph over communism. In fact, the military sector continued to enjoy a privileged position in the economy in the 1980s, thanks to huge increases in spending on military hardware in the Carter and Reagan administrations. In the Los Angeles basin, white suburbs like Irvine grew at lightning speed thanks to high-tech industry, much of it fueled by military spending. It was largely the older black working-class neighborhoods like Watts, Compton, and South Central that lost heavy industry and were abandoned like Vietnam. Ironically in *Falling Down*, the only person with whom D-fens identifies is an out-of-work black veteran who stages a one-man picket line in front of a bank and whose sardonic picket sign reads "Not Financially Viable." Despite this rapport, D-fens is fearful and resentful of the multicultural city. Getting off the freeway, perhaps for the first time, he is armed only with his anger. Honed by thirty years of conservative attacks on affirmative action, this sense of victimization empowers the angry white male with a deep resentment at the challenge to his privilege presented by minorities and women. In *Falling Down,* as in *Rising Sun,* the rage of the angry white male and the dispossessed African American male show black and white men as equal victims of Orientalized capitalism.

Menace II Society is a film of raw brutality about the struggle for survival among young black men in Watts. Made in response to the sentimentality of *Boyz 'n the Hood,* the Hughes brothers' film paints a bleak picture, focusing not on the potentially good boyz but on the already bad ones. When Caine, a young drug dealer who is the film's narrator, is asked by the grandfather who has raised him, "Do you want to live or die?" Caine can only reply, "I don't know." The deadly encounters in these movies between Asian American grocers and their assailants are the product of a global political economy that has a direct effect on race relations in contemporary LA. The history of this new world order and its local effect are elided as historical meaning is stripped from the category of race, and race as performance becomes the focal point.

Despite or because of its new multiracial constituency, nowhere in this dystopian Los Angeles does a public sphere—a space where different positions, identities, and histories can be negotiated—survive. In *Falling Down* and in *Menace II Society,* as in *Rising Sun,* the possibility of national rebirth is embedded in a narrative of family. The state, represented here only by the police, is largely absent from both films. In *Menace II Society* Caine mainly fears rival street "gangstas," not the police, despite being savagely beaten by police officers. In the end, even though they have been sent the video from the convenience store, the police never arrest O-Dog or Caine. When Caine finally prepares to leave LA to rebuild his life with a new family in Georgia, it is not the police who kill him but rival gangstas in a drive-by shooting. In *Falling Down,* the state appears not only to have abandoned its faithful servant but to have turned on him. The state has interfered with his right to control his family, the source of his private identity. In both these films, the state's abandonment of the black family on the one hand, and its interference with the white family on the other, have led to social collapse.

The immediate cause for rage in both films is the breakdown of family in the post-Fordist crisis. D-fens's wife, fearing his deepening insanity, has gotten a court restraining order keeping him from the home and their child. D-fens suffers a psychological breakdown when he is prohibited from attending his daughter's birthday party. In *Menace II Society,* the Korean storekeeper's remark reminds O-Dog of his drug-addicted mother's abandonment of him and sends him on a murderous rampage.

On the mean streets of Los Angeles, Asian immigrant store owners are the tethered goat of post-Fordist capitalism. D-fens's victim is the operator of a small neighborhood convenience store. The Korean shopkeeper, seemingly petty and hard, represents alienated capitalism, capital literally given into the hands of the alien. *Falling Down* invokes the mere gook rule when Pendergast (Robert Duvall), a detective who is tracking D-fens, simply assumes his Japanese American partner can communicate with the Korean store owner.

In *Menace II Society,* the encounter between the black youths and Asian merchants in the 'hood is even more brutal and ends in murder. The Asian store clerk and his wife are made to bear the full price of the post-Fordist capitalist transformation. Their murders delineate the ideological roles of Asian and black. By commenting that he pities the mothers of the black youths, the Asian shopkeeper enacts the model minority stereotype and indirectly invokes the accusation that black poverty is due to the failure of the black family. Bringing mothers into the verbal exchange crosses a boundary in black street culture from which the outsider is forbidden. The alien is executed for his inadvertent trespass; there was a widespread resentment of perceived rude treatment on the part of many patrons of transgression.

Falling Down mobilizes white middle-class resentment through the comedic strategy of excessive violence. The audience is prompted to laugh at the excessiveness of D-fens's response to each encounter with urban dystopia. Since the context—of D-fens's encounter with the Asian American shopkeeper, or any stereotypes that represent the victimization of the white middle-class—goes unexamined, the audience is given to understand and sympathize with D-fens's perspective that the new world is, by turns, threatening and incomprehensible. It is the excessiveness of D-fens's reactions to these encounters—smashing up the convenience store with a baseball bat, shooting up a McDonald's with a submachine gun, blowing up a truck that is blocking traffic with a Stinger missile—and not his rage, that is inappropriate and therefore comedic. Only when D-fens's rage turns against his own family, in particular his daughter, is the audience cued to a more anxious reading. As D-fens's mental collapse becomes increasingly acute, the audience is distanced from his violence and relieved of the burden of guilt by association. The audience can simultaneously cheer him on and cluck at his violent excess, excusing it as mental illness.

In *Menace II Society*, it is the surveillance video of the event and its replay that are excessive; they divert our attention from an interrogation of the murders as a product of the brutal political economy of Watts, LA, and the Pacific Rim, and redirect it to the poverty of black culture and the pathology of the black underclass. At first, the naive viewer might think that O-Dog's taking the video is simply a strategy of survival, a matter of hiding the evidence of the crime and the identity of the killer. However, the audience is soon made aware of other uses of the video. Almost immediately, O-Dog begins to show the video to his friends as evidence, not of his crime, but of his hypermasculinized selfhood. O-Dog himself becomes absorbed in watching the video, replaying it and reliving the homicide as a supremely masculinizing moment.

O-Dog's fetishization of the murder video mimics the televised fetishization of racial violence in the mainstream mass media. It mimics the plethora of "real life" cop shows, which invariably show the mainly white police stopping, chasing, and bringing to ground mainly black criminals. O-Dog's continuous replay of the murder video mimics precisely what network television has done with the videotaped recordings of the murder of Latasha Harlins, the beatings of Rodney King and Reginald Denny, the burning of Koreatown, the actions of black looters and shotgun-toting Korean merchants. Lauren Berlant has noted that "it is now commonplace in television criticism to say that the structure of televisual experience promotes the annihilation of memory and in particular, of historical knowledge and political self-awareness."[30] These scenes of racial violence were endlessly replayed, constantly fragmented, and spliced into a thousand different shows. Constant repetition decontextualized the events and detached the violence from the class and racial crises of LA. Racial and class violence is thus stripped of historical meaning and aestheticized and, whether for the news or entertainment divisions of the multimedia corporation, transformed into performance. In a recent essay, David Palumbo-Liu brilliantly deconstructs a news photo of a young Korean-American man holding a handgun and wearing a Malcolm X t-shirt emblazoned with the slogan "by any means necessary." In the background is a burning store. Palumbo-Liu points out that the photo of the armed Korean (one of many similar images that flooded the nation in the wake of the riots) now poses the Asian immigrant as a stand-in for white property rights.[31] Such fragmented and decontextualized images of race are central to a narrative that treats the urban violence of Los Angeles not as a material result of the global restructuring of capital that has polarized the city between the rich and poor (in which Asian Americans are posed in the middle), but as a black and white clash of civilizations, transformed into a war of black against yellow.

Rising Sun, Falling Down, and *Menace II Society,* despite their quite different vantage points, share a narrative of beset nationhood and a postmodern anxiety about the harsh and unforgiving new world of global capitalism, transnational culture, and multiracial communities. All three films attempt to restore national unity by creating nostalgic narratives of revived patriarchy. The enormous contempt mobilized against the careerist (feminist) mother who has abandoned her child and husband in *Rising Sun* is transformed in *Falling Down* into sympathy for D-fens, abandoned by his spouse in his hour of need and then denied the right to see his daughter on her birthday (at least until he himself becomes a threat to the family). In *Menace II Society,* sympathy shifts to the sentimental role of the young mother who, struggling to raise her five-year-old son while his father is in jail, is Caine's only counsel. Her plan to leave LA to take a job in Atlanta, a plan that Caine shares until he is shot dead at the moment of departure, may be read as a nostalgic and utopian attempt to reconstruct a patriarchal and pastoral life. In none of the films do we see the patriarchy actually restored; this is the task to be accomplished.

Disobedient Citizenship:
Deconstructing the Oriental

n contemporary narratives of American collapse and national revival, capital itself is Orientalized. In the contemporary labor market, globalized capital is the new yellow peril that threatens to reduce the American worker to the wage levels of Third World workers. The new identification of capital with foreign cultures, from the Indonesian banking conglomerates to the Korean greengrocer, enables the U.S. to camouflage its own leading role in the reorganization of a globalized capitalist economy. The Oriental is, once again, constructed as the alien agent.

The 1990s embodiment of the Asian American as agent of foreign capital is, of course, John Huang. To be sure, it was only with the blessing of his mentors at both the multinational Lippo Group and the Democratic National Committee that he attempted to arrange the marriage between Democratic party politics and the interests of global capital. This marriage had after all had long been a dream of the business-oriented Democratic Leadership Council, which has dominated the Democratic party since the election of the DNC's founding father, Bill Clinton, as president. The payoff for the Asian American matchmakers was supposed to be a greater voice in the public sphere—in particular, a voice in the debates on policy issues of critical concern to Asian American communities (such as immigration). This attempt to buy into American politics as a special-interest group demonstrates how limited is the liberal multiculturalist approach in establishing a place for Asian Americans in the body politic. The

223

attempt to transform Asian American concerns into simple interest-group politics relied on a theory of ethnic assimilation. It ran aground because it ignored the historical construction of Asian Americans as an alien race. As Thomas Oliphant's cartoon and the *National Review*'s cover both make painfully clear, without challenging the Orientalist representation and the structure of racial ideology on which it is built, Asian Americans are always vulnerable to being seen as the alien minion of a foreign power.

In 1943, the same year that Gunnar Myrdal published *An American Dilemma,* Carlos Bulosan published *America Is in the Heart.* Bulosan, a Filipino immigrant, chronicled the struggle of the Pinoys, the approximately 45,000 Filipino migrant workers in the fields, orchards, and canneries of California, Oregon, and Washington. Bulosan gave witness to the degrading living conditions, exploitative wage system, corrupt labor practices, racist brutality, and moral despair that faced the Pinoys.

Like Myrdal, Bulosan also believed in an American creed, but he understood it differently. While Myrdal saw the American creed as a set of ideals that had already shaped the course of American history, Bulosan understood America as a contradiction between the promise of justice and the historical reality of oppression. For Bulosan, the American creed could only be realized through a fierce class struggle for democracy. Such a struggle required understanding of the deep connections between colonialism and capital, between power and privilege. As a writer, Bulosan understood the necessity of creating a powerful counter-narrative as a critique and strategy for resistance.

> It is for the workers that we must write. . . . We must interpret their hopes as a people desiring their fullest fulfillment of their potentialities. We must be strong of voice, objective of criticism, protest and challenge. There is no other way to combat any attempt to suppress individual liberty.[1]

A half century later, we are left asking, "How can Asian American culture assert itself against a popular culture that constructs the Asian American as a stand-in for Orientalized capital?" Mira Nair's 1995 film *Mississippi Masala* suggests precisely such a critique and an alternative imaginary. *Mississippi Masala* tells the story of cross-racial romance between Mina, a young Indian-American woman (Sarita Choudhury) and Demetrius, a young African-American man (Denzel Washington). Nair explores the different and conflicting racial trajectories of Asian, black and white that come together in contemporary Mississippi. The film maps the contradictions within and between political economies structured by race, class, sex, and immigration status. *Mississippi Masala* illustrates the diasporic character of the contemporary Indian-American community and elaborates the transnational histories of Asians as middleman minorities in racially stratified colonial and capitalist societies. Finally, *Mississippi Masala* works as a meditation on the problem of political consciousness and resistance at the intersection of the global and the local.

The film begins in 1972, on the eve of the expulsion of the Indian community from Uganda. Okelo, a black Ugandan, urges his best friend Jay, an Indian Ugandan, to leave the country. Jay asks, "Why should I go? Uganda is my home." Okelo answers with a pained expression, "Africa is for Africans now—black Africans." Coming from his closest friend, someone who has just saved his life from dictator Idi Amin's police, Okelo's answer forces Jay to see that the Indian diaspora in Uganda has come to an end. This recognition is so bitter that despite Okelo's continued devotion and his great affection for Jay's wife Kinnu (Sarmila Tagore) and daughter Mina (Sarita Choudhury), Jay can not bring himself to speak to his friend again.

While the departure scene generates great sympathy for the uprooted Indian families, Nair takes pains to emphasize that the Indian community in Uganda, although now politically vulnerable, has enjoyed a century of economic privilege under British colonialism. Jay's home in the hills above Kampala is a large comfortable bungalow built in classic British colonial style. The serene comfort of the home stands in sharp contrast to the heat and dust of Kampala. In a scene that reveals the distance between the Indian and black communities in Uganda, soldiers force Kinnu off the bus carrying Indians to the airport. The first thing that falls out of her suitcase is a cherished photo of Jay in his barrister's robes and powdered wig, an obvious reminder of the complicity of the Indian community in British colonial rule. A soldier tosses the photo into the mud. Another soldier pulls out a cassette tape player, which plays a Hindi pop tune whose lyrics include the refrain, "my perfume may be French and my hat may be Russian, but my heart is Hindi, Hindi, Hindi." After being stripped of her gold necklace, a humiliated Kinnu is allowed back on the bus full of terrified Indians. The scene reveals not only the present helplessness of the disenfranchised Indian community but also the political privilege (the photo) it had been granted, the cultural isolation (the Hindi tape) it had cultivated, and the wealth (the necklace) it had accumulated.

The film's contemporary plot opens in the parking lot of a Piggly Wiggly supermarket in the small town of Greenwood, Miss., in 1990. The new racial and class dynamics of contemporary Mississippi are suggested when Mina smashes her cousin's car into a van driven by Demetrius, which in turn rear-ends a truck driven by a white redneck. The heated arguments—which in an earlier day would have either been unthinkable or have resulted in violence—are mediated here in the New South by a black police officer.

In a story of downward mobility familiar to hundreds of thousands of other Asian immigrants whose training has not fit the U.S. labor market or its licensing requirements, Jay is unemployed and spends his time petitioning the Ugandan government for the return of his property; Kinnu runs a small and clearly marginal liquor store in the black part of town; and Mina cleans rooms and works the desk at the Monte Cristo motel owned by her uncle. Underscoring the poverty of their now transient and much-reduced lives, the family lives at the Monte Cristo at the sufferance of their relatives.

The garish and somewhat sleazy Monte Cristo Motel is at once quintessentially American and symbolically Indian. It joins the myth of American mobility to the rootlessness of diaspora. The motel industry, which requires little capital but intensive labor, is heavily staffed by immigrant entrepreneurs. The Monte Cristo is the site of struggles of class, ethnicity, sex, and generation in the Indian community of Greenwood.

In an American community where the divide between white and black defines virtually all social relations, skin color is revealed to be a central concern in the diasporic Indian community. Although it resembles the concern over skin color among African Americans, color consciousness in the diasporic Indian community is historically linked both to caste hierarchies in the old homeland and to racial hierarchies in the new homeland. Mina's mother hopes that Mina will attract the favorable attention of Harry Patel, the community's most eligible bachelor. In response, Mina tells her, "Face it, ma, you got a darkie daughter. Harry Patel's mother doesn't like darkies." At a wedding reception, the mothers of two other girls articulate the traditional calculus of color and class, dismissing Mina's chances with young Harry. "You can be dark and have money, or be fair and have no money, but you can't be dark and have no money and still expect to get Harry Patel." The formulation simultaneously exposes the status anxiety of the community and reveals their tacit recognition that race is a social construct.

The romantic relationship between Mina and Demetrius, which drives the plot of *Mississippi Masala* is set in a complex dynamic of Asian, black, and white relations of class and race configured by different but converging histories of slavery, colonialism, and immigration. The presence of Asian Americans disrupts the black and white racial narrative. When Demetrius' partner, Tyrone, meets Mina for the first time, he is attracted to her "exotic" sex appeal. First, he mistakes her for Mexican; then, when she explains that she is Indian, he mistakes her for an American Indian.

In a later scene, a white motel owner has to explain to another who wants to send the Indians "back to the reservation" that "they aren't that kind of Indian."

Mina's transnational history is mapped when she is invited to Sunday supper at Demetrius's house. The brief conversation over supper sketches out the commonalties and differences of the black and Asian diasporas. In response to the curiosity of Demetrius's younger brother, Dexter (Tico Wells), Mina explains that she was born and lived in Africa but, just as he has never been to Africa, she has never been to India. When Mina explains the Indians had been brought to Uganda to build the railroads, Dexter responds, "like slaves." To which Mina, recalling the privileges that the Indian community had come to enjoy, answers weakly, "Not exactly." The history of Indian labor in Uganda, with its origins in the railroads, their transformation into a commercial class, and status as a middleman minority in a racially stratified society is immediately recognizable to us as resembling the racial trajectory of other Asians, notably the Chinese, in the United States.

The inclusion of Indian Americans and other south Asians in the category of Asian American is by no means a foregone conclusion, the *Thind* ruling notwithstanding. Nair establishes a direct link between the new Asian immigrant community and an older Asian community in Mississippi with the introduction of an elderly local Chinese man, a regular customer at the Monte Cristo motel. In the 1870s, Chinese workers were brought to the Mississippi Delta as contract labor to replace the newly free African Americans in the cotton fields. After their contracts ended, most left the plantations, and many managed to become grocers or run small businesses. They intermarried with both black and white and became a third, intermediate community in the black and white race relations of the post-reconstruction South.[2]

In a reversal of the stereotype, it is Demetrius, the owner of his own carpet cleaning business, who is cast as the model minority in this film. Demetrius, not Jay, embodies the Protestant work ethic. While Mina refuses to go to college out of pride since her parents are poor, Demetrius has chosen not to go to college out of a sense of familial obligation; he has decided to look after his elderly widowed father. Demetrius takes great pride in his status as a business owner, which defines his self-identity. It is the first thing that Demetrius tells Mina about himself. Entrepreneurship is not without its cost. Demetrius understands his success to be built on his hard work alone, and this leads him to take a reproachful and self-righteous attitude toward his younger brother, who is an easygoing dreamer, prone to blaming others—particularly whites and "the system"—for his chronic unemployment. Dexter is less a fool than a foil for showing Demetrius as rigid and constrained. Demetrius's identity as a petty capitalist is as much an iron cage as it is for Mina's uncles and cousins, the motel owners.

Demetrius's status as entrepreneur is also contrasted to his elderly father (Seneca Wells), who works long past retirement age as a waiter in the rundown local hotel. He works for a demanding and patronizing white woman, a holdover from the Old South. When Demetrius picks up his father at the hotel, she remarks to a friend, "He's the good one." She takes credit for Demetrius's success, saying that is she who has "vouched for him with the bank." Even as we can see the contrast between Demetrius and his father, we are reminded that it is the whites who control the political economy of Greenwood.

When Demetrius and Mina are discovered sleeping together in the nearby town of Biloxi, the carefully skirted contradictions of race, class, and sex explode into the public sphere. In "new" Mississippi as in Uganda, the power relationships between racialized communities have been rendered invisible; in this case the civility of an official but shallow multiculturalism has allowed the citizens to avoid referring to race or power. No racial slurs were exchanged during the auto accident involving Demetrius and the white working-class truck driver. In the fisticuffs that ensue when Mina's cousins attack Demetrius, claiming sovereignty over "our women," there are no racial taunts (although it is Demetrius and Mina who are arrested). When Mina expresses her anger at racial bigotry, Demetrius observes "racism—only now it's called tradition."

In the wake of Mina's and Demetrius' transgression, a cross-racial network of gossip-mongering becomes the public sphere. Each community interprets this private relationship of desire across races to be a public offense that has disrupted the carefully plotted narrative of multicultural but racially separate harmony. Each racialized community is revealed to have a stake in the racial status quo.

Like Korean groceries, Chinese restaurants, and many other middleman minority enterprises, the Monte Cristo is only a marginally successful business. Despite their ostentation and great pride of ownership in their aging Lincoln, Mina's motel-owning relatives are not wealthy. The car that is the pride and joy of her cousins is big and shiny but hardly new. The motel owner and his sons are thus constantly worried about money. They panic when one cousin warns that "here [in America] everybody sues."

In a scene reminiscent of Spike Lee's *Do The Right Thing*, where the Korean storekeeper saves his store with a sign saying "Asians are black too," Mina's uncle tries to persuade Demetrius not to sue over the accident that Mina has caused. "Black, brown, yellow, Mexican, Puerto

Rican, all the same. As long as you are not white, means you are colored. . . . United we stand, divided we fall."³ This self-serving appeal to racial unity is exposed as the empty rhetoric of a liberal multiculturalism that papers over the real and conflicting relations of power that are present in the exchange. The transparency of the ploy becomes patently evident when the Indian community later punishes Demetrius by canceling their contracts with him.

The conflict between the Asian and black communities reveals the historical continuity of white control over the economy. The white motel owners play off one minority against the other. One white motel owner calls an Indian counterpart to ask rhetorically, "I hear you're having nigger problems now." The white hotel owner withdraws her endorsement of Demetrius, and the loan on his van is called. The white banker asserts that calling the loan is only a matter of business. He disingenuously insists that the successful loan applicant must demonstrate "character, capital, and collateral." Leaving the bank, Demetrius knowingly adds "color" to the qualifications.

It is only through confrontation with the nostalgic myths of diaspora that these contradictions can be resolved. Pressing Mina to end her relationship with Demetrius, Jay asserts that he is not a racist and that he wants only to protect Mina from racism and the pain that he has experienced. "In the end," he says, "after thirty-four years, it came down to the color of my skin." Mina challenges her father's narrative of "why we left Uganda," reminding him, "Okelo risked his life to save yours, I don't know what more proof you need of his love. I remember when he came to say good-bye, you would not even look at him."

Mina identifies with the black community when she declares herself a "darkie," and she takes Harry Patel to the Leopard Lounge, a black club where she feels at home. Her rejection of Harry at the Leopard Lounge consciously demolishes her mother's dream of a "good marriage." In rejecting the socially desirable Harry Patel even before she begins the relationship with Demetrius, she has taken a radical step in asserting control over her body with respect to future marriage. (This is contrasted to the sexually dysfunctional arranged marriage of her cousin.) Mina is conscious that achieving historical agency requires a self-awareness not only in terms of race and sex but of class as well. When Mina offers to join Demetrius, it is to share his economic as well as his romantic life. She tells Demetrius, "I can be your partner—I know how to clean rooms."

The second confrontation is between Jay and Demetrius. When Jay tries to refer to his own experience as victim of racism, Demetrius explodes. "Struggle, struggle" he mimics, "Look, I'm a black man born and raised in Mississippi, not a damn thing you can tell me about struggle." He

continues with a scathing indictment of the Indian community in Greenwood, telling the other side to the diasporic story.

> You and your folks can come down here from God knows where and be
> about as black as the ace of spades and as soon as you get here, you start
> acting white and treating us like your our doormats. I know that you and
> your daughter ain't but a few shades from this right here [pointing to his
> own face], *that* I know.

This confrontation forces Jay to recognize that in constructing his nostalgic narrative of diaspora, "after thirty-four years, it came down to the
color of my skin," he has reproduced the same reductionist logic of race
that he so bitterly assigns to Idi Amin. This racial narrative has repressed
his own political consciousness, his own understanding of the complicity
of Indians in Uganda's exploitation and its subsequent dictatorship. In a
flashback to his final evening in a Kampala bar, Jay recalls that he had
admonished his Indian drinking partners, "We helped create Idi Amin.
Most people are born with five senses. We are left with only one—sense
of property."

After Mina and Demetrius leave Greenwood, Jay finally returns to
Uganda alone. Kinnu will not return with him. On his return, Jay discovers his house in ruins, and worse, that Okelo had been killed shortly after the Indians had left. Jay realizes that years of nostalgic mythmaking
about his homeland have been an illusion. Jay writes to Kinnu in Greenwood, "Home is where the heart is, and my heart is with you," a declaration that is trite except in the context of diaspora. In the final scene of
the film, Jay returns to the Kampala marketplace, the scene of his family's
departure from their "homeland." It is now filled with color and vi-
brancy. There, he watches young Ugandans dancing, and he picks up
and tenderly holds an African baby, a child who symbolizes both a global
future and his own future grandchild. He can only hold on to this future
after he has jettisoned his nostalgic past.

On its surface, *Mississippi Masala*'s utopian ending may seem sentimental, even to the point of being maudlin, but it would be a mistake to
let such a reading distract us from the radical potential of Nair's work.
Mississippi Masala's utopian resolution can only be imagined on the basis of a class struggle through a materialist engagement with history. Such
a utopian vision is resonant of another Asian American narrative of
struggle, Carlos Bulosan's *America Is in The Heart*. Bulosan understood
America's promise in terms of the legacies of colonialism, the violence of
race, the inequities of sex, and class exploitation. He also understood that
political consciousness—the consciousness of the histories of peoples
in struggle—was the necessary first step to realizing the promise of
freedom.

A half century ago, Bulosan wrote:

America is not a land of one race or one class of men. We are all Americans that have toiled and suffered and known oppression and defeat, from the first Indian that offered peace in Manhattan to the last Filipino pea pickers. America is not bound by geographical latitudes. America is not merely a land or an institution. America is in the hearts of men that died for freedom, it is also in the eyes of men that are building a new world. America is a prophecy of a new society. . . . The old world is dying but a new world is being born. It generates inspiration from the chaos that beats upon us all.[4]

Notes

Preface

1. On these settlements, see Marina Espina in Fred Cordova, ed., *Filipinos: Forgotten Asian Americans* (Seattle: Demonstration Project for Asian Americans, 1983), 1–7.

2. "Grisly Account of Ly Killing Believed Penned by Suspect," *Los Angeles Times,* Orange County edition, March 7, 1996. Even the racially motivated murder of Asian Americans is slow to provoke other Americans to think of Asians Americans as fellow citizens. The murder of Vincent Chin, a Chinese American engineer, became newsworthy only when Asian Americans organized to protest the fact that Chin's murderers, two white autoworkers, were fined and given no jail sentences because they were otherwise considered good citizens. Despite the fact that the killer of five Cambodian children in a Stockton schoolyard in 1989 confessed to the crime, citing as his inspiration the Vietnam revenge movie *Rambo,* the national media chose to treat the Stockton schoolyard killings not as hate crimes but rather as a problem of the availability of automatic weapons.

3. See the National Asian Pacific Legal Consortium, "Audit of Violence Against Asian Pacific Americans: The Consequences of Intolerance in America," Third Annual Report (Washington, D.C., 1996), 1.

4. See Karl Marx, "The Eighteenth Brumaire of Louis Napoleon," in Robert C. Tucker, ed., *The Marx Engels Reader* (New York: W. W. Norton, 1978), 595.

Introduction: Yellowface

1. Non-Asians fined by the Federal Election Commission for illegal contributions to the Clinton-Gore re-election campaign included Simon Fireman, who was fined $6 million (the largest such fine ever levied), and Thomas Kramer, a German national who was fined $323,000. See "Petition of the National Asian Pacific American Legal Consortium et al. to the United States Commission on Civil Rights," September 10, 1997, reprinted at http://www2.ari.net/oca/camp/complain.html.

2. *Takao Ozawa v. United States,* 260 U.S. 178 (1922).

3. Mary Douglas, *Purity and Danger: An Analysis of the Concepts of Pollution and Taboo* (London and New York: Ark Paperbacks, 1966), 54.

4. *Ozawa,* and *United States v. Bhagat Singh Thind,* 261 U.S. 204 (1923). For an analysis of these cases, see Philip Tajitsu Nash in Hyung Chan Kim, ed., *Asian Americans and the Supreme Court* (Hamden, Conn.: Greenwood Press, 1993), and Jeff H. Lesser, "Always Outsiders: Asians, Naturalization and the Supreme Court: 1740–1944," *Amerasia Journal* 12 (1985): 83–100.

5. See "Petition of the National Asian Pacific American Legal Consortium et al. to the United States Commission on Civil Rights."

6. For a detailed analysis of the media coverage of the John Huang affair, see Frank Wu and May Nicholson, "Racial Aspects of Media Coverage of the John Huang Matter," *Asian American Policy Review* 7 (1997): 1–37.

7. An alternative view, which locates the image of the Chinese immigrant in America in the constellation of racial images in nineteenth-century American culture, is Ronald Takaki, *Iron Cages: Race and Culture in Nineteenth-Century America* (Seattle: University of Washington Press, 1979). Takaki's view, like Alexander Saxton's in *The Rise and Fall of the White Republic* (London and New York: Verso, 1990), is a Gramscian class analysis.

8. For a succinct review of these debates, see John Storey, *An Introductory Guide to Cultural Theory and Popular Culture* (Athens, Ga.: University of Georgia Press, 1993).

9. Jurgen Habermas argues that the idea of the citizen came into being in the public sphere that emerged in the seventeenth and eighteenth centuries in bourgeois drawing rooms, salons, and cafes. This public sphere was a social space between the realm of the state and the realm of civil society (composed of the private family sphere and the sphere of commodity exchange and social labor). The public sphere is the realm in which the individual is constituted as public citizen and where he (the bourgeois male, in Habermas's historical account) makes his interests heard by the state. See Jurgen Habermas, *The Structural Transformation of the Public Sphere: An Inquiry into a Category of Bourgeois Society,* translated by Thomas Burger (Cambridge: Massachusetts Institute of Technology Press, 1989). Habermas's focus on a single public sphere defined by the political emancipation of the bourgeois male has been challenged by Nancy Fraser and others, who argue for the existence of multiple public spheres whose participants include the disenfranchised and the marginalized: women, racial minorities, and the working class. See Nancy Fraser, *Power, Discourse, and Gender in Contemporary Social Theory* (Minneapolis: University of Minnesota Press, 1989), and "What's Critical about Critical Theory? The Case of Gender," in *Unruly Practices* (Minneapolis: University of Minnesota Press, 1990); and Craig Calhoun, "Populist Politics, Communications Media, and Large Scale Societal Integration," *Sociological Theory* 6 (no. 2, 1988): 219–241.

10. On the significance of saloon, boardwalks, and popular theater see, respectively, Roy Rosenzweig, *Eight Hours for What We Will: Workers and Leisure in an Industrial City, 1870–1920* (New York: Cambridge University Press, 1983); Kathy Peiss, *Cheap Amusements: Working Women and Leisure in Turn-of-the-Century New York* (Philadelphia: Temple University Press, 1986); and Sean Wilentz, *Chants Demo-*

cratic: New York City & the Rise of the American Working Class, 1788–1850 (New York: Oxford University Press, 1984).

11. The notion of hegemony comes, of course, from Gramsci. For a critique that emphasizes the incomplete and contested nature of hegemony, see James Scott, *Domination and the Arts of Resistance: Hidden Transcripts* (New Haven: Yale University Press, 1990).

12. The thesis that sovereignty rests in the privatized body is John Locke's. See the chapter "On Property" in *The Second Treatise of Government,* edited by Thomas P. Reardon (Indianapolis: Bobbs-Merrill, 1952), 16–30. On the "abstract citizen," see also Lisa Lowe, *Immigrant Acts: On Asian American Cultural Politics* (Durham, N.C.: Duke University Press, 1996), 2.

13. Sociologists Michael Omi and Howard Winant argue that race cannot be explained as simply a subcategory or an epiphenomenon of another single social dynamic such as class formation or ethnicity, but instead exists as a separate category of social difference. They argue that the production and reproduction of race is historically contingent, decentered, and contested. Michael Omi and Howard Winant, *Racial Formation in the United States: From the 1960s to the 1990s,* 2nd ed. (New York and London: Routledge, 1994), 53–76 passim.

14. On the family as ideological structure, see Stephanie Coontz, *The Way We Never Were: American Families and the Nostalgia Trap* (New York: Basic Books, 1992).

15. In Habermas's reconstruction of the bourgeois public sphere, the patriarchal family operated as a private realm in which the bourgeois male could establish his individualized selfhood and enter into the public sphere (and presumably represent the interests of the family).

16. David Bell, "The Secret of Asian American Success," *The New Republic,* July 15–22, 1985: 24–31.

17. See David Roediger, *The Wages of Whiteness: Race and the Making of the American Working Class* (London and New York: Verso, 1991).

18. Alexander Saxton, *The Indispensable Enemy: Labor and the Anti-Chinese Movement in California* (Berkeley, University of California Press, 1971).

19. Lothrop Stoddard, *The Rising Tide of Color Against White World-Supremacy* (New York: Charles Scribner's Sons, 1920).

20. See, for example, T. J. Jackson Lears, *No Place of Grace: Antimodernism and the Transformation of American Culture, 1880–1920* (New York: Pantheon Books, 1981).

21. Of the many and varied periodizations of American economic history, the one I have found most useful for this study is the analysis of changes in the labor market and the social structure of accumulation by David M. Gordon, Richard Edwards, and Michael Reich, *Segmented Work, Divided Workers: The Historical Transformation of Labor in the United States* (New York: Cambridge University Press, 1982). They examine the relationship between long cycles of economic activity and the social structure of accumulation. They outline three periods in the development of American capitalism with regard to labor:

- Initial proletarianization, from the 1820s to the 1890s.
- Homogenization, from the 1870s to the onset of World War I, during which the labor markets became more competitive and the dominance of skilled

crafts positions was diminished by the large-scale introduction of semiskilled labor.

• Segmentation, from the 1920s to the present, during which political and economic forces have produced qualitative differences in the organization of work and three distinct labor markets: a secondary labor market, plus a primary labor market divided into independent and subordinate sectors.

Gordon et al. link these broad periods to long swings (on the order of twenty-five years) in global economic activity, each associated with a distinct social structure of accumulation, the institutional environment in which capital accumulation takes place. For a periodization shaped by both economy and culture, see Herbert Gutman, *Work, Culture, and Society in Industrializing America: Essays in American Working-Class and Social History* (New York: Knopf, 1976), 1–78.

22. I use "emergent" here in the same counterhegemonic sense that Raymond Williams uses the term in *Culture and Society* (London: Penguin, 1971).

23. See Ella Shohat and Robert Stam, *Unthinking Eurocentrism: Multiculturalism in the Media* (London: Routledge, 1994), 178.

24. British theorist T. H. Marshall identifies three elements of citizenship in a social democracy: civil rights, political rights, and social rights. T. H. Marshall, *Citizenship and Social Class* (Cambridge, England: Cambridge University Press, 1950), 12–27. On the struggle to broaden definitions of citizenship in American history, see James A. Morone, *The Democratic Wish: Popular Participation and the Limits of American Government* (New York: Basic Books, 1990).

28. Sucheng Chan, *Asian Americans: An Interpretive History* (Boston: Twayne, 1991), 90. See also Hyung Chan Kim, ed., *Asian Americans and the Supreme Court;* Sucheng Chan, ed., *Entry Denied: Exclusion and the Chinese Community In America, 1882–1943* (Philadelphia: Temple University Press, 1991); and Charles J. McClain, *In Search of Equality: The Chinese Struggle Against Discrimination in Nineteenth-Century America* (Berkeley, Calif.: University of California Press, 1994).

29. Lowe, *Immigrant Acts,* 29.

One: The "Heathen Chinee" on God's Free Soil

1. "What Was Your Name in the States?" reprinted in Richard A. Dwyer and Richard E. Lingenfelter, *The Songs of the American West* (Berkeley and Los Angeles: University of California Press, 1968), 313.

2. Dwyer and Lingenfelter, *The Songs of the American West.*

3. Nicholas E. Tawa, *A Music for the Millions: Antebellum Democratic Attitudes and the Birth of American Popular Music* (New York: Pendragon Press, 1984), 18.

4. Regarding music as linguistic codes and group solidarity, see Mary Douglas, *Natural Symbols: Exploration in Cosmology* (London: Barrie & Jenkins, 1973), 22.

5. Ronald L. Davis, *A History of Music in American Life, Volume I: The Formative Years, 1620–1865* (Malabar, Florida: Robert Krieger Publishing Company, 1982), 242.

6. Tawa, *A Music for the Millions,* 6.

7. Russell Sanjek, *American Popular Music and Its Business: The First Four Hun-*

dred Years, Volume II, 1790–1909 (New York and Oxford: Oxford University Press, 1988), 145.

8. "Ho! For California!" Text: *Book of Words of the Hutchinson Family* (New York: Baker, Godwin & Co., 1851); Music to "De Boatman Dance," *American Songs;* reprinted in Richard A. Dwyer and Richard E. Lingenfelter, eds., *The Songs of the Gold Rush* (Berkeley: University of California Press, 1964), 15–16.

9. Emmett wrote for and performed on the minstrel stage and was adamantly opposed to both secession and abolition. In addition to a number of well-known minstrel songs, such as "Blue Tail Fly" and "Old Dan Tucker," Dan Emmett is popularly credited with having written "Dixie."

10. Robert Gordon, Richard Edwards, and Michael Reich, *Segmented Work, Divided Workers: The Historical Transformation of Labor in the United States* (Cambridge and New York: Cambridge University Press, 1982).

11. Henry George, *Progress and Poverty: An Inquiry Into the Cause of Industrial Depressions and of Increase of Want With Increase of Wealth* (New York: Walter J. Black, 1942), 51.

12. In *The Condition of Postmodernity: An Enquiry Into the Origins of Cultural Change* (Cambridge, Mass.: Blackwell, 1990), cultural geographer David Harvey gives an important critique of postmodernism as a response to the transition from Fordist capitalist production to a stage of capitalism he calls "flexible accumulation." Harvey writes that flexible accumulation is experienced culturally as a collapse of spatial and temporal boundaries. I believe that the transition into industrial capitalism occasioned a similar boundary crisis. See also Stephen Kern, *The Culture of Time and Space, 1880–1918* (Cambridge, Mass.: Harvard University Press, 1983).

13. Herbert Gutmann, *Work, Society and Culture in Industrializing America* (New York: Vintage, 1977), 29.

14. John Walton Caughey, *Hubert Howe Bancroft: Historian of the West* (Berkeley: University of California Press, 1946); Hubert Howe Bancroft, *California Inter Pocula* (San Francisco: The History Company, 1888), 274.

15. Ibid., 275.

16. Ibid., 270.

17. Ibid., 275.

18. Ibid., 263–264.

19. See Robert G. Lee, "The Origins of Chinese Immigration to the United States 1848–1882," in *The Life, Influence, and History of the Chinese in the United States, 1775–1975* (San Francisco: Chinese Historical Association of America, n.d.), 183–193; also Kil Young Zo, *Chinese Emigration to the United States, 1850–1880* (New York: Arno Press, 1978).

20. Thomas Chinn, Mark Lai, and Philip Choy, eds., *A History of the Chinese in California: A Syllabus* (San Francisco: Chinese Historical Society of America, 1969), 9–10.

21. Ibid., 15.

22. Mary Roberts Coolidge, *Chinese Immigration* (New York: Henry Holt and Co., 1958), 498.

23. *California China Mail and Flying Dragon* (March 1, 1867), 1.

24. William Issel and Robert W. Cherny, *San Francisco, 1865–1932: Politics, Power, and Urban Development* (Berkeley: University of California Press, 1986), 10.

25. Ibid., 15.

26. See Lee, "Origins," 190.

27. David Montgomery, *The Fall of the House of Labor: The Workplace, the State, and American Labor Activism, 1865–1925* (Cambridge: Cambridge University Press, 1987), 73.

28. Bancroft, *California Inter Pocula*, 275–276.

29. Issel and Cherny, *San Francisco*, 14.

30. Ibid., 277.

31. An account of Helper's career as a Southern racist abolitionist is in George M. Fredrickson, *The Arrogance of Race: Historical Perspectives on Slavery, Racism and Social Inequality* (Middletown, Conn: Wesleyan University Press, 1988).

32. Ibid.

33. John A. Stone and G. P. Knauff, "California Ball," published in *Golden Songster*, reprinted in Dwyer and Lingenfelter, *The Songs of the Gold Rush*, 127.

34. Hinton R. Helper, *The Land of Gold: Reality Versus Fiction* (Baltimore: Henry Taylor, 1855), 60.

35. Ibid., 57.

36. Issel and Cherny, *San Francisco*, 14.

37. *Billy Rice's Ethiopian Comic Songster* (New York: New York Popular Publishing Co., 1883).

38. Edward Said, *Orientalism* (New York: Vintage, 1979), 55.

39. Charlotte Elizabeth Smith, "West Meets East: Exhibitions of Chinese Material Culture in Nineteenth-Century America" (master's thesis, University of Delaware, 1987), 7.

40. Hongs were the Chinese companies licensed to do business with foreign merchants in Canton. The Hong merchant Howqua was reputedly one of the wealthiest men in the mid-nineteenth-century world. Since American merchants often lacked sufficient funds to purchase Chinese goods, Howqua was often paid in stocks of New England companies. He had interests in a number of New England textile factories and invested in the railroad development of the Midwest. See, for example, John K. Fairbank, *Trade and Diplomacy on the China Coast: The Opening of the Treaty Ports, 1842–1854* (Cambridge: Harvard University Press, 1953); Yen-ping Hao, *The Comprador in Nineteenth-Century China: Bridge between East and West* (Cambridge: Harvard University Press, 1970).

41. Smith, "West Meets East," 8.

42. Ibid., 32.

43. James S. Moy, *Marginal Sights: Staging the Chinese in America* (Iowa City: University of Iowa Press, 1993).

44. See Jennifer Jang, "Freaks of Culture: Siamese Twins and Raising the Specter of the Eurasian" (unpublished paper, Brown University, 1990); John Kuo Wei Tchen, "Believing is Seeing: Transforming Orientalism and the Occidental Gaze," in *Asia/American: Identities in Contemporary Asian American Art*, Curator Margo Machida (New York: The Asia Society Galleries and the New Press, 1994);

and Leslie Fiedler, *Freaks: Myths and Images of the Secret Self* (New York: Simon and Schuster, 1978).

45. With specific reference to East Asia and the Pacific, see the essays in Part II of Vincent Rafael, ed., *Discrepant Histories: Translocal Essays on Filipino Cultures* (Philadelphia: Temple University Press, 1995).

46. Mary Douglas, *Purity and Danger: An Analysis of the Concepts of Pollution and Taboo* (London and New York: Ark Paperbacks, 1966), 116.

47. Joanne Pope Melish, "Disowning Slavery: Gradual Emancipation and the Cultural Construction of 'Race' in New England, 1780–1860" (Ph.D. dissertation, Brown University, 1996).

48. The literature on Blackface minstrelsy is voluminous. See Robert C. Toll, *Blacking Up: The Minstrel Show In Nineteenth-Century America* (New York: Oxford University Press, 1974); Eric Lott, *Love And Theft: Blackface Minstrelsy And The American Working Class* (New York: Oxford University Press, 1993); and Alexander Saxton, *The Rise and Fall of the White Republic: Class Politics and Mass Culture in Nineteenth-Century America* (London and New York: Verso, 1990).

49. Alexander Saxton, *The Rise and Fall of the White Republic*, 165–181.

50. David Roediger, *Towards the Abolition of Whiteness: Essays on Race, Politics, and Working Class History* (London: Verso, 1994).

51. Douglas, *Purity and Danger*, 44.

52. *"Bones," His Gags and Stump Speeches: Nigger and Dutch Stories and Dialogues, "Broken China" Dialect Pieces, and Other Conundrums* (New York: Wehman Bros., 1879), 38.

53. J. L. Dillard, *Black English: Its History and Usage in the United States* (New York: Random House, 1972). See also Anton Bauer, *Das Kanton-Englisch: ein Pidginidiom als Beispiel fur ein soziolinguistisches Kulturkontaktphanomen* (Bern: Herbert Lang; Frankfurt: Peter Lang, 1975).

54. *Nick Gardner's Two Ring Circus Songster* [publisher, date unknown].

55. Chas A. Loder, *Chas A. Loder's Hilarity Songster: Containing a Collection of All the Favorite Songs as Sung by This Great German Comedian* (New York: New York Popular Publishing Company, 1885).

56. Luke Schoolcraft, *Shine On: Remembrances of the South*, arranged by John Braham, music by Luke Schoolcraft (Boston: Louis P. Goullaud, 1874).

57. Anne Norton, *Alternative Americas: A Reading of Antebellum Political Culture* (Chicago and London: Univ. of Chicago Press, 1986), 204.

58. Cited in Carroll Smith-Rosenberg, *Disorderly Conduct: Visions of Gender in Victorian America* (New York and Oxford: Oxford University Press, 1985), 98.

59. Ibid., 97.

60. Schoolcraft, "Heathen Chinee," in *The Wedding of the Chinee and the Coon* (publisher and date unknown), 6.

61. *Billy Rice's Chinese Ball and Other Songs* (New York: New York Popular Publishing Co., n.d.). "Meuse" is a shortened version of *gemeuse*, the German word for vegetable.

62. Gary Scharnhorst, ed., *Bret Harte's California: Letters to the "Springfield Republican" and "Christian Register," 1866–67* (Albuquerque: University of New Mexico Press, 1990), 113.

63. Carl I. Wheat, ed., "California's Bantam Cock: The Journals of Charles De Long," *California Historical Society Quarterly* 8:3 (September 1929), 345.

64. On the history of scalping among Native Americans, French, and English colonists, see James Axtell, *The European and the Indian: Essays in the Ethnohistory of Colonial North America* (New York: Oxford University Press, 1981), 207–244; and Ellen Rawson Wood, *Californians and Chinese, The First Decade* (master's thesis, University of California, Berkeley, 1961), 37–39 *passim*.

65. Schoolcraft, *Shine On*, 14.

66. "Hong Kong," in *Nick Gardner's Two Ring Circus*.

67. Hinton R. Helper, *The Land of Gold: Reality versus Fiction* (Baltimore: Henry Taylor, 1855).

68. Ibid., 88.

69. Ibid., 88–89.

70. Ibid., 86.

71. Ibid., 86.

72. Stone, *Put's Original California Songster*, 29.

73. "John Chinaman," reprinted in Dwyer and Lingenfelter, *The Songs of the Gold Rush*, 121.

74. Helper, *The Land of Gold*, 77.

75. Eric Foner, *Free Soil, Free Labor, Free Men: The Ideology of the Republican Party Before the Civil War* (New York: Oxford University Press, 1970), 17–23.

75. Thomas Jefferson, *Notes on the State of Virginia*, ed. William Peden (New York: Norton, 1954),137–138.

76. Joanne Pope Melish, "Disowning Slavery: Gradual Emancipation and the Cultural Construction of 'Race' in New England, 1780–1860" (Ph.D. dissertation, Brown University, 1996), 2–5.

77. 15 March 1848. Cited in Lucile Eaves, *A History of California Labor Legislation* (Berkeley: The University Press, University of California Publications in Economics, 1910), 82.

78. March 25, 1848. Cited in Ibid., 83.

79. Ibid., 84.

80. Ibid., 84.

81. Ibid., 85–86.

82. Ibid., 85.

83. Ping Chiu, *Chinese Labor in California, 1850–1880: An Economic Study* (Madison: State Historical Society of Wisconsin, 1967), ix.

84. The "long tom," a simple but relatively inefficient placer frame, was identified as principally a device used by the Chinese in *The Miner's Own Book, Containing Correct Illustrations and Descriptions of the Various Modes of California Mining, Including All the Improvements Introduced from the Earliest Day to the Present Time* (San Francisco: Hutchings & Rosenfield, 1858).

85. Dwyer and Lingenfelter, *Songs of the American West*, 309.

86. Hyung-chan Kim, *Asian Americans and the Supreme Court* (Westport, Conn.: Greenwood Press, 1992), 404.

87. Ibid., 6.

88. Helper, *Land of Gold*, 95–96.

89. "The Days of '49," text and music E. Zimmer (San Francisco: Sherman and Hyde, 1876); reprinted in Dwyer and Lingenfelter, *Songs of the American West,* 127.

Two: The Coolie and the Making of the White Working Class

1. The *Wasp* (November 7, 1885), 16; reprinted in Philip P. Choy, Lorraine Dong, and Marlon K. Hom, *Coming Man: 19th Century American Perceptions of the Chinese* (Hong Kong: Joint Publishing Co., 1994),123.

2. David Roediger, *The Wages of Whiteness: Race and the Making of the American Working Class* (London and New York: Verso, 1990), 59–60; see also Alexander Saxton, *The Rise and Fall of the White Republic: Class Politics and Mass Culture in Nineteenth-Century America* (London and New York: Verso, 1990).

3. David M. Gordon, Richard Edwards, and Michael Reich, *Segmented Work, Divided Workers: The Historical Transformation of Labor in the United States* (Cambridge: Cambridge University Press, 1982), 67.

4. Ibid., 69.

5. Ibid., 68.

6. Ibid., 69.

7. Ibid., 113.

8. David Roediger, *Wages of Whiteness,* 87.

9. David Montgomery, *Workers' Control in America: Studies in the History of Work, Technology and Labor Struggles* (Cambridge: Cambridge University Press, 1979), 58.

10. Ibid., 60.

11. Marcus Cunliffe, *Chattel Slavery and Wage Slavery: The Anglo-American Context, 1830–1860* (Athens: University of Georgia Press, 1979).

12. For a biography of Burritt, see Merle Curti, *The Learned Blacksmith: The Letters and Journals of Elihu Burritt* (New York: Wilson-Erickson, 1937).

13. Elihu Burritt, *A Plan of Brotherly Copartnership of the North and South, for the Peaceful Extinction of Slavery* (New York: Dayton and Burdick, 1856), 48.

14. Ibid., 47.

15. Bill Ong Hing, *Making and Remaking Asian America through U.S. Immigration Law* (Stanford: Stanford University Press, 1994), 239.

16. Elmer Clarence Sandmeyer, *The Anti-Chinese Movement in California* (Chicago: Illinois Studies in the Social Sciences, 1939) reprinted with foreword and supplementary bibliographies by Roger Daniels, University of Illinois Press, 1991, 25. Sandmeyer's remains the best organizational study of the official movement.

17. Alexander Saxton's *The Indispensable Enemy: Labor and the Anti-Chinese Movement in California* (Berkeley: University of California Press, 1971) details the rise of Kearny and the Workingman's Party of California and the party's complicated relationship to the labor movement.

18. *The Blue and Grey Songster* (San Francisco: S. S. Green, 1877), 16–17.

19. Ibid.

20. Terrence Powderly, the first president of the Knights of Labor, dissolved Chinese assemblies that had been established in New York City. Powderly later was appointed the first U.S. Commissioner of Immigration, which offered him

the opportunity to rigorously enforce the Chinese Exclusion act. See Philip Foner, *American Socialism and the Black Worker, From the Age of Jackson to World War II* (Hamden, Conn.: Greenwood Press, 1977), 375; and Philip Foner and Daniel Rosenberg, eds., *Racism, Dissent, and Asian Americans from the 1880s to the Present: A Documentary History* (Westport, Conn.: Greenwood Press, 1993).

21. An account of the Rock Springs Massacre is found in Roger Daniels, *Asian America: Chinese and Japanese in the United States Since 1850* (Seattle: University of Washington Press, 1988), 59–62.

22. On anti-Chinese violence in the nineteenth century generally, see Roger Daniels, ed., *Anti-Chinese Violence in North America* (New York: Arno Press, 1978).

23. Ping Chiu, *Chinese Labor in California* (Madison: University of Wisconsin Press, 1963), 47.

24. Ibid., 50.

25. Lucy Cohen, *Chinese in the Post–Civil War South: A People Without a History* (Baton Rouge: Louisiana State University Press, 1984).

26. See Kristen Farmelant, "The Coming of the Chinese to North Adams," (unpublished paper, Brown University, 1992).

27. Renqiu Yu, *To Save China, To Save Ourselves: The Chinese Hand Laundry Alliance* (Philadelphia: Temple University Press, 1992), 9.

28. Philip Foner, *American Socialism and Black Americans: From the Age of Jackson to World War II* (Westport, Conn.: Greenwood Press, 1977), 378.

29. Ibid., 67.

30. L. Perry Curtis, *Apes and Angels: The Irishman in Victorian Caricature* (Washington, D.C.: Smithsonian Institution Press, 1971).

31. *The Berkshire Eagle* (March 14, 1868).

32. Gary Scharnhorst, ed., *Bret Harte's California: Letters to the Springfield Republican and Christian Register, 1866–67* (Albuquerque: University of New Mexico Press, 1990), 114.

33. *Hide and Leather* 3: 43 (July 1869).

34. *North Adams Transcript* (August 1, 1875).

35. Ibid. (August 8, 1875).

36. For differing views on Irish racial attitudes, see Noel Ignatiev, *How the Irish Became White* (New York: Routledge, 1995); Roediger, *The Wages of Whiteness;* and Theodore Allen, *The Invention of the White Race* (New York: Verso, 1994).

37. "John Chinaman," in *The Blue and Gray Songster* (San Francisco: S. S. Green, 1877), 16–17.

38. P. J. Downey, *A Workingman's Thoughts Songster* (New York: New York Popular Publishing Co., 1881), 53.

39. Despite the cost and discomfort of trans-Pacific travel and increasing American immigration regulations that made it risky to leave the United States if one wanted to return, there was considerable circular travel between China and the United States as well as to Australia, Canada, and Southeast Asia. This may have inflated the number of exits from U.S. ports.

40. See Sucheng Chan, "Asian and European Immigration Compared," in *Immigration Reconsidered: History, Sociology, and Politics,* Virginia Yans-McLaughlin, ed. (New York and Oxford: Oxford University Press, 1990).

41. Sucheng Chan, ed., *Entry Denied: Exclusion and the Chinese Community in America, 1882–1943* (Philadelphia: Temple University Press, 1991).

42. J. L. Dillard, *Black English: Its History and Usage in the United States* (New York: Random House, 1972)

43. Jack Kuo Wei Tchen, "Quimbo Appo's Fear of Fenians: Anglo-Irish-Chinese Relations in New York City," in Ronald H. Bayor and Timothy Meagher, eds., *New York Irish, 1625–1990* (Baltimore: Johns Hopkins University Press, 1996).

44. Ibid., 11.

45. Charles MacCabe Jr., *New York by Sunlight and Gaslight* (New York: George MacCabe, Jr., 1882).

46. Roediger, *The Wages of Whiteness,* 154–155.

47. "Hay Sing, Come From China," in Richard E. Lingenfelter, Richard A. Dwyer, and David Cohen, eds., *Songs of the American West* (Berkeley: University of California Press, 1968), 304.

48. "Marriage of John Chinaman," in J. Walter Connor, *Connor's Irish Song Book* (San Francisco: D. E. Appleton & Co., 1868), 60–61.

49. T. S. Denison, *Patsy O'Wang: An Irish Farce With a Chinese Mix-Up* (Chicago: T. S. Denison, 1895).

50. Ibid., 3.

51. Ibid., 2.

52. Ibid., 5.

53. Ibid., 30.

54. Ibid., 32.

55. Louis J. Beck, *New York's Chinatown: A Historical Presentation of Its People and Places* (New York: Bohemia Publishing Co., 1899), 250–260.

56. Ibid., 261.

Three: The Third Sex

1. Philip P. Choy, Lorraine Dong, and Marlon K. Hom, *Coming Man: 19th Century American Perceptions of the Chinese* (Hong Kong: Joint Publishing Co., 1994).

2. Dale Baum, "Woman Suffrage and the 'Chinese Question,'" *New England Quarterly* 56 (March 1983): 60–77.

3. Kathryn Kish Sklar, "The Historical Foundations of Woman's Power in the Creation of the American Welfare State, 1830–1930," in Seth Koven and Sony Michel, eds., *Mothers of a New World: Maternalist Politics and the Origins of Welfare States* (New York and London: Routledge, 1993), 51.

4. Peggy Pascoe, *Relations of Rescue: The Search for Female Moral Authority in the American West, 1874–1939* (New York and Oxford: Oxford University Press, 1990).

5. Marjorie Garber, *Vice Versa: Bisexuality and the Eroticism of Everyday Life* (New York: Simon & Schuster, 1995).

6. See, for example, essays in Andrew Parker et al., eds., *Nationalisms and Sexualities* (New York and London: Routledge, 1992). With regard to Asian Americans, see essays by Eric Reyes, Mona Oikawa, Jennifer Ting, Martin Manalansan,

and Alice Hom in Gary Y. Okihiro et al., eds., *Privileging Positions: The Sites of Asian American Studies* (Pullman, Wash.: Washington State University Press, 1995).

7. Stephanie Coontz, *The Social Origins of Private Life: A History of American Families 1600–1900* (London: Verso, 1988).

8. The distinction and complex relationship between the homosocial and the homosexual is discussed in Eve Kosofsky Sedgwick, *Between Men: English Literature and Male Homosocial Desire* (New York: Columbia University Press, 1985): 1–5, 21–27.

9. See, for example, Christine Stansell, *City of Women: Sex and Class in New York, 1789–1860* (New York: Knopf, 1986); and Kathy Peiss, *Cheap Amusements: Working Women and Leisure in Turn-of-the- Century New York* (Philadelphia: Temple University Press, 1986).

10. Coontz, *The Social Origins of Private Life,* 224–236.

11. The literature on the West as a gendered, imaginary space is large. See Richard Slotkin, *Regeneration Through Violence: The Mythology Of The American Frontier, 1600–1860* (Middletown, Conn.: Wesleyan University Press, 1973); *The Fatal Environment: The Myth of the Frontier in the Age of Industrialization, 1800–1890* (New York: Atheneum, 1985); and *Gunfighter Nation: The Myth of the Frontier in Twentieth-Century America* (New York: Atheneum, 1992). See also Annette Kolodny, *The Land Before Her: Fantasy and Experience of the American Frontiers, 1630–1860* (Chapel Hill: University of North Carolina Press, 1984); and *The Lay of the Land: Metaphor as Experience and History in American Life and Letters* (Chapel Hill: University of North Carolina Press, 1975).

12. Carroll Smith-Rosenberg, *Disorderly Conduct: Visions of Gender in Victorian America* (New York: Knopf, 1985) 60.

13. Sedgewick, *Between Men,* 21–27.

14. Kolodny, *The Land before Her;* Henry Nash Smith, *Virgin Land: The American West as Symbol and Myth* (New York: Vintage, 1950).

15. Peiss, *Cheap Amusements,* Chapter 3.

16. Barbara Meil Hobson, *Uneasy Virtue: The Politics of Prostitution and the American Reform Tradition* (Chicago and London: University of Chicago Press, 1987).

17. Lucie Cheng Hirata, "Free, Indentured, Enslaved: Chinese Prostitutes in Nineteenth Century America," *Signs* 5:1 (1979), 3–29.

18. Helen Campbell, *Darkness and Daylight: Lights and Shadows of New York Life, A Pictorial Record* (Hartford, Conn.: The Hartford Publishing Company, 1898).

19. Anne Butler, *Daughter of Joy, Sisters of Misery: Prostitutes in the American West* (Champagne-Urbana: University of Illinois Press, 1985), 6.

20. Workingman's Party of California, Anti-Chinese Council Investigating Committee, *Chinatown Declared a Nuisance!* (San Francisco, March 10, 1880).

21. Lydia Maria Child, *The History of the Condition of Women in Various Ages and Nations, Volume 1: Comprising the Women of Asia and Africa* (Boston: Otis, Broaders and Company, 1838).

22. Peggy Pascoe, *Relations of Rescue: The Search for Female Moral Authority in the American West, 1874–1939* (New York and Oxford: Oxford University Press, 1990).

23. Ambrose Bierce, "The Haunted Valley," *Overland Monthly* 7:1 (July 1871),

91; Mary Mote, "Poor Ah Toy," *The Californian Overland Monthly,* 2:5 (April 1882), 371–382.

24. William Wu, *The Yellow Peril: Chinese Americans in American Fiction 1850– 1940* (Hamden, Conn.: Archon Books, 1982), 50.

25. Ibid., 52.

26. Ibid., 53. The *Overland Monthly* suspended publication in 1875. Between 1880 and 1883, it was published under the title *The Californian.* It was under that imprint that "Poor Ah Toy" was published. The magazine resumed publication as *The Overland Monthly* in 1883 and continued until 1935.

27. See his editorials in Ambrose Bierce, *Collected Works of Ambrose Bierce* (New York: The Neale Publishing Co., 1909–12).

28. Cathy Davidson, *The Experimental Fictions of Ambrose Bierce: Structuring the Ineffable* (Lincoln and London: University of Nebraska Press, 1984); and Cathy Davidson, ed., *Critical Essays on Ambrose Bierce* (Boston: G. K. Hall & Co., 1982).

29. Cathy Davidson, *The Experimental Fictions,* 142.

30. Ambrose Bierce, "The Haunted Valley," *Overland Monthly* 7:1 (July 1871), 91. A later version of the story has the following: "Ah Wee—Chinaman. Age unknown. Worked for Jo Dunfer. This monument is erected as a warning to Celestials not to take on airs. Devil take 'em! She was a Good Egg." Ambrose Bierce, *Can Such Things Be?* (New York: Albert & Charles Boni, 1924), 137.

31. Ambrose Bierce, "The Haunted Valley," *Overland Monthly,* vol. 7, no.1 (July, 1871), 93.

32. See, for example, Bierce's entry on religion in Ambrose Bierce, *The Devil's Dictionary* (New York: printed for the members of the Limited Editions Club, 1972).

33. Ambrose Bierce, "The Haunted Valley," 89. The later version underscores the racial meaning of the last passage when it substitutes "mightn't treat him White" for "mightn't treat him well."

34. Ralph Mann, "Community Change and Caucasian Attitudes Towards the Chinese: The Case of Two Chinese Mining Towns, 1850–1870," in *Explorations in American Labor and Social History,* ed. Milton Kantor (Westport, Conn.: Greenwood Press, 1979), 397–492.

35. Ambrose Bierce, "The Haunted Valley," 89.

36. Ibid., 88.

37. Mary Douglas, *Purity and Danger: An Analysis of the Concepts of Pollution and Taboo* (London and New York: Ark Paperbacks, 1966), 116.

38. Ambrose Bierce, "The Haunted Valley," 90.

39. Glenna Matthews, *Just A Housewife: The Rise and Fall of Domesticity in America* (New York and Oxford: Oxford University Press, 1987), 92.

40. Mary Mote, "Poor Ah Toy," *The Californian Overland Monthly,* 2:5 (April 1882), 371–382; Charles Nordhoff, *California: For Health, Pleasure, and Residence; A Book for Travellers and Settlers* (New York: Harper & Bros., 1872).

41. Mote, "Poor Ah Toy," 371.

42. Ibid., 372.

43. Ibid., 372.

44. Ibid., 372.

45. Ibid., 373.

46. Ibid., 374.

47. Ibid., 374.

48. G. M. Goshgarian, *To Kiss the Chastening Rod: Domestic Fiction and Sexual Ideology in the American Renaissance* (Ithaca and London: Cornell University Press, 1992).

49. Mote, "Poor Ah Toy," 378.

50. Ibid., 379.

51. Ibid., 379.

52. Ibid., 378.

53. Ibid., 379.

54. Ibid., 379.

55. Ibid., 380.

56. Ibid., 382.

57. Ibid., 382.

58. Ibid., 382.

59. "The Irish Widdy Woman," in J. Walter Conner, *Conner's Irish Song Book: Comprising the Original & Selected Songs of the Distinguished Delineator of Irish Character* (San Francisco: D. E. Appleton & Co., 1868), 30.

60. *Quong Wing v. Montana,* cited in Alice Kessler-Harris, "The Gendered Content of Free Labor," in Noralee Frankel and Nancy S. Dye, eds., *Gender, Class, Race and Reform in the Progressive Era* (Lexington, Ky.: University Press of Kentucky, 1991), 91.

61. Alice Kessler-Harris comes to a similar conclusion with regard to the principle of "common regard" and the social construction of gender. This "common regard" principle is also used the Supreme Court in determining the status of race in the 1920s. See Chapter Five.

Four: Inner Dikes and Barred Zones

1. Howard K. Beale, *Theodore Roosevelt and the Rise of America to World Power* (New York: Collier Books, 1956), 142.

2. Alfred Thayer Mahan, *The Influence Of Sea Power Upon History, 1660–1783* (Boston: Little, Brown and Company, 1895) and *The Problem of Asia and Its Effect Upon International Politics* (Boston: Little, Brown, & Co., 1900).

3. See for example, Jack London, "Yellow Peril," in *Revolution and Other Essays* (New York: Macmillan, 1912); and Homer Lea, *The Valor of Ignorance* (New York: Harper & Bros., 1909).

4. The phrase "Yellow Peril" *(die jelbe Gefahr)* was coined at the end of the century by Kaiser Wilhelm of Germany to justify Germany's grab for concessions in China. To illustrate his point, in 1895 the Kaiser commissioned a painting of the nations of Europe, dressed as female warriors, defending Christiandom from the Yellow Peril. This he had reproduced and sent to various European heads of state and to William McKinley. For an analysis of the painting and its ideology, see Gary Okihiro, "Perils of Mind and Body" in *Margins and Mainstreams* (Seattle and London: University of Washington Press, 1994), 118–147.

5. Finley Peter Dunne, "On the Anglo-Saxon," in *Mr. Dooley in Peace and in*

War (Boston: Small, Maynard and Co., 1898), reprinted at http://www. maxwell. syr.edu/unofficial/students/fjzwick/ailtexts/gompers.html, from Jim Zwick, ed., *Anti-Imperialism in the United States, 1898–1935,* http://web.syr.edu/~fjzwick/ ail98–35.html (January 1996).

6. It was not until the passage of the McCarran-Walters Immigration and Naturalization Act of 1952 that the principle of the right to naturalization regardless of race was legislated.

7. Stuart Creighton Miller, *The Unwelcome Immigrant: The American Image of the Chinese, 1785–1882* (Berkeley: University of California Press, 1969), 11–14.

8. Sucheng Chan, "Asian and European Immigration Compared," in *Immigration Reconsiderd: History, Sociology, and Politics,* ed. Virginia Yans-McLaughlin (New York and Oxford: Oxford University Press, 1990).

9. Prior to the Naturalization Act of 1870, Chinese had applied for naturalization with mixed success. In the late 1850s and 1860s, they were routinely denied citizenship in California, while Chinese appplicants in Massachusetts were commonly granted citizenship. See Dale Baum, "Woman Suffrage and the 'Chinese Question': The Limits of Radical Republicanism in Massachusetts, 1865–1876," *New England Quarterly* 56 (March 1983), 75.

10. For a summary of Japanese, Filipino, Indian, and Korean immigration, see Sucheng Chan, "European and Asian Immigration into the United States in Comparative Perspective, 1820s to 1920s" in *Immigration Reconsidered, History, Sociology, and Politics,* ed. Virginia Yans-McLaughlin (New York: Oxford University Press, 1990), 37–78.

11. See Bill Ong Hing, *The Making and Remaking of Asian America Through U.S. Immigration Law* (Stanford, Calif.: Stanford University Press, 1993); Milton Konvitz, *The Alien and Asiatic in American Law* (Ithaca, N.Y.: Cornell University Press, 1946); Sucheng Chan, ed., *Entry Denied: Exclusion and the Chinese Community in America, 1882–1943* (Philadelphia: Temple University Press, 1991); and Joan Jensen, *Passage From India* (New Haven, Conn.: Yale University Press, 1988).

12. The literature on American imperialism at the turn of the century is voluminous. Standard accounts of this debate over the Spanish American war include Ernest R. May, *Imperial Democracy: The Emergence of America as a Great Power* (New York: 1961), and Walter LaFeber, *The New Empire: An Interpretation of American Expansion, 1860–1898* (Ithaca, N.Y.: Cornell University Press, 1963).

13. Stuart Creighton Miller, *"Benevolent Assimilation": The American Conquest of the Philippines, 1899–1903* (New Haven and London: Yale University Press, 1982).

14. Andrew Carnegie, *Distant Possessions: The Parting of the Ways From The Gospel of Wealth* (New York: The Century Co., 1901). Originally published in the *North American Review* (Aug. 1898); reprinted at http://www.maxwell.syr.edu/unofficial/students/fjzwick/ailtexts/gompers.html, in Zwick, *Anti-Imperialism in the United States.*

15. C. Vann Woodward, *The Strange Career of Jim Crow,* third ed. (New York: Oxford University Press, 1974), 73.

16. David Starr Jordan, "Colonial Expansion," in *Imperial Democracy* (New York: D. Appleton and Co., 1899), reprinted in Zwick, *Anti-Imperialism.*

17. Ibid.

18. See Robert L. Beisner, *Twelve Against Empire: The Anti-Imperialists, 1898–*

1900 (New York: McGraw-Hill, 1968). On Ben Tillman's career as a populist and racist, see C. Vann Woodward, *Origins of the New South, 1877–1913* (Baton Rouge: Louisiana State University Press, 1951), 352, 369.

19. Benjamin Tillman, "The White Man's Burden," reprinted at http://www.maxwell.syr.edu/unofficial/students/fjzwick/ailtexts/tillman.html, in Jim Zwick, ed., *Anti-Imperialism in the United States.*

20. Samuel Gompers, "Imperialism—Its Dangers and Wrongs," in *Republic or Empire? The Philippine Question,* ed. William Jennings Bryan et al. (Chicago: The Independence Co., 1899); reprinted at http://www.maxwell.syr.edu/unofficial/students/fjzwick/ailtexts/gompers.html, in Zwick, *Anti-Imperialism in the United States.*

21. Frank Dumont, *The King of the Philippine Islands, A Ludicrous Afterpiece* (New York, Chicago, San Francisco, and London: M. Witmark and Sons, 1900).

22. Ibid., 11.

23. Cecilia Elizabeth O'Leary, "Blood Brotherhood: The Racialization of Patriotism, 1865–1918," in *Bonds of Affection, Americans Define Their Patriotism,* ed. John Bodner (Princeton, N.J.: Princeton University Press, 1996), 53–81.

24. The ferocity with which the insurgency was suppressed is well documented in Miller, *"Benevolent Assimilation."*

25. Walter Benn Michaels, "Race into Culture," *Critical Inquiry* 18 (Summer 1992), 656 *et passim.*

26. Ibid., 658.

27. Frank Dumont, *The King of the Philippine Islands,* 12.

28. Kathryn Kish Sklar, "The Historical Foundations of Woman's Power in the Creation of the American Welfare State, 1830–1930," in *Mothers of a New World: Maternalist Politics and the Origins of Welfare States,* ed. Seth Koven and Sony Michel (New York and London: Routledge, 1993).

29. Eileen Boris, "Restructuring the 'Family': Women, Progressive Reform, and the Problem of Social Control," in *Gender, Class, Race and Reform in the Progressive Era,* ed. Noralee Frankel and Nancy S. Dye (Lexington, Ky.: 1991), 75.

30. Boris, "Restructuring the "Family," 81; and Alice Kessler-Harris, "The Gendered Content of Free Labor," in *Gender, Class, Race and Reform in the Progressive Era,* ed. Noralee Frankel and Nancy S. Dye (Lexington, Ky.: University Press of Kentucky, 1991), 91.

31. See Alisa Klaus, "Depopulation and Race Suicide: Maternalism and Pronatalist Ideologies in France and the United States" in *Mothers of a New World: Maternalist Politics and the Origins of Welfare States,* ed. Seth Koven and Sony Michel (New York and London: Routledge, 1993), 188–211.

32. Cited in Ibid., 190.

33. Sax Rohmer [pseud. Arthur Ward], *The Insidious Dr. Fu Manchu* (New York: Pyramid Books, 1913).

34. William F. Wu, *Yellow Peril: Chinese Americans in American Fiction, 1850–1940* (Hamden, Conn.: Archon Books, 1982).

35. Edward Said, *Orientalism* (New York: Vintage, 1979), 32.

36. Rohmer, *The Hand of Fu Manchu* (New York: A. L. Burt Co., 1917), 20.

37. Rohmer, *The Insidious Dr. Fu Manchu,* 117.

38. Ibid., 37. The career of the turn-of-the-century China expert, Sir Edmund Backhouse, was similarly built on a mix of fact and fantasy. See Hugh Trevor-Roper, *Hermit Of Peking: The Hidden Life Of Sir Edmund Backhouse,* 1st American ed. (New York: Knopf, 1977).

39. Ibid., 37.

40. On late Victorian anxiety about masculinity and the restoration of a martial spirit, see T. J. Jackson Lears, *No Place of Grace: Antimodernism and the Transformation of American Culture 1880–1920* (New York: Pantheon, 1981), 97–141. On regeneration through violence as a theme in American history, see Richard Slotkin, *Regeneration Through Violence: The Mythology Of The American Frontier, 1600–1860* (Middletown, Conn.: Wesleyan University Press, 1973); also Ronald Takaki, *Iron Cages: Race and Culture in Nineteenth Century America* (Seattle: University of Washington, 1979), 253–289.

41. Amy Kaplan, "Romancing the Empire: The Embodiment of American Masculinity in the Popular Novel of the 1890s," *American Literary History* 2:4 (Winter 1990), 659–690.

42. Ibid., 6.

43. Rohmer, *The Hand of Fu Manchu,* 37.

44. Rohmer, *The Insidious Dr. Fu Manchu,* 93.

45. The best analysis of the racial ideology of *The Birth of A Nation* and a detailed account of the close relationship between Thomas Dixon, D. W. Griffith and Woodrow Wilson are found in Michael Paul Rogin, *Ronald Reagan, The Movie and Other Episodes of Political Demonology* (Berkeley, University of California Press, 1987), 190–235.

46. John Higham, *Strangers in the Land: Patterns of American Nativism, 1860–1925* (New York: Atheneum, 1985), 285–299.

47. Lary May, *Screening Out the Past: The Birth of Mass Culture and the Motion Picture Industry* (Chicago: University of Chicago Press, 1980), 31.

48. Since movie theaters were largely segregated in both the South and the North, African Americans had their own theaters, and an African American film tradition developed somewhat independently of the white tradition. See Manthia Diawara, ed., *Black American Cinema: Aesthetics and Spectatorship* (New York: Routledge, 1993).

49. Robert S. Lynd and Helen Merrell Lynd, *Middletown: A Study in Contemporary American Culture* (New York: Harcourt, Brace, and Company, 1929).

50. On middle-class anxiety over weightlessness and inauthentic experience, see Lears, *No Place of Grace.*

51. Cited in Mary P. Ryan, "The Projection of a New Womanhood: The Movie Moderns in the 1920s," in *Our American Sisters: Women in American Life and Thought,* compiled by Jean E. Friedman and William G. Shade (Lexington, Mass.: D. C. Heath, 1982), 507.

52. Scott Simmon, *The Films of D. W. Griffith* (Cambridge and New York: Cambridge University Press, 1993).

53. Nick Browne, "Orientalism as an Ideological Form: American Film Theory in the Silent Period," *Wide Angle* 11:4 (October 1989), 23–31.

54. Boris, "Restructuring the 'Family,'" 81.

55. Gina Marchetti, *Romance and the Yellow Peril: Race, Sex, and Discursive Strategies in Hollywood Fiction* (Berkeley: University of California Press, 1993), 14.

56. Ibid., 10.

57. Ibid., 18.

58. Ibid., 21. Gina Marchetti makes this point in a somewhat different way, suggesting that Tori becomes neither excludibly alien nor assimilated, hence impotent.

59. Mari Yoshihara, *Women's Asia: American Women and the Gendering of American Orientalism, 1870s–WWII* (Providence, R.I.: Unpublished Ph.D. dissertation, Brown University, 1997) 34–102.

60. Gina Marchetti, *Romance and the Yellow Peril*, 18.

61. Eileen Boris, "Restructuring the 'Family,'" 73–87.

62. Cited in Said, *Orientalism*, 149.

63. Linda Gordon, *Heroes in their Own Lives: The Politics and History of Family Violence* (Boston: Virago, 1988), 219.

64. Ibid., 223.

65. *Broken Blossoms*, D. W. Griffiths, dir.

66. Ibid., 149.

67. Gordon, *Heroes*, 216.

68. Ibid., 225.

69. Lothrop Stoddard, *The Rising Tide of Color against White World-Supremacy* (New York: Scribner's Sons, 1920), 20.

70. Ibid., 20.

71. Ibid., 226.

72. *United States v. Bhagat Singh Thind*, cited in Kim, ed., *Asian Americans and the Supreme Court*, 536.

73. Stoddard, *The Rising Tide of Color*, 240.

74. Ibid., 236.

75. Ibid., 240.

76. Ibid., 235.

77. Ibid., 240.

78. Ibid., 220.

79. Ibid., 219.

80. Ibid., 220.

81. Sucheng Chan, ed., *Entry Denied: Exclusion and the Chinese Community in America, 1882–1943* (Philadelphia: Temple University Press, 1991); and Jeffery Lesser, "Always Outsiders: Asians, Naturalization and The Supreme Court, 1740–1944," *Amerasia Journal* 12:1 (1985–86), 83–100.

82. John Higham, *Strangers in the Land: Patterns of American Nativism 1860–1925* (New York: Atheneum, 1985).

83. Cited in Yuji Ichioka, "The Early Japanese Immigrant Quest for Citizenship: The Background of the 1922 Ozawa Case," *Amerasia Journal* 4:2 (1977), 1–22.

84. Reprinted in Kim, *Asian Americans and the Supreme Court*, 315.

85. Ibid, 528.

86. *Takao Ozawa v. United States*, cited in Hyung-chan Kim, ed., *Asian Americans*

and the Supreme Court: A Documentary History (Westport, Conn.: Greenwood Press, 1992), 528.

87. See Sucheta Mazumdar, "Colonial Impact and Punjabi Emigration to the United States," in *Labor Immigration Under Capitalism: Asian Workers in the United States before World War II,* ed. Lucie Cheng and Edna Bonacich (Berkeley: University of California Press, 1984), 316–336; and Joan Jensen, *Passage From India: Asian Indian Immigrants in North America* (New Haven: Yale University Press, 1988).

88. *United States v. Bhagat Singh Thind,* cited in Kim, *Asian Americans and the Supreme Court,* 536.

89. Ibid., 540.

90. Ibid., 540.

91. Ibid., 541.

92. *Morrison v. California,* cited ibid., 410.

Five: The Cold War Origins of the Model Minority Muth

1. Frank Chin et al., eds., *Aiiieeeee! An Anthology of Asian-American Writers* (Washington, D.C.: Howard University Press, 1974).

2. In this case, the goal was not to meet a real threat to national security but to ease anxieties about the government's preparedness and to mobilize support for policies of austerity and sacrifice. See, for example, Michi Weglyn, *Years of Infamy: The Untold Story of America's Concentration Camps* (New York: William Morrow & Co., 1976); and Peter H. Irons, *Justice at War: The Story of the Japanese American Internment Cases* (Oxford: Oxford University Press, 1983).

3. "How to Tell Japs from the Chinese," *Life,* December 19, 1941, 14; "How to Tell Your Friends from the Japs," *Time,* December 22, 1941, 33.

4. "How to Tell Japs from the Chinese," 14.

5. Ibid., 14.

6. *Korematsu v. United States* in Hyung-chan Kim, ed., *Asian Americans and the Supreme Court,* 833–867. Under "strict scrutiny," discrimination by the state on the basis of race is held to be illegitimate unless the state can show an overriding national interest. This ruling, that race is a "suspect category," became a much-cited justification of subsequent rulings against racial discrimination. Under *coram nobis,* Korematsu, Hirabayashi, and Yasui were granted a new trial in 1984. In 1986, Hirabayashi was vindicated, and the government decided not to contest the other cases. See Yasuko I. Takezawa, *Breaking the Silence: Redress and Japanese American Ethnicity* (Ithaca: Cornell University Press, 1995).

7. Fred Warren Riggs, *Pressures on Congress: A Study of the Repeal of Chinese Exclusion* (New York: King's Crown Press, 1950).

8. Reference to Asiatic Barred Zone of 1917. Asian immigration was "normalized" under the provisions of the Immigration Act of 1924, which had established a system of national quotas. Each country was assigned a quota of visas equivalent to 5 percent of the total number of immigrants from that country of origin who resided in the United States in 1905. The resulting quota for Chinese visas was a mere 105 per year, and Indian and Filipino visas were limited to 100 for each country.

9. William Peterson, "Success Story: Japanese-American Style," *New York Times Magazine* (January 9, 1966), 38; "Success Story of One Minority in the U.S.," *U.S. News and World Report* (December 26, 1966), 73.

10. Lee Rainwater and William Yancey, *The Moynihan Report and the Politics of Controversy* (Cambridge: Massachusetts Institute of Technology Press, 1967), 79.

11. Ibid., 124.

12. Ibid., 49. The likelihood that Moynihan also drafted Johnson's speech does not negate the point that the speech and the report reflect two quite different ideological tendencies.

13. "Success Story of One Minority in the U.S.," 73–78.

14. Yasuko I. Takezawa, *Breaking the Silence: Redress and Japanese American Ethnicity* (Ithaca, N.Y.: Cornell University Press, 1995).

15. See H. Mark Lai, "The Chinese Marxist Left in America to the 1960s," in *Chinese America: History and Perspectives* (San Francisco: Chinese Historical Association of America, 1992), 3–82.

16. See Bill Ong Hing, *Making and Remaking of Asian America through Immigration Policy, 1850–1990* (Stanford: Stanford University Press, 1993); Robert G. Lee, "The Hidden World of Asian Immigrant Radicalism," in *The Immigrant Left in the United States*, ed. Paul Buhle and Dan Georgakas (Albany: SUNY Press, 1996), 256–288.

17. George Lipsitz, *Rainbow at Midnight: Labor and Culture in the 1940s* (Urbana and Chicago: University of Illinois Press, 1994).

18. David M. Gordon, Richard Edwards, and Michael Reich, *Segmented Work, Divided Workers: The Historical Transformation of Labor in the United States* (New York: Cambridge University Press, 1982), 170.

19. Claudia Goldin, *Understanding the Gender Gap* (New York: Oxford University Press, 1990), 152.

20. George Lipsitz, *Rainbow at Midnight*, 69–95.

21. Laurence H. Shoup and William Minter, *Imperial Brain Trust: The Council on Foreign Relations and United States Foreign Policy* (New York: Monthly Review Press, 1977).

22. In 1960, the United States still enjoyed a favorable balance of trade of six billion dollars.

23. Cited in Noel J. Kent, *Hawaii: Islands under the Influence* (New York: Monthly Review Press, 1983), 95.

24. Noel Kent claims that in this period the United States' direct investment abroad grew by approximately 10 percent annually, or twice as fast as the U.S. economy as a whole. Ibid., 97.

25. Gunnar Myrdal, *An American Dilemma: The Negro Problem and Modern Democracy* (New York: Harper & Brothers, 1944), lxxii.

26. See, for example, Franz Schurmann, *The Logic of World Power: An Inquiry Into the Origins, Currents, and Contradictions of World Politics* (New York: Pantheon Books, 1974), 16–19, 91–114, and *passim*.

27. Mary L. Dudziak, "Desegregation as a Cold War Imperative," *Stanford Law Review* 41 (November 1988): 105.

28. Ibid., 110.

29. Rainwater and Yancey, *The Moynihan Report*, 79.

30. Ibid., 47; the full text of Glazer's essay is in Nathan Glazer, *Affirmative Discrimination: Ethnic Inequality and Public Policy* (New York; Basic Books, 1975).

31. E. Franklin Frazier, *The Negro in the United States*, rev. ed. (New York: Macmillan, 1957), 681.

32. Milton Gordon, *Assimilation in American Life* (New York: Oxford University Press, 1964), 249.

33. John D'Emilio and Estelle B. Freedman, *Intimate Matters*, 282.

34. Ibid., 292–293.

35. Elaine Tyler May, *Homeward Bound: American Families In The Cold War Era* (New York: Basic Books, 1988), 102–104. See also Guy Oakes, *The Imaginary War: Civil Defense And American Cold War Culture* (New York: Oxford University Press, 1994).

36. Bok-Lim Kim, "In the Shadows: Asian Wives of U.S. Servicemen," *Amerasia Journal* 4 (1977): 97–98. See also Michael C. Thornton, "The Quiet Immigration: Foreign Spouses of U.S. Citizens, 1945–1985," in *Racially Mixed People in America*, ed. Maria P. P. Root (Newbury Park: Sage Publications, 1992), 64–76.

37. David M. Reimers, *Still the Golden Door: The Third World Comes to America* (New York: Columbia University Press, 1985), 21–28.

38. Hing, *Making and Remaking Asian America*, and Kim, *Asian Americans and the Supreme Court.*

39. For a somewhat different view of the theme of homeroticism in *Sayonara*, see Marchetti, *Romance and the Yellow Peril*, 136–143.

40. This is a significantly revisionist response for 1957. One might note that the less forgiving *Bridge on the River Kwai* beat *Sayonara* for the Academy Award for best picture that year.

41. Although Pocahontas was a historical figure, the legend of her relationship to John Smith is fiction. Rayna Green establishes an Orientalist folkloric tradition for the Pocahontas legend itself. She traces the legend to popular medieval tales about the European adventurer captured in an "Oriental" land and his rescue by the Pasha's or Sultan's daughter who has fallen in love at the very sight of the pale and handsome stranger. The princess follows the stranger back to his country, where he is about to marry a noble woman of his own people. Once reminded of her presence, the stranger throws over his intended to marry the darker beauty. In most versions, the princess converts to Christianity and the two live happily ever after. "The Pocahontas Perplex," in *Unequal Sisters: A Multicultural Reader In U.S. Women's History*, ed. Ellen Du Bois and Vicky Ruiz (New York: Routledge, 1990), 17.

42. For an account of Pocahontas as archetypal of the exotic ethnic American woman, see Mary Lawlor, "Exoticization," in *The Oxford Companion to Women's Writing in the United States*, ed. Cathy Davidson and Linda Wagner-Martin (New York and Oxford: Oxford University Press, 1996), 290.

43. Simon van de Passe, *Pocahontas* (1616), published in John Smith, *Generall Historie* (1624), reprinted in William M. S. Rasmussen and Robert S. Tilton, *Pocahontas: Her Life and Legend* (Richmond: Virginia Historical Society, 1994), 11.

44. *Time*, December 13, 1958, 51.

45. "The Stage: The Peaceable Kingdom," *Commonweal,* April 14, 1959, 57.

46. *The New Yorker,* December 13, 1958, 73.

47. For a similar reading of this dance scene, see Peter Feng, "Looking Down on Chinatown: Musical Discourses in *Flower Drum Song*" (unpublished paper presented at Ohio University Film Conference, 1992).

48. Despite its universalist claims, liberalism is historically identified with the Enlightenment tradition and the democratic states of the West as "the outstanding doctrine of Western civilization." Harold J. Laski, *The Rise of European Liberalism: An Essay In Interpretation* (London: Unwin Books, New York: Barnes & Noble Inc., 1962).

Six: The Model Minority as Gook

1. See, for example, Bennett Harrison and Barry Bluestone, *The Great U-Turn: Corporate Restructuring and the Polarizing of America* (New York: Basic Books, 1988).

2. David Harvey, *The Condition of Postmodernity: An Enquiry Into the Origins of Cultural Change* (Oxford [England] and Cambridge [Mass.]: Blackwell, 1989), Chapters 9–11 *passim.*

3. Paul Ong, Edna Bonacich, and Lucie Cheng, eds., *The New Asian Immigration in Los Angeles and Global Restructuring* (Philadelphia: Temple University Press, 1994), 14.

4. Harrison and Bluestone, *The Great U-Turn,* 29.

5. Francis Fox Piven and Richard A. Cloward, *The New Class War: Reagan's Attack on the Welfare State and Its Consequences* (New York: Pantheon, 1982) and Barry Bluestone and Bennett Harrison, *The Deindustrialization of America: Plant Closings, Community Abandonment and the Dismantling of Basic Industry* (New York: Basic Books, 1982).

6. David M. Gordon, Richard Edwards, and Michael Reich, *Segmented Work, Divided Workers,* 160.

7. Harvey, *The Condition of Postmodernity,* 201–301 and *passim.*

8. Howard Winant, *Racial Conditions: Politics, Theory, Comparisons* (Minneapolis: University of Minnesota Press, 1994). See also Thomas Byrne Edsall with Mary D. Edsall, *Chain Reaction: The Impact of Race, Rights, and Taxes on American Politics* (New York: W. W. Norton, 1991).

9. See David A. Bell, "The Triumph of Asian Americans," *The New Republic,* July 15–22, 1985, 24–31.

10. Ibid., 30.

11. Stephen G. Graubard, "Why Do Asian Pupils Win Those Prizes?" *The New York Times,* January 29, 1988, A35.

12. "The New Whiz Kids," *Time* Magazine, August 31, 1987, 47.

13. The U.S. Census Bureau estimates that by the turn of the century, twelve million Asian Americans will make up 4 percent of the national population, and by the middle of the next century Asian Americans will account for 10 percent of the U.S. population.

14. See Bill Hing, *Making and Remaking of Asian America: Yen Espiritu, Asian-American Pan-Ethnicity, Bridging Institutions and Identities* (Philadelphia: Temple University Press, 1992), and Ong et al., *The New Asian Immigration.*

15. See Hing, *Making and Remaking Asian America.*

16. U.S. Census Bureau Report, 1994.

17. See Lowe, *Immigrant Acts,* 154–173; and Ong et al., *The New Asian Immigration,* 164–196.

18. 1994 U.S. Census Reports.

19. 1994 U.S. Census Reports.

20. Bluestone and Bennett, *The Great U-Turn;* David Gordon et al., *Segmented Work, Divided Workers;* and Joyce Kolko, *Restructuring the World Economy* (New York: Pantheon Books, 1988).

21. Ong et al., *The New Asian Immigration.*

22. Gina Marchetti, *Romance and the "Yellow Peril,"* 212.

23. See Susan Jeffords, *The Remasculinization of America: Gender and the Vietnam War* (Bloomington: Indiana University Press, 1989).

24. Lee Iacocca, *Iacocca, An Autobiography* (New York: Bantam, 1984), 315.

Seven: After LA

1. See, for example, the various readings in Robert Gooding-Williams, ed., *Reading Rodney King, Reading Urban Uprising* (New York and London: Routledge, 1993).

2. Peter Kwong, "The First Multicultural Riots," *The Village Voice* 9 (June 1992): 29, 32; and Edward Chang, "America's First Multiethnic Riots," in *The State of Asian America: Activism and Resistance in the 1990s,* ed. Karin Aguilar–San Juan (Boston: South End Press, 1994), 101–117.

3. Miyamoto Musashi, *The Book Of Five Rings,* translated by Thomas Cleary (Boston: Shambhala: distributed in the United States by Random House, 1994).

4. Karel van Wolfren, The Japanese Enigma (New York: Alfred Knopf, 1989).

5. Samuel P. Huntington, "The Clash of Civilizations," *Foreign Affairs* 72:3 (Summer 1993), 22–49.

6. Ibid., 29.

7. Ibid., 24

8. Ibid., 25

9. Ibid., 27.

10. Samuel P. Huntington, "If Not Civilizations, What? Paradigms of the Post–Cold War World," *Foreign Affairs* 72:5 (November 1993), 186–194.

11. Ibid., 190.

12. Ibid., 191.

13. Ibid., 191.

14. See Nicholas Mills, *Arguing Immigration, The Debate over the Changing Face of Immigration* (New York: Simon and Schuster, 1993); "Demystifying Multiculturalism" issue of *National Review,* February 21, 1994; William F. Buckley and Allen Brimelow, "Why Kemp and Bennett are Wrong on Immigration," *National Review,* November 21, 1994, 36–45, 76, 78; and Allen Brimelow, *Alien Nation: Common Sense About America's Immigration Disaster* (New York: Random House, 1995).

15. Brimelow, *Alien Nation,* 271–272.

16. Michael Crichton, *Rising Sun* (New York: Alfred Knopf, 1992); *Rising Sun* (Peter Kaufman, Twentieth Century Fox, 1993).

17. Michael Crichton, *Rising Sun,* 393.

18. Ibid., n.p.

19. Ibid., 109.

20. Ibid., 110.

21. Ibid., 327.

22. Ibid., 13.

23. Ibid., 40.

24. Ibid., 136.

25. Ibid., 200.

26. Ibid., 200–203.

27. Pyong Gap Min, *Caught in the Middle: Korean Merchants in America's Multi-ethnic Cities* (Berkeley: University of California Press, 1996). See also Nancy Abelmann and John Lie, *Blue Dreams: Korean Americans and Los Angeles* (Cambridge, Mass.: Harvard University Press, 1995); and Edna Bonacich and Ivan Light, *Immigrant Entrepreneurs, Korean Immigrants in Los Angeles* (Berkeley and Los Angeles: University of California Press, 1988).

28. Cited in *CAAV Voice, Newsletter of the Committee Against Anti-Asian Violence* 2 : 1 (Spring 1991), 1–2.

29. Cited in Sumi Cho, "Korean Americans vs. African Americans: Conflict and Construction" in Robert Gooding-Williams, ed., *Reading Rodney King,* 199.

30. Lauren Berlant, *The Queen of America Goes to Washington City: Essays on Sex and Citizenship* (Durham: Duke University Press, 1997), 30.

31. See David Palumbo-Liu, "Los Angeles, Asians, and Perverse Ventriloquisms: On the Functions of Asian America in the Recent American Imaginary," *Public Culture* 6 (1994), 365–381.

Eight: Disobedient Citizenship: Deconstructing the Oriental

1. Carlos Bulosan, *America Is in the Heart* (New York: Harcourt Brace, 1943; reprint, Seattle: University of Washington Press, 1983), 188.

2. Lucy M. Cohen, *Chinese in the Post-Civil War South: A People Without a History* (Baton Rouge: Louisiana State University Press, 1984); James W. Loewen, *The Mississippi Chinese: Between Black and White* (Cambridge: Harvard University Press, 1971); and Robert Seto Quan in collaboration with Julian B. Roebuck, *Lotus Among The Magnolias: The Mississippi Chinese,* foreword by Stanford M. Lyman (Jackson: University Press of Mississippi, 1982).

3. *Do the Right Thing* (1989, dir. Spike Lee).

4. Carlos Bulosan, *America Is in the Heart,* 189.

Index